THE ELECTRONIC COTTAGE

Joseph Deken

WILLIAM MORROW AND COMPANY, INC.

New York 1982

Library of Congress Cataloging in Publication Data

Deken, Joseph.
  The electronic cottage.

  Bibliography: p.
  Includes index.
  1. Computers. 2. Electronic data processing.
I. Title.
QA76.D3336   001.64   81-14016
ISBN 0-688-00664-7   AACR2

Printed in the United States of America

CONTENTS

1

Welcome to the Age of Logic

There is a revolution underway, whose scope will exceed that brought about by the invention of printing. This revolution will come about because of the advent of cheap and powerful logical devices. The primitive precursors are here: stone-age hand tools such as pocket calculators, lumbering computer-dinosaurs the size of rooms, and rococo hardware with spinning wheels, tapes, and paper. But look through the clutter, the hype, and the trivia and the maze of gadgets that make your airline reservation or limit your exhaust emissions. The ice age of thought is thawing, and channels for the flow of minds are opening daily like the geometric emergence of the new branches of a great tree. Now is the time to tune in to the current. It will soon be all around you.

The coming decade will be a pivotal period in the development of this computer revolution. The primary phenomenon of the next decade, simply put, will be the advent of widespread **computer literacy.** Other developments will continue to take place and have their impact. Notably, the size (not physical!) of large computers and the sophistication of their uses will continue to increase. But the most pervasive change will be that computers will leave the realm of the academic, military, and business elites and become tools and companions of the everyday educated person.

This computer revolution is inherently more fundamental than other revolutions which may mark this decade. It promises to change not only the way we live, but ultimately the way we think. Compare this with the energy revolution which will inevitably occur with the increasing scarcity of oil. The energy revolution will certainly produce more powerful effects, at least initially. The potential list of casualties includes not only individuals, but the foundations of entire economies and governments. Provided we survive it, however, the energy revolution's long term effects will be primarily external. If alternative energy sources can be developed, and international pressures kept under control, the net effect may simply be that oil and other fossil fuels are replaced by more durable resources. Even if the "short term" effects are disastrous, the real measure of a revolution is not its casualty count, but its effects on the survivors.

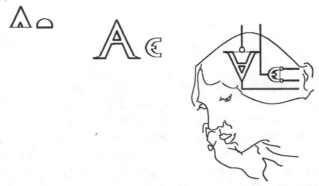

The computer revolution will not simply produce a change in lifestyles, but an entirely new mental ecology for humans.

Ways of thinking which are effective and rewarding in this new environment will flourish. Skills which no longer are relevant will no longer be cultivated, and will gradually vanish. Modern humans would find it useless to compete in raw muscle power with tractors or combines; it is equally futile to compete in raw memory power with a bank of videodiscs. Farming for pleasure notwithstanding, the human role is management, values, and vision. New priorities of mental tasks will shape our minds in the same way that new priorities in physical strengths have shaped our bodies. When our predecessors moved from the trees to the open ground, locomotive skill became central. Two legged motion proved superior, the hands were freed, and the result was no less than a fork in the evolutionary tree. We are again at the crossroads.

Talk of revolution is common enough. Depending on your prophet, the computer worldchange may have had its dates pushed back several times already. For the time being, you only need to understand what my point of view is. Whether this viewpoint has any reference to reality is a question you will have to decide for yourself. My view, that the technology of computers and other logical devices is moving us to an evolutionary crossroads, explains what kind of book this is. It is not another of the "gee whiz, what will they think of next?" treatises that flourish in pulp. It is not a chronicle of what "they" are going to be doing with computers in the near future, "they" being Uncle Sam, Harvard, or even General Motors. What "they do with computers" has largely been the story in the past.

**The story of the future is what *you*
will be able to do with computers.**

My evolutionary viewpoint means that this book attempts to be more than a catalog of toys and gadgets you can expect to see on the market soon, organized by which room you can use them in. These trinkets illustrate the trend. They do not define it. Their development is often no more useful than the crass profit motive of a manufacturer. By maintaining a higher level (post-crass?), you will be able to discern larger patterns, and develop a more durable and adaptable conceptual framework.

     Despite the fact that "computer" is now a household word, you may be one of the millions of otherwise well educated people for whom the whole subject is shrouded in magic and ritual. Perhaps you have accepted the computer as a new species and attempted to fathom the psychology and motivations of this new being. Popular toy manufacturers ("educational" included), movie scriptwriters, and novelists find it profitable to maintain the image. In reality, a computer is more like an electronic *tabula rasa* or blank slate than any of the fictitious robot movie stars would lead you to believe. If you write nothing on the slate, nothing happens. If you can discover the right kind of patterns to put on the slate, though ...

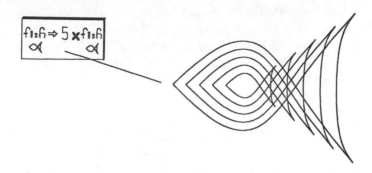

...the maze of electrical connections within the "slate" will enable your patterns to produce dynamic effects.

In particular, you will find much more discussion here of patterns or **programs** for communicating with computers than of the machines' internal electronics and architecture.

The hype and the myths will be adding their flavor to our perception of computers for a long time to come. Better metaphors, such as Seymour Papert's description of the "computer as movie camera," have all the excitement with greatly improved accuracy. Computers are an unprecedented medium for **language,** allowing our words to produce effects both in the medium which carries them and in the world beyond. With this radical new view, our task is to become "literate." At present, the state of computer literacy is that:

- There are a small number of **experts,** (ranging in age mainly from high school upwards) who both understand the principles by which computers operate and possess the technical facility to use them productively at a fundamental level.

- A much larger group, the **consumers,** consciously use computers and logical devices developed by other people, but have little flexibility to develop or adapt these computers and devices.

- The remainder of the populace, by far the largest group, are **uninitiates,** who do not understand or actively use computers, but keep running into them, pleasantly or otherwise, in things from bank accounts to airline tickets to automobile ignition systems.

By the end of the current decade, the distribution of skills outlined above will change radically. The opportunities available to those who become educated consumers—not to mention the new experts—will be so great, that to remain uninitiated will be functional illiteracy. The recognition of this fact has made computing an explicit or *de facto* part of university curricula all over the country. As full fledged computers become ever more available to *individuals*, the importance of learning the possibilities for using them will soar.

This book will provide you with essential information about computers and the myriad ways you can make personal use of them. You will see:

- a few of the important strategies humans use for dealing with computers.
- a fundamental description, without technical jargon, of how computers remember and make decisions.
- a wide sampling of the potential uses you might make of the computer you are likely to have in your home within the next few years.

You will not find here a hardware manual, technical reference, or consumer buying guide, although information in these areas will be provided somewhat in the last chapter. In describing computing machines themselves, I emphasize the fundamental structures common to all logical devices. When you understand these structures, you can more accurately judge for yourself the capabilities and limitations of computers, even if you have no further technical interest. You will be impelled to find out more, if you have the bent to be an experimenter or hobbyist. The range of possibilities you will have for using computers in the near future is limited only by your own imagination. The sampling of these possibilities, which takes up the major portion of this book, does little more than indicate some places to start. In describing what you can do with computers, I have avoided any effort to amaze you unnecessarily. Rather, I describe, at a conceptual rather than a technical level, the strategies behind each computer use. These strategies are not tied down to (and hence do not require you to understand) specific computer designs or electronic hardware. Much of the detail is described in terms of modular structures or "black boxes" which you can eventually examine more closely, if you ever need to. Based on this approach, I think you will find the book interesting, non-technical, and fundamentally useful reading. You will ultimately find your own level of computer literacy. It's a good bet that it will be much higher than you now imagine it could be.

What Computers Do Well

The great strengths of computers are speed and reliability. Nowadays, no one is astonished if a computer performs a million logical operations in a second. The only surprise would be if the computer did any of the million operations incorrectly. By using appropriate computer languages to express data of all sorts, as well as our ideas for transforming things, these ideas take on not only unequalled speed of use but an entirely new quality of "functionality."

Functionality of language, as made possible by computers, can hardly be imagined by those who have not experienced it. The computer *does* what you say. Whether the unexpected results are new discoveries and startling insights or utter nonsense depends simply on your ability to plan your commands and say what you mean. **Cooperative language** is the essence of computing; your own literacy is the key.

The single word "functionality" conveys a whole spectrum of capabilities:

- "transportability"—Information as computers deal with it can be sent across the country by telephone or across the world by satellite.
- "negotiability"—Computerized information can go directly to work for tasks from finding oil to building automobiles.
- "consistency"—Large and complex computing projects are assembled by combining the work of many individuals.

Unlike human communications, computer messages are conveyed and remembered *without distortion*. The "telephone" game, where a message is whispered in turn to many players, shows a wide variety of interesting and often humorous ways that a message changes when it is passed among several people. You would not be as amused by similar random changes in your bank balance, a Shakespeare text, or other information which you have asked a computer to store and transmit.

Computer speed is used in a host of ways. The most obvious way is that when a computer can be set up to do things in roughly the same way that people do them, the computer will do the job at an astonishing (on a human scale) speed, and with untiring accuracy. Arithmetic is the classic example. A computer will do all the daily accounting for your small business, or recompute your income tax in six different ways, in a matter of minutes. People are so impressed that they often mistakenly think that arithmetic must be the ideal use of computers.

A second, more subtle way that the computer's speed can be used is that if a complex task can be broken down into a large number (even a ridiculously large number) of similar pieces, it will be feasible to have the computer do the task, because the simple pieces of the task can be done so rapidly.

For instance, if you are faced with putting a few last pieces into a jigsaw puzzle, you would not find it difficult. Typically, you would examine the holes left in the puzzle, select one of the unused pieces, and try to insert it. Rarely would you have to try more than a few orientations of the piece, and it would be even more unusual if the first or second piece tried would not be the correct one. This type of human performance, where the right piece to try is almost instantly found, involves **recognition of perceptual patterns**, and is inherently much more difficult for a computer than arithmetic. If you are not a master of computer techniques, or a researcher in artificial intelligence, it is reassuring to know that you can still solve puzzles with the computer by **breaking the task down into simpleminded components.** All you have to do is make the computer try every unused piece, taking each piece in turn and trying to fit it into all remaining holes (*e.g.,* put the center of the piece over the center of a hole, and rotate it clockwise in small steps until its boundary matches the boundary of the hole. If none of the rotations of the piece make its boundary match up with that of the hole, then move the piece over another hole and repeat the procedure). Although this strategy would drive most people berserk with boredom long before the puzzle was complete, a computer will not only not become bored, but will do all the positionings and rotatings at the rate of thousands per second, so that it might even finish the puzzle faster than a "smart" human. Examples like this abound, where...

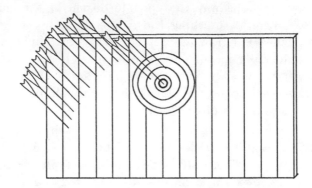

...lowly "trial and error" strategies become respectable, when trials can be done rapidly by
the thousands.

Researchers have even gone so far as to dub this newly respectable
trial and error method by a more impressive name—"heuristic search
in solution space."

The computer's ability to "try, try again," pressing on with
blinding speed and completely undaunted by failure, is not limited
to tasks like finding missing puzzle pieces, or more common jobs
like searching through and updating mailing lists. The notions of
pattern matching and **function application** enable the computer to *generate* "lists" as well as search in them, then do specific
operations, tailored specifically to fit each individual case it finds,
even without knowing beforehand what it will find in each case. As
an illustration, a common use of computers is to go through a file of
documents and do such things as:

- find all sentences which contain a specific word.
- find all documents which contain a specific phrase.
- find all documents whose *title* contains a specific word or
  phrase.

And so on. A doctor may use a computer in this fashion
to find the latest research on gallstones, or a lawyer might search
for legal cases involving intoxicated pets. All sorts of forays into the
library or into the ocean of technical literature are becoming more
and more manageable because of this capability.

Such simple fetching and retrieving is just the tip of the
iceberg. Once you know a little about functions and pattern matching (read on, read on...), you will also learn that the computer could

just as easily take the individual documents in a large file, one by one, and retrieve from each one all occurrences of whatever happened to be the most common word *in that document.* (Of course, words like "the," "and," "of," and other bits of connective tissue in the document would be ignored.) An even more clever search is possible: The computer might retrieve only the occurrences of *unusually* frequent words (e.g., "proton" would be an unusually frequent word, if it were frequent in an article, unless the article appeared in some publication such as the *Journal of Proton Studies.*) By retrieving sentences containing such key words, a rough "abstract" of every document in the file could be rapidly and automatically produced. By the way, since we're a little bit below the surface here looking at the rest of the iceberg, you may as well unhinge your notion of computers from the restricted context of documents, files, and numbers:

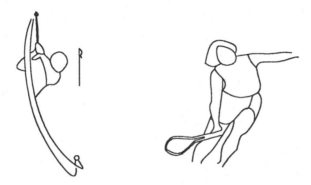

The documents stored, generated, or searched through by the computer might well be pictures of faces, or stop-action sports scenes.

In this case, the "abstract" generated by the computer would in fact be line drawings or cartoons or movie animation frames. Such techniques have already produced results ranging from improved modeling of cardiac function to new world records in the shotput. Soon you will be able to put these methods to your own use.

Fast Machines Take Slow Motion Pictures

Another area in which the computer's speed is used with great success is in so-called "real-time" applications, or applications where the computer has to take in problems at a high rate of speed, and solve each one before the next one is given, so that no backlog piles up. For example, computers inside aircraft automatically sense the position and angle of the craft, and this information represents the following problem: How should the controls of the aircraft be set, to either maintain or correct the plane's position? New position readings arrive every fraction of a second or so, and the plane's controls (flaps, engine speed, etc.) must automatically respond. Unless you want the computer to be trying to pull you out of that climb over Kansas when in fact you are now diving toward Duluth, the corrective signals to the controls must be generated by the computer just as quickly as the position signals come in. The name "real time" is used for these applications to distinguish them from typical "pretend time" computer studies. For example, a pretend-time study might have the computer figure out all of the forces on an airplane, and the deformation of its structure, when it maneuvers by turning and diving. In pretend time, you may simply stop the clock, wind, gravity and whatever else you have to, while the calculations are being completed. "Real time" is hardly that cooperative.

A key idea behind the computer's success in "real time" is that if the status of an object (like an airplane) is sampled very rapidly, you can get away with some simplifying assumptions about its behavior. You may crudely assume that its status in one sample will be roughly the same as it was in the previous sample. Better yet, you can assume that the status in a current sample will just be a straightforward continuation of the trend represented by the difference between the previous two samples: If you've taken your pet turtle outside, and want to keep an eye on him so that he doesn't wander off, it would certainly suffice to take a look every fifteen seconds or so, looking in the neighborhood of wherever you saw him last and mentally noting his new position. You wouldn't use this "four looks per minute" strategy on a quicker pet, such as your canary, but a computer attached to a television camera could do it easily, simply by taking a new look every thousandth of a second. Even with film from an ordinary home movie camera taking sixteen looks per second, you will see little difference in the image from one frame to the next. To the typical computer, performing millions of operations per second, events on a human time scale appear to be extreme "slow motion."

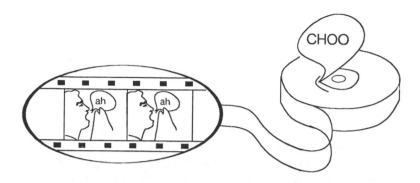

The slow motion effect caused by a computer's speed means that, from its point of view, there are long "dead spots," interacting with humans.

In chess exhibitions, a grandmaster or other strong player can play on perhaps ten or twenty boards simultaneously, since he needs much less time to think about his responses than his opponents. In a simple exchange of information with a human, the computer is operating perhaps tens of thousands of times faster. Like the chess grandmaster, the computer can talk to many humans at once, perhaps hundreds simultaneously on a large computer and where the human requirements (like storing and fetching information) are not very demanding. This "simultaneous tournament" strategy abounds in computing and in modern data communication, under names like "multiplexing," "multitasking," and "timesharing."

Even when you have your own personal computer, and never dream of letting its mind wander to someone else, multiprocessing is a valuable way to improve efficiency. With a good **operating system** on your computer, you can carry out such chores as monitoring your home temperatures, searching newspapers or library files for interesting items and advertisements, and perhaps even carry on some revenue-generating business operations, *simultaneously* with your own use of the computer in such slow operations as reading or composing. Despite your great "speed" of 80wpm, and your impression that the machine awaits every character you type with rapt interest, the fact is that a gaggle of parallel activities can be occupying most of the machine's productive capability, while it waits out the "interminable silence" between your keystrokes.

A valuable lesson which humans learn quickly from interacting with such a multiplexed computer is that their own organization of tasks should involve several projects running simultaneously. In the "old days," a computer programmer might have been content to watch every step, as a process being tested slowly traversed the tortuous path of translation to machine instructions and eventually returned its few crumbs of new results or output (along with page after page of print which conveyed no non-predictable information). Nowadays, it is more likely that the instructions for the computer will be set up and launched into the processing mill to fend for themselves, with the resulting output sent to a temporary electronic "file" and never printed at all. The programmer moves on to other things during this processing, and later scans over the temporary file with a high speed television display, quickly finding just the new information needed. In environments with such high speed displays and editing facilities, complex plans for controlling computers are being developed today which would have buried the writers in paper and punched cards a few years ago.

Free Flowing Information

The **reliability** of computers, and the adaptability and transportability of information as they deal with it, is a direct consequence of the extreme simplemindedness of elementary computer components. The computer version of a human neuron, the switch or **gate,** has neither the neuron's regenerative and metabolic capacity, nor any similar long range susceptibility to ambience or the activities of its fellow cells. An important result of the computer's simplemindedness is that extreme **space compression** of computers is theoretically possible, allowing their components to operate on a scale which is vanishingly small compared to that of the human neuron. **Information**, which, you will see, is the inherent entity for these devices, resides not in any particular physical property of a system, but only in the *differences* which are possible in whatever physical property of the system you choose to look at. The more different patterns which can be made with any structure, the more information the structure holds.

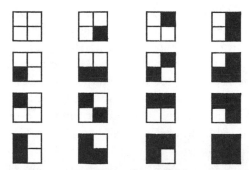

The number of possible patterns which can be made with four black or white tiles arranged in a square is sixteen...

...regardless of the size of the tiles.

Since a modern computer's components are oblivious to such considerations as food, rest, crowded conditions, and so on, computers can be constructed to function routinely and reliably in extremely small scale or in environments uninhabitable by humans. Computer "pills," which can traverse your digestive tract, provide a variety of information and exit unnoticed in one day without chemically polluting you have already been developed. For compelling reasons such as reduction of space and energy usage, computers are capable of being made smaller and smaller. The ultimate limit is only reached at the atomic level, where the states of matter itself become uncertain.

If computers are becoming smaller almost daily, the amount of information accessible to them is increasing at an even faster rate. **Computerized data**, or data in **machine-readable form** (which punched cards, magnetic tapes, and magnetic discs are, but your handwriting usually is not) can be transported, stored, and retrieved indefinitely without degradation. Thus, it is possible to collect and compile larger and larger collections of information, and make this information accessible to many users. A modern lawyer, for example, can access electronic legal "libraries" which consist of more than two billion English words, and search these libraries automatically for topics, sentences, or even words. Electronically stored information can be distributed widely and effectively, enabling information developed in one place to be saved and transmitted directly to other users for many other purposes. For example, the typesetting process, by which written material gets translated into printed books, now typically involves an intermediate step where the manuscript is translated into machine-readable form, perhaps on magnetic tape. A publisher may originally develop this tape to run a typesetting computer, but can then find many other uses for it, from "recording" books for the blind, to in-house analysis, to abstracting and foreign translation and publishing.

A final word in praise of the computer's simplemindedness (the brickbats will be brought out in a minute) is that computers are inherently unprejudiced and non-judgmental. Any human being with a good mind, regardless of race, religion, emotional preferences, or physical limitations, can function effectively using computers. There are no built-in checks in a computer to see where you got your education, if you have one, or whether your socks match. If you can speak its language and write programs, a computer will deal with you solely on that basis, oblivious to any other considerations. A great area of promise for computer development is in providing aids for those who are physically limited. The information stored by computers has a simple, homogeneous form, whether this information comes from a Shakespeare passage, a symphony recording, or television pictures from the moon. **Cross-sensory perception,** by which people are enabled to see sound, hear light, and so on, is not a science fiction fantasy, but a current computer technique which is giving "eyes" to the blind, "ears" and speech to the deaf, and bringing these groups of people into the mainstream not just of computing, but of society at large. It may be months or years before you discover that a "pen pal," political adversary, or co-worker with whom you interact over a computer network, is blind, deaf, or of multiply exotic ethnic origin. When you do, it will be irrelevant.

The Human Perils of Computer Evolution

The most significant danger in the evolution of computers, which should not be either sensationally overstated or in any way minimized, is that the more powerful computers become, the more disastrous will be the human consequences of letting them get out of control. It is entirely beyond the scope of computers or computer programs of our era to be in any conscious sense *hostile* to humankind at large; that particular worry should remain in the province of science fiction for a long time to come. For the foreseeable future, the danger from computers will be when they are consciously directed by one human against another, or when computer systems are recklessly given a great deal of power, perhaps imperceptibly increasing over a period of time, without adequate development of "fail-safe" controls for human monitoring and takeover when necessary. Computers in this sense are no different from any other machines. Only an incorrigible optimist would claim that modern "transportation machines" have had entirely beneficial effects, unless the results of modern air warfare count as benefits, or tens of thousands of automobile accident deaths in a country can be dismissed as minor drawbacks. My discussion of the threats of computing here is an effort in consciousness raising, I would hope, rather than hysteria mongering. (It is worthwhile, I think, to show a group of ebullient and carefree new teenage drivers a realistic movie which starts with innocuous enough drinking, carelessness, showing off, and so on, and ends in a horrible automobile accident. It would not be similarly worthwhile to show them Gothic episodes of cars prowling around eating babies.)

Leaving science fiction to its imaginative practitioners, let's look at a few of the clear and present dangers produced by computer usage, as well as some of the most undesirable trends in the near term development of this use. In the immediate present, it is already true that computers are used (and in fact *must* be used) to keep track of bodies of data which are too large or too rapidly developing to be processed by ordinary humans. Such bodies of data occur in contexts ranging from banking or a national census to the maintenance and activation of intercontinental missiles. Unless a great deal of care is used, we may be put in the uncomfortable position of having no independent checks on the computer's functioning, or being completely helpless when the system malfunctions or is disabled. You may naïvely believe that the high salaries paid to computer professionals are due to these people's unique mental capabilities. It would often be more accurate to recognize these high payments as subtle forms of ransom.

When a computer system generates a false alarm of enemy missile attacks, it makes the newspapers. When another system indicates that you are unfit to be given a loan, it probably will not

be as newsworthy to the general public. It is vitally important for
us *all* to become critical of the answers generated by computerized
analysis, and break the habit of accepting answers "from the computer" which we would not accept from a person or an organization.
As you will realize instantly when you see the output from the first
program you write, "from the computer" is shorthand for "by the
rules of the person who wrote the program." In contemporary par-
lance, "that's how the computer does it" is often simply an easy cop
out, to avoid the necessity of understanding (or explaining) the rules
and procedures which are being used.

> For any computing procedure, there must always be
> a human or group of humans who originated this
> procedure, in human terms and irrespective of any
> particular computing machine.

Computer programs are so easy to communicate, buy and
sell, that a program's original writer (and design) are often long forgotten when the program gets put into its nth generation of use by
your bank, supermarket, or city planners. It should be obvious, even
if economically often hard to live by, that the *availability* of programs does not imply their *suitability* for any particular application.
Computer programs (regardless of how "good" the technical staff
which produced them) that can not be explained to company executives, sales people, accounting agents, customers, or other interested
and affected parties should simply be barred from any public use.

- When identical deposit and withdrawal records over a few
  months' time fail to produce the same final balance in any
  two of a group of banks studied, all nominally using the
  same rules of computing interest, there is simply something
  wrong. The fault lies not with the particular computing
  machines being used, but with the failure of the *humans*
  who have conceived and executed the procedures involved
  to communicate unambiguously with each other and their
  customers, and translate their procedures to the machines.
- If you do not know *why* all of those recent false alarms of
  enemy missile attacks could occur in the computer systems
  involved, you can have little assurance that the situation
  has been corrected, or any real confidence that more serious
  errors will not occur in the future.

- If you trust that the "experts" know, you can only hope that this assumption does not pervade the entire establishment you are dealing with, up to the point where some single programmer's humanly undecipherable code is actually controlling the computer.

The power of computers is also increasing in a purely physical, rather than an abstract, sense. More and more, whether controlling manufacturing and industrial processes or switching devices in homes, computers are beginning to directly **do and act.** There is no need for a panel switch, waiting for the human to push it when the computer lights it up. The computer simply throws the switch itself. Computers of the current generation are frequently said to have "crashed" when internal problems or external physical reverses render them non-communicative and unable to function without having their internal mental patterns completely rebuilt from scratch. Computers of the future, with their extensive abilities to take direct physical action, must not be allowed to render the term significantly more apt. Fail-safe and error-correcting mechanisms, as well as constant human oversight of critical decisions, must become integral parts of computer systems.

Is it worth the risk? Would it be desirable, and how is it even possible, to restrict the real-world functioning of computers? If we are dealing with a specific computer, it is essential that protective features be built in. Humans are ridiculously overqualified for every factory job ever invented. Even if safety procedures are deficient, humans have sufficient interest in their own well being and are capable enough of evaluating danger and injury to themselves and others that the vast majority of potential accidents are avoided. Accidents which do occur provoke immediate and usually remedial response. Not so for the factory robot/computer. Simple economics—never mind theoretical difficulties—preclude making the robot any more humanlike than its specific task requires. At any level more global than that task, the robot is guaranteed to be disoriented and idiotic. For safety, it may be desirable to have every single instruction to the "active" computer transmitted in an error-correcting form. Certainly, every active device must have a clearly defined "box," not only in physical space but in terms of surrounding conditions, outside of which it cannot function. The device must instantly revert to some "fail-safe" mode when it encounters the boundaries of this "box," or upon command from outside. We are all familiar with the safety standards for home electrical devices, at least enough to look for tags such as "U.L. listed" or "U.L. approved" before buying an appliance. As intelligent home devices become more common, it is essential that similar standards become developed to prevent these devices from operating incorrectly or dangerously.

You might conclude overall that the risks associated with more and more active computers simply outweigh the advantages, and fight tooth and nail to prevent computer devices from being used. If the history of technological innovation is any guide, that fight will be futile. To be effective, we must rather act, intelligently and with conviction, to guide the development of computing devices into channels which are the most beneficial to humans. When human safety or prerogatives are involved, computer activities should be explicitly limited. In particular, programs which have direct contact with the public will eventually have to be explicitly regulated, much as business accounting systems are designed to make a company's practices accessible to independent audit. The United States Department of Defense, for example, has decided, to require a single language, Ada, to be used for all of its computer programs. Whether the "common language" approach furnishes the ultimate solution or not, the days of the "incomprehensible computer" in the public arena must be brought consciously and rapidly to a close.

Dependency and Addiction

Many potential dangers of the "logical age" are the common heritage of all effective advanced technologies. Without close attention, we may find ourselves, at the level of individuals, companies, or countries, dangerously dependent on the services (and even the particular suppliers) of computer devices and programs, simultaneously suffering the effects of no longer doing things for ourselves that we should be. (If you are at least a little flabby from an overdose of modern transportation, and/or have complained about the price of gasoline recently, the "dependency" theme should strike a resonant chord.) In our strictly private use of computers, it must remain true that "our thoughts are our own." Nonetheless, the point of view taken toward computers and their use by social organizations such as libraries and schools will shape students of all ages, exerting far more influence than traditional policies such as the choice of textbooks and physical facilities.

Educators who supply their schools with "personal computers" should be aware of the fact that the **programs** they choose to buy, and not the wires and plastic of the computers themselves, are the crucial elements. If we are forced to admit realistically that the most immediately attractive thing about a computer to many students is the ability it gives them to participate in fantasy treasure hunts or intergalactic war games, these activities should be seen as a starting point rather than a *de facto* "computer literacy" curriculum. (In more familiar terms, it would not be wise to either deny the affinity of youngsters for comic books and fan magazines on the one hand, or on the other to try and emulate these approaches entirely in curriculum materials.) The current spectre of television zombies unable to read and unwilling to find any more challenging entertainment than sitcoms exists despite glowing early predictions of television's educational value. The prospect of citizens who need a pocket calculator to remember their birthday and spend every free minute playing interactive electronic shootout lurks beneath similar optimism about the *potential* intellectual benefits of widespread computer use.

If future uses and development are based on conscious choice and public policy rather than chance or commercial expedience, the dangers of computer power need not outweigh (or even compare with) the potential for human development this power presents. There are few of us who see the ability to trip and fracture our skulls as sufficient motivation to wish to be paralyzed to avoid it.

Making the Machine Do What You Want

In addition to the overriding concern that computers not become too powerful and influential without human direction, there are a number of problems involved with simply dealing with computers on a day to day basis. Fortunately, the prospects for reducing or eliminating most of these problems are very good. By designing computer systems to adapt to people's preferences, rather than trying to redesign humans, many of the day to day problems of using computers are being reduced and eliminated.

A major problem with computers has been the difficulty ordinary humans have had communicating with them.

At the grass roots level, computer languages are completely rigid and unable to cope with such human amenities as context and connotation. Computers have been around at least since Schickad's digital calculator which he built for the astronomer Johannes Kepler (1571–1630), or Pascal's calculator of 1642, but in such a hidebound form that only the mathematical (and perhaps mechanical) experts could get anything useful from them, and even that most likely in small chunks. Things only began to loosen up a little with Charles Babbage, who is generally acknowledged to be the originator of modern techniques of computing, where many calculations can be performed successively and automatically under program control.

In his pioneering effort to construct an Analytical Engine (1834–1846), Babbage had all the ideas and incorporated most of the features of a "real" computer, including a memory, arithmetic capabilities, punched card input and output of data, and automatic sequencing of operations (also governed by punched cards). Unfortunately, he had to work with mechanical wheels and levers rather than electronics. The precision required to construct the mechanical computer was beyond the reach of 19th-century craftsmen, and the construction of Babbage's engine was never completed. Even if you could have obtained a working version of Babbage's engine, odds are it would have wound up in your attic. The amount of effort to formulate any substantial problem, "code" it for this machine, and painstakingly punch the required cards would probably have exhausted your patience (and your interest in the original problem). Nowadays, "analytical engines" in the form of programmable electronic pocket calculators are mass produced by the thousands, and are routinely used by everyone from engineers to high schoolers.

Unless you are fond of figures for mathematics, business, gambling, or whatever, even the best calculators may still leave you cold. The big story about personal computing revolves around machines that go far beyond calculators. These new "personable computers" are capable of dealing with words, pictures, and a host of other symbols just as easily as with numbers; are more and more "conversational" in their interaction with humans; and easily connected into large information sources and communication facilities. The major improvements in today's computers, although interrelated with each other, can be classified as:

- Physical improvements in the way computing devices are made (so-called "hardware" improvements).
- Improvements in computer programs ("software") to make computer systems more comprehensible and manageable by humans.
- Development of effective communities of users to exchange ideas and solve common problems.

Hardware: the Incredible Shrinking Mind

Hand-held calculators of the early eighties, battery operated and blithely carried everywhere, are equivalent in computing power to early computers which would have needed to use rooms of space, rows of electron tubes, and more electricity than you could afford. The technology of miniaturization and mass production is discussed in more detail later. The point here is that this technology is radically affecting people's use of computers. You would not have carried around an old fashioned calculating machine, even if you could have afforded to own one. You may now be wearing such a machine on your wrist. If you are not particularly interested in numbers, you will nonetheless probably become seriously interested in computers before the end of the 1980s, when full fledged computers, capable of sophisticated display such as pictures and text, with memories large enough to hold entire volumes of books, appear widely in personal, portable form. The **dynabook**, conceived of as a powerful computer small enough to be carried and read like a book, may have seemed like science fiction when it was first proposed by Alan Kay. With the technologies available today, including the ability to place millions of circuit components on a single "chip," high density magnetic memory, and permanent storage systems which need no power to retain their information, the question for the dynabook is not "if," but simply "when."

Part of the reason for recent advances in the physical design of computers has been that this design itself can now be carried out with the assistance of existing computers. Given a fairly simple and humanly comprehensible plan, CAD (computer-assisted design) systems are capable of **automatically generating** the complicated networks of components necessary to realize that plan in a working electronic device. This capability marks a theoretical watershed comparable to John von Neumann's pioneering insight that the **instructions** telling a computer what to do could be treated in exactly the same fashion as the **numerical data** computers were originally designed to process. That insight, that **programs can create programs,** has put computers on their present path of development as powerful intellectual tools rather than special-purpose mathematical calculators.

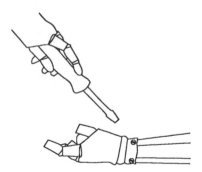

A new fact, whose impact can only be dimly imagined, is that *programs can create new computing machines.*

Theoretical considerations aside, the fact that present computers can be programmed to create other computers has enormous practical significance. An effect which is being felt already is that it is possible to cheaply mass produce many **special purpose** electronic devices. These "dimestore computers" can be custom tailored to the needs of particular individuals and/or applications, with most of the necessary instructions and features built in right along with the manufacturing process. The *tabula rasa*, general-purpose computer will of course still flourish, but it may take an entrepreneurial and economic back seat to thousands of "dimestore" devices. Once they are put into mass production, "custom computers" become widely available and usable by anyone, without the need for any training or knowledge of the computer's internal operation.

Perhaps without realizing it, you have already used such special-purpose computers, in devices like toys, wristwatches, and electronic games. Not only can you expect to see much more, and more sophisticated "fun and games," but you can also count on special purpose computers in a whole spectrum of "down to business" uses like application of energy and management of its consumption, home and personal security and medical devices, communication networks, and advanced television and hi-fi equipment. Not only will you not have to be a "programmer" to use and benefit from such devices, you will simply plug in and forget many of them.

Software: Common Sense for Computers

The most annoying thing about computers to a beginning user has been their literalmindedness. There is a unique feeling of frustration that comes about when your very first program, carefully thought out and artfully designed, fails miserably, mysteriously, and inexplicably because of something like an extra blank space in your typing or a missing comma. No more, you say! Rather than lapsing into frozen silence or hopeless garble when you say something unexpected, a modern computer may reply with: "Did you mean 'rotate picture four in the northwest corner?' " or some equally intelligible prompting. If that's what you meant, there will be no need to repeat it all; just say "yes." If you say "no," you may receive something like a numbered (short) list explaining your further options—just pick a number. Many modern computer programs (including some which will tutor you in writing your own computer programs) are completely **menu driven.**

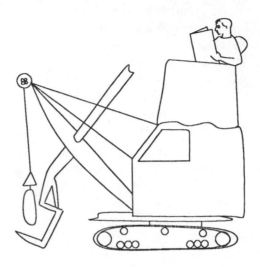

To communicate with a computer using a *menu-driven* system, you simply make a sequence of selections, one by one, from a "menu" which the computer shows you at each step.

The selections may assist you to develop anything from an architect's model to a program for your home alcohol still. Like any helpful waiter, the system will give further explanations of any items which seem obscure to you, as well as simply take your order without a menu, if you are in a hurry, and/or are quite familiar with the selections already.

Communication and Cooperative Effort

As the personal computing market grows in size, the accessibility of products and services will be further enhanced. Whether you judge it from the number of owners of personal computers, the readership of computer-related magazines and books, or any other measure, the size of the "computer literate" populace is growing explosively. Many useful programs are now going to be developed for personal computers, simply because of the ever increasing marketplace. Any hotshot programmer can take a look around at the needs and available products, and find a niche for him or herself. Good programming techniques make it possible to produce scores of slightly different program versions, starting from a single approach or idea, so that the entrepreneurial hotshot can rapidly turn a brainstorm into a whole catalog of "custom-made" programs. To the individual user, this means the development of a vast array of program tools and components which "plug in" perfectly to his or her machine, ready to go to work instantly.

As computer *networks* develop, enabling you to connect your home computer to the telephone, your problems or suggestions you might have for improving a program can be transmitted directly to the author.

In a matter of minutes or hours, you could have a response, or even a "tailored alteration" suggested for your use. As you will see from suggestions in this book, you can do a great deal of additional stitching and tailoring yourself.

Much has been said about the economic value of information and you may wish to become literate primarily to acquire the new coin of the realm. Beyond that, the active and literate use of computers offers a new ethic of production and cooperative active communication, reaching far beyond commerce into science and art. Read on, not to find out how the computer fits into a stale consumerist milieu, but how you might use it to shape something better.

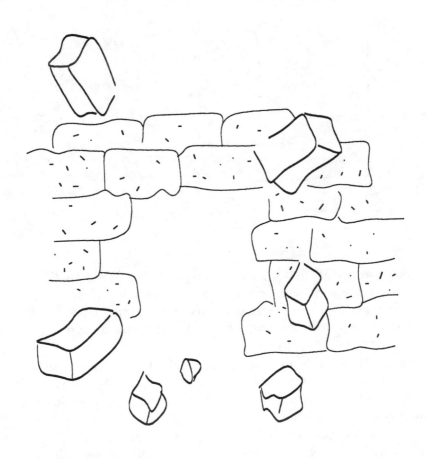

2

Breaking the Language Barrier

If you have ever cooked from a recipe, you should be able to talk to a computer. You have a lot in common. The process of following a recipe is the essence of a computer's existence: To take a specific and limited set of instructions, combine the ingredients required, and make logical decisions, as called for, in the process. You may be surprised to know that a computer could conceivably cook. Such applications today are called "process control," and they account, among other things, for large quantities of canned soup. (Suspend judgment about canned soup, if this application bothers you.)

Programs **are sets of instructions that tell the computer what actions to take and how to make decisions based on its own current state and previous actions which have been taken.**

Programs and Substitution

Imagine for a moment that you have hired an excellent cook. In order to have any dish prepared, you only have to give this cook a recipe. Computing is very much like that. You get what you want from your computer, provided you can find the right recipe to give it. You needn't know how cooks, food processors, or computers do their job, as long as you can provide the right input.

**Peanuts in—Peanut Butter out. Cashews in—
Cashew Butter out. Garbage in—Garbage out.**

Once you learn how to **communicate** your plans, to be translated into the innards of a computer, you can get all sorts of projects done the way you want them, without ever literally or figuratively looking inside the "black box." If you want to get a feeling for the present customs and methods of communicating with computers, a good place to start is by looking at the kind of recipes (from now on we'll call them **programs**, like everybody else) which computers deal with. In this chapter you will see some examples of programs, and learn how to use them to have a computer do what *you* want it to do. A useful thing to know is that you can accomplish quite a bit, and tailor-make instructions for the computer to suit your own interests to a large extent, even without understanding the language in which the computer's programs are written.

Obviously, there will be a lot left unsaid in this chapter about how a typical computer actually translates the instructions or programs given to it and carries them out. The point here, which you should find encouraging and even surprising, is that you can graduate almost immediately from total ignorance to a workable knowledge and understanding.

An easy first approach to writing computer programs is by the idea of **substitution**. Imagine that you have just been given a set of instructions, written in fluent cuneiform, which tell a delivery boy to go to the marketplace and pick up three chickens. Your problem is that:

- You don't understand cuneiform.
- Delivery boys don't understand anything but cuneiform.
- What you need from the marketplace is not three chickens but three loaves of bread.

You could, of course, just keep handing over the instructions to the delivery boy, without understanding cuneiform at all, and hope to trade off the resulting flood of chickens with your neighbors for some bread. We're going to suppose, though, that you are tired of chicken, and don't have any neighbors to trade with.

A relatively easy solution, if you don't have time to learn cuneiform before you starve to death, is to find out the words in cuneiform for "chicken" and "bread." Now simply copy the set of instructions you have, but everywhere you see the conglomeration of symbols that means "chickens," replace this with the symbols which mean "bread." Needless to say, you don't have to know a bit of grammar (or such fine points as how to pronounce the symbols you've written down), in order to get the job done. The analogy with computing is fairly direct. You may think of these computers as high powered delivery boys, whose native languages are quite esoteric. (The better educated ones are gradually learning a type of pidgin English, and the situation will improve as time goes on.) If you don't have the time, talent, or inclination to add such a language to your repertoire, substitution is the method for you.

Here is a quick example, with a real computing language called BASIC. If the language seems basic to you, that's fine. If it doesn't, no matter. The program which I am going to list below sets up the computer to play a jumbled word game. The computer will give you the scrambled letters of a secret word, and ask you to guess the word or quit. If you guess, the computer will congratulate you if you are right, and if you are wrong, it will ask you if you wish to guess again or quit. If you say "quit," the computer will type out the secret word. Here is the program...

```
10 read a$
20 l=len(a$)
25 dim p(40)
30 for i=1 to l: p(i)=i: next i
55 for i=1 to l-1
60 j=(l-i+1)*rnd(1)+1
65 t=p(i)
70 p(i)=p(j)
80 p(j)=t
90 next i
100 for i=1 to l
110 print mid$(a$,p(i),1);
120 next i
125 print
130 print "Guess or quit?"
140 input c$: goto 160
150 print "Sorry. New guess or quit?"
155 input c$
160 if c$="quit" then print a$: goto 210
170 if c$=a$ then print "Congratulations!": goto 210
190 goto 150
200 data CARROT
210 end
```

If you have a computer handy which speaks BASIC, you can type in the above program word for word, (or rather symbol for symbol, since most of it doesn't even look like words), whether you understand it or not, and the computer will play the jumbled word game with you.

Just in case you don't have a computer yet, or if you have one which doesn't speak BASIC, or you didn't feel like typing in the program, I'll let you in on a secret: the secret word is "carrot." You are going to have very little long term interest in this particular program. Once the secret word is not secret anymore, there is no point in playing, or inviting your date up to your apartment to try it out. It's easy though, to *change* the program and give it a new secret word. If you want the secret word to be "carat" instead of "carrot," all you need to do is retype the program, and substitute "carat" for "carrot" wherever it appears. (You will find it in the line numbered 200.) At the risk of boring you, let me show the result:

```
10 read a$
20 l=len(a$)
25 dim p(40)
30 for i=1 to l: p(i)=i: next i
55 for i=1 to l-1
60 j=(l-i+1)*rnd(1)+1
65 t=p(i)
70 p(i)=p(j)
80 p(j)=t
90 next i
100 for i=1 to l
110 print mid$(a$,p(i),1);
120 next i
125 print
130 print "Guess or quit?"
140 input c$: goto 160
150 print "Sorry. New guess or quit?"
155 input c$
160 if c$="quit" then print a$: goto 210
170 if c$=a$ then print "Congratulations!": goto 210
190 goto 150
200 data CARAT
210 end
```

This substitution method, simple as it seems, can be very powerful. What makes it even nicer is that the substitution itself can be handled quickly and effortlessly by a computer. Computer programs which do this type of thing are known generically as **editors**.

Any computer system you are seriously planning to buy or use should have an editor program supplied with it.

Rather than retype the whole program every time you want to change the secret word, you just tell the editor in your computer to change the word "carrot" to whatever it is you want.

If you are daring, you will realize that you are not restricted to just changing the secret word. You could have the computer be more acid when the guess is wrong, by changing the phrase "Sorry," in line 150, to something such as: "That's a terrible guess. Do you want to rest for a while?" On the other hand, you might want to be more effusive when the player guesses correctly, saying something like: "Wow, that was a great guess. You really have a talent for this!", etc., by changing line 170. The "manuscript" of this book itself was developed with the help of several computer editors and shuffled back and forth between many different computer programs in the course of writing, typesetting, and graphic composition.

To illustrate how much fun you can have with a computer editor, I will give some news stories below. One is a real news story, and the others are takeoffs, obtained by various substitutions. The reader may decide which version is more "real" or more interesting. Since you will soon have a computer at home which can communicate over the phone lines, you will be able to subscribe to an electronic version of your favorite newspaper. If you find certain stories typically depressing or moronic, you can have your computer make remedial substitutions in the text, before you even read it. Here are the news stories:

***

The Good Guys were accused yesterday of running a vast eavesdropping operation from the roof of the Bad Guy embassy in the second Bad Guy press attack on alleged Good Guys' spying this week. The government newspaper *Slanderia* charged that the Good Guy agents involved in the operation, code-named Cobra Ace, were regularly listening in on Bad Guy communications in the Bad Guy area.

The United States were accused yesterday of running a vast eavesdropping operation from the roof of the Moscow embassy in the second Soviet press attack on alleged United States' spying this week. The government newspaper *Isvestia* charged that the American agents involved in the operation, code-named Cobra Ace, were regularly listening in on Soviet communications in the Moscow area.

The Bad Guys were accused yesterday of running a vast eavesdropping operation from the roof of the Good Guy embassy in the second Good Guy press attack on flagrant Bad Guys' spying this week. The government newspaper *True News* charged that the Bad Guy agents involved in the operation, code-named Cobra Ace, were regularly listening in on Good Guy communications in the Good Guy area.

***

Computer editing programs are so flexible nowadays that

you can often make good substitutions in text or programs even without knowing beforehand exactly what you will be replacing, what you want to put in, or where you need to make the substitutions. This kind of capability goes under the name of "pattern matching," and is useful in a wide variety of contexts. If you have such a pattern-matching editor, you can automatically "highlight" a text you are reading, for example by having all sentences containing both the words "computer" and "vision" automatically extracted, copied into another file, underlined, and replaced in their original position in the text. The new file you have created would contain a list of references to "computer vision," and these references would also jump out at you as you read the amended text. With automatic pattern matching, you might also quickly "equalize" books and other traditionally sexist forms of writing. If you find an author's exclusive use of masculine pronouns to be distracting or offensive, you can simply instruct your text editor to **filter** the text before you read it, changing all unattached pronouns to a democratic she/he form, or entirely to the feminine gender, or to a random choice of masculine or feminine, as you prefer. Whether your methods are this simple or perhaps more sophisticated, your computer editor can help you automatically remove a great deal of subconscious sexism from what you read (and write.)

The substitution method will not do a thing for you if you do not have an original program to substitute into. For this and other reasons, you will want to eventually pick up the fundamentals of at least one computer **programming language**. When you buy your first computer for personal, professional, or business use, for example, it is essential to realize that there are two interdependent considerations:

- **hardware** choices—How good is the physical electronic gear?
- **software** choices—What languages and **operating system** are available to you, to set up in the hardware memory and transform the "blank slate" into a friendly and manageable interactive device?

There are, if anything, too many computer languages rather than too few, and unfortunately many hardware salespeople are not helpful or sufficiently knowledgeable when it comes to software. As a result, you may find that they emphasize hardware issues and minimize your concerns about languages and the operating system. If a computer were just another appliance like a stereo or television set, you might well concentrate on hardware. The fundamental difference with computers is that a computer's value lies not just in *what it can do*, but more importantly in *what you can do with it*. The computer is a new tool (the evolutionary descendant of both the pen and the engine), and languages, operating systems, and other interfaces are its "handle." You may care very little if the knobs on your stereo do not work: If things are arranged wisely, you hardly need to use them. If your shovel handle is broken or your typewriter keys stick, the situation is entirely different. (Although, if the manufacturer goes on and on about his shovel's stainless steel blade, you may be distracted enough to overlook the rubber handle.) In Chapter Twelve we will look at both hardware and software in more detail. For the moment, the analogy of hardware as blade and software as handle for the computer-shovel will not be pressed further than to emphasize the importance of both components.

A specific example of mistaken emphasis, which you should be aware of, occurs when vendors promote simplicity and "ease of use," of a system, while hampering its ultimate flexibility. Limited menus and plug-in modules are fine to break the ice, but you will not become literate in the new language of programs, planning, and functions if you restrict yourself to only this simplest kind of interaction. Many microcomputer manufacturers would present the impression to a novice that BASIC (the language used in the word game example on pp. 29–31) is **the** language for their computer. That is hardly ever true. The mass-market micro vendors are still largely pushing BASIC, and there are a large number of programs around in BASIC for you to plug in and use substitution on. Nonetheless, BASIC is a primitive language, which can tie your head in knots when other modern and more streamlined languages such as Pascal or LISP would keep you well in control, or friendly languages such as LOGO would keep you much more interested. Similarly, you would be ill-advised to preserve the clumsy and difficult operating systems of many personal computers. Powerful and streamlined systems such as Digital Research's **CP/M** and Bell Laboratories' **UNIX** or one of its lookalikes could be easily installed in your hardware instead. Knowledgeable buyers of personal computers often buy their machine **hardware** from one (the cheapest, or best service in the area, or whatever) manufacturer, and go to a completely different company for the **software** to set the machine up internally.

No one but the rawest novice can manage for long without

becoming familiar with some languages and other software. The point of substitution though, is that you can be "tapping into" scores of computer languages directly, and fiddling directly with the innards of perhaps hundreds of programs to make these recipes more to your liking, long before you learn your first BASIC (or LISPing, or whatever) words. The art of adroit substitution is all you need to know. You may produce some bizarre results, and even (temporarily) wreck a few programs with this "try it and see" approach, but you will learn a lot. Any sensible computing system provides mechanisms for undoing whatever changes you make. If the "tangled web we weave" becomes hopeless, we can take our lumps and lessons, and start again with a new plan from the original program.

> # Computers Don't Hold Grudges

It is often true that if you have a computer, or have access to one by some communication link like telephone or cable television, the program to do whatever it is you want to do has already been written. More to the point, it is almost certain that a program to do *almost* what you want to do, or several programs each of which do *part* of what you want to do, not only have been written, but are easily accessible to you, in printed form, or on cassette tape, or on magnetic discs, or over telephone networks. (More details on these and other computerized communication methods are given in Chapter Ten.) With such availability, and a little bit of imagination, you have painless access to computing power and enjoyment. Just wade in there and substitute.

You might have a program which provides a color display of fighter planes in battle. Once this program is transmitted and stored inside your computer, you can begin to modify it to your liking, changing anything from the shape of the planes to the color of the sky and the rockets' red glare, bombs bursting in air, etc. A rather bland "conversational" program (there is a famous one named PARRY which mimics a schizophrenic) can have its dialog changed anywhere in the range from sententious to scurrilous. Good programmers put comments, in plain English, in their programs, that are often dead giveaways as to what words, numbers, and other symbols in their program can be easily, effectively, or uncautiously fiddled with. You may feel somewhat less than 100 percent literate, using only substitution, but that should only motivate you to learn more. From the very start, you have greater flexibility than the 0-level user, who knows only where to plug in the modules, and that when the computer says "type yes or no" he should type "yes" or "no."

Pitfalls with Substitution: The Idea of a Function

Going back to the example of the market instructions in cuneiform, you could take the clay tablets or whatever the instructions were written on, and make a note to yourself on the top:

"Instructions to Get Three Chickens from the Market"

To use the substitution method, you only need to know the word for "chickens" in cuneiform. You can quickly go through the tablet and underline every place this word appears, for future reference. If you then found out the cuneiform symbols for "bread" or "eggs" or "goat cheese," you could substitute any of these for the symbols you have underlined as meaning "chicken." With a little luck, you could give any one of these new versions of the tablet to a messenger, and he would return from the market with the right thing.

Suppose, however, that the original instructions had been for the messenger to go to the fair and buy a horse. Using the substitution method, you find out the word for horse, and substitute the word "chicken" for the word "horse" everywhere it appears. Will the messenger return from the fair with a chicken? Maybe not. Suppose that the original instructions (translated) were:

> "Get on your horse and ride south to the fair. There
> you will find an old man in a red bandana with horses
> on it who sells horses. Buy a horse from him for no
> more than twenty measures of corn and return with it
> before dark."

Blithely applying the substitution method, you will produce the following set of instructions, which will probably not get you a chicken and will almost certainly lose you a messenger:

"Get on your chicken and ride south to the fair. There you will find an old man in a red bandana with chickens on it who sells chickens. Buy a chicken from him for no more than twenty measures of corn and return with it before dark."

What's the problem here? Simply put, the problem is that the word "horse" in the original message has many roles, from the vehicle for the messenger to a description of the seller to the object of the purchase. Indiscriminate substitution has led you to throw the baby out with the bathwater. There is no general way out of this dilemma without learning cuneiform, unless the original writer of the instructions gives you some help.

Functions to the Rescue

A good way to avoid the confusion above would be for the writer of the instructions to label them:

"**Instructions to Get Two—| horses |— from the market.**"

In the text of the message itself, only those occurrences of the word "horses" which referred to the horses-to-be-bought would be marked by —☐—. The message is now a **function**, and it has one **argument**: —| horses |—. We might call it the get-from-the-market function. To get chickens, for example, with this function, you only substitute "chickens" in the message for those occurrences of "horses" marked by —☐—. (This would be called "applying the get-from-the-market function with the argument 'chickens.' ") Once you have the idea of functions, the whole business of substitution (putting new words in old messages) becomes very precise and streamlined. You may simply say to your delivery boy (or to a computer using any one of a number of modern languages):

"**get-from-the-market(chickens).**"

The delivery boy or the computer can then go through its whole (possibly large) collection of "functionalized" messages, see if there is one called "get-from-the market," and then do the substitution of "chickens" for —☐—in that message. You will often see functions called "subroutines" and said to be "called," rather than "applied." For a beginner, the idea is the same, whether you say you are "applying the **get-from-the-market** function with the argument chickens," or "calling the subroutine **get-from-the-**

market with the argument chickens." If you have a capable delivery boy or computer, the results are the same. Here is a little example in code of a **get-from-the-market** function:

get-from-the-market (—⟨SLIHVH⟩—)

Usage: Use this to get two—⟨horses⟩— from the market.

TVG LM BLFI SLIHVH ZMW IRWV HLFGS
GL GSV NZIPVGKOZXV. GSVIV BLF DROO
URMW Z NZM DSL HVOOH—⟨SLIHVH⟩—. YFB
GDL —⟨SLIHVH⟩— UILN SRN, ULI ML NLIV
GSZM GDVMGB NVZHFIVH LU XLIM.
IVGFIM DRGS GSV—⟨SLIHVH⟩— YVULIV WZIP.

Two things to notice about the above bizarre message are that "SLIHVH" evidently means "horses," but the first occurrence of "SLIHVH" is to be left alone, since it isn't marked —⟨☐⟩—. Here are a few other words and their codes which might be useful to put in for—⟨SLIHVH⟩— :

bread—YIVZW   chickens—XSRXPVMH
tamales—GZNZOVH   cows—XLDH

This example is obviously contrived. Nonetheless, a completely new computer language, which you are looking at for the first time, might be nearly as mysterious. (Writing a program so that the computer can read it is often called "coding"—not without reason.) But when a program is explicitly given as a **function,** you can use it and tailor-make it to your needs, without fear of sending the messenger off to market on a tamale. By the way, the code here is relatively easy to crack. If you haven't guessed it already, it is a letter-substitution code, and the letters to be substituted are just obtained by writing the alphabet down backwards:

The Backwards-Alphabet Code																									
text	a	b	c	d	e	f	g	h	i	j	k	l	m	n	o	p	q	r	s	t	u	v	w	x	y	z
code	Z	Y	X	W	V	U	T	S	R	Q	P	O	N	M	L	K	J	I	H	G	F	E	D	C	B	A

The decoded message is thus:

"get on your horses and ride south to the marketplace.
there you will find a man who sells—| horses |—. buy
two—| horses |— from him, for no more than twenty
measures of corn. return with the—| horses |— before
dark."

The basic idea behind all of this, whether you think in
terms of programs and possible substitutions or functions and possible arguments, is the notion of **a pattern, a method, or a
paradigm.** Once you have the pattern or the method, you may
be able to apply it in many situations. For example, if you know
how to go to the market and get horses, you may know how to get
chickens or tamales using the same pattern. The pattern or method
is embodied in a **function,** and the things which may vary are explicitly indicated as **arguments.** The pattern itself is fixed and
rigid. (If there are no chickens sold at the market, but only horses,
then applying the "get-from-the-market" function with "chickens"
as the argument will be futile.) But power and flexibility are built
up steadily and enormously by linking many functions together, as
you will have opportunity to see.

Structured Programming—A Plan for Planning

Deep down in their innermost workings, computers are
incredibly simpleminded. (Their redeeming feature is that they are
very, very fast. Any simpleton who can do millions of calculations
per minute is not to be sneezed at.) If you ever take a look at
the final, lowest level batch of instructions which guide a computer
through even the simplest task, you will find a welter of unexpected
details. Everything has to be exactly where it's expected to be,
and in exactly the form required. We all have to take our great
plans for using computers and somehow eventually cope with this
fundamental simplemindedness.

So far, the only strategy we have discussed is the substitution method—let someone else do the grubby details. The dedicated
substituter just carries around his or her bunch of arguments, and
looks for good functions to apply to them. Often, this strategy will

work straight off. With a little planning, it can be made to work more often. (Suppose you need a new mailbox at the end of your driveway. You will probably be disappointed if you thumb through mail order catalogs, looking for a mailbox that can be "applied" to your driveway in a single complete package, especially if you would like your name and address printed on it. Nor would you want to reinvent metal containers, 4 x 4's or posthole diggers especially for the occasion.)

If you break the problem down into four pieces as mailbox & lettering & pole & hole though, you will find all the pieces ready-made, and simply obtain and "apply" them.

If you want to use computing creatively without getting bogged down in a welter of detail right from the start, you should learn to think hierarchically. If you have some task which you want the computer to do for you, you must successively play a variety of roles. To switch from a military to a corporate analogy, you will start out as Harvey M. Biggey, president of the company, and give instructions to your trusted vice presidents, Winken, Blinken, and Nod. When you give the instructions, you should plan things so that all of Winken's tasks are related to each other, and none of them could be done better by Blinken or Nod, and similarly for the other vice presidents. In your role as president, it would be inappropriate for you to consider the mundane details of *how* the tasks you set are actually going to be accomplished by the subordinates, although you must know fairly well (from experience or reliable sources) *what* they are capable of. It would be perfectly reasonable for you to ask Winken to find the cheapest collection of materials which could be used to make an automobile, Blinken the lightest collection, and Nod the strongest, and let them worry about how to find and test possible materials. On the other hand, it doesn't pay to be unrealistic in your demands, especially considering that your term as president will be over as soon as you have assigned all the tasks.

You must then successively become Mr. Winken, Mr. Blinken, and Mr. Nod, and prepare instructions for further subordinates to carry out. As Mr. Winken, for example, you must take your instructions from old man Biggey and break them down for suitable consumption by the lower classes, such as the manager trainees Ho, Hum, and Drum. Notice that you don't need to concern yourself too much with how Ho, Hum, and Drum will do their subtasks, but you should organize the subtasks well. A further burden lifted from your shoulders is that as Mr. Winken, you also don't have to concern yourself with what Biggey told to Blinken and Nod.

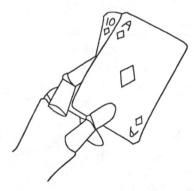

Suppose you wish to write a program so that your computer will be the dealer in a game of blackjack.

Your high level "program" might be:

- **Deal the initial cards.** (First Task)

- **Display the cards in play.** (Second Task)

- **Ask players if they wish more cards.** (Third Task)

- **Deal more cards as requested.** (First Task, again)

- **Display the cards in play.** (Second Task, again)

- **Give the dealer more cards, if needed.** (Fourth Task)

- **Display the cards in play.** (Second Task, again)

- **Determine the amounts won and lost.** (Fifth Task)

- **Display the results.** (Sixth Task)

It's a safe bet that no computer on earth will take the words written above as a program and begin to play blackjack. (About as safe a bet as that your mail order catalog doesn't advertise a mailbox with your name and address on it, along with a hole for the end of the driveway.) Nonetheless, the six tasks given above are the essentials from which a complete program can ultimately be made. The strategy is to divide and conquer. If you like buzz words, you can refer to your strategy as the **top-down approach**, and feel like a real programming insider. The Second Task, the **display**, for example, is used in several places, but with a wise division of labor, it need only be thought through once. The tasks are separate from one another, so that they can be dealt with one at a time, then assembled later. Pursuing the divide and conquer strategy, each of the tasks can be successively broken down to further detail. For example, for the Fourth Task above, we might have:

Fourth Task: Give the dealer more cards, if needed.
  Total the cards in the hand   (Task A)
  If the total is 16 or less, take a card (Task B)

And in Task A, we will have to know whether to count an ace, if there is one, as 1 or 11, which gives two possible ways to total the hand, and so on. As you can imagine, the hierarchical planning, top-down approach can be carried out down to many, many levels. If interest or necessity compels you, you will eventually be playing Mr. Jot and Ms. Tittle. The virtues of this planning strategy are:

- You don't have to think of little details at the same time you're trying to decide major issues.
- You may never have to think of little details at all, since low level tasks are common to many applications, and are quite likely to have been set up already by someone else.

Pursuing the corporate analogy, we expect that somewhere in the collection of tasks set in motion by Mr. Biggey, it will be necessary for someone to write a letter. Safe to say, though, that no one in the corporation will be involved with typewriter design. At this point, the task is at such a common level that a typewriter designed by almost anyone (provided they supply the correct alphabet, etc.) will do. The optimal solution in terms of time, errors, and efficiency is to get a ready-made one and use it. In the same way, you will start out at the top level to tell the computer what you need done, then move into more and more minor roles, until at some point your tasks reduce to things that either the machine you are working with knows how to do immediately, or can be done by a program which has been written by someone else. With hierarchical planning, you thus put yourself effectively in command of the literal hordes of useful but limited programs being constantly produced.

If you find thinking in terms of managers, executives, and other such human agents much more congenial than dealing with standard computing entities such as subroutines, block structures, and arrays, you are certainly not alone. Not only do many skilled programmers engage (even secretly) in these mentally prophylactic analogies, but entire languages, such as ACTOR, SMALLTALK, and LOGO, are built up on the idea of setting up mutually cooperative and communicating entities within a computer system. You can call your entities "managers," "turtles," or "Hussars," as you please; their behavior develops along lines you specify. Not only would such languages know what a "manager" is, but even what to expect from Ho, Hum, and Drum, once you describe them.

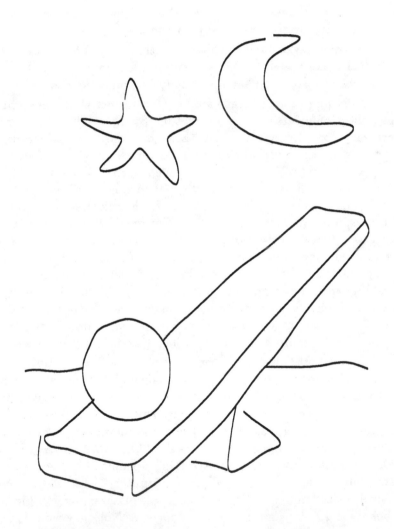

3

How Machines Make Decisions

A panel is discussing their nominations for the greatest invention of all times. The first panelist says that she believes that fire was the greatest discovery, since it was the basis of so much of humankind's ability to survive and produce. The second panelist says that he believes that the wheel was the greatest invention, because of its effect on people's mobility and its role in so many mechanical devices. The third panelist, a philosopher, proclaims that the greatest invention of all is the thermos bottle. "The thermos bottle?" asks the moderator in disbelief. "The thermos bottle—" replies the philosopher, "it keeps *hot* things *hot* and *cold* things *cold*." "So what?" the moderator asks. His gaze lost in wonder, the philosopher ponders, "Yes, but how does it know?"

One of the messages that it is important to understand about computers and other logical devices, is that it is often not necessary (and even positively distracting) to know in exhaustive detail how they work, if you are trying to use them creatively. After all, the number of people who have used a telephone successfully is far greater than the number who understand electronics or acoustics. At the level of the most recalcitrant reader, that means that you may skip this chapter, if you wish, without losing the ability to understand anything else in the remainder of the book.

Congratulations! If you're reading this paragraph, bravo for your inquisitive spirit! On the other hand, maybe you've still got half a mind to skip the chapter, so let me talk you out of it. In this chapter, I'm going to describe *concepts* rather than the details of specific electronic gear ("hardware" as it's called). What I will try to explain at a fundamental level is, "How does it know?" ("it" being the computer in this case.) After all, how *does* some mechanical/electrical device think, remember, make decisions, or any of the thousand other things observed of, or imputed to, computers? If you understand, at least in principle, how such things are possible, you will dispel a lot of silly fantasy and mystery about computers, at least in your own mind, and possibly be able to help some of the uninitiated as well.

Like it or not, computers are going to be important in shaping the planet from now until, or possibly after, humankind becomes extinct. Some of the ways in which computing could be developed would be harmful and dehumanizing, other ways positively exhilarating and liberating. Human beings will decide how computers should develop, at least initially. Such decisions cannot be made wisely without knowing the fundamental makeup of computers and what they are and are not capable of.

At the end of this chapter, you should be no more awed by a computer thinking than you are by a typewriter writing. You will even know why it is that computers are likely to be affected by a cosmic ray, but not by such things as their operator's cursing because twelve hundred empty pages have just mistakenly spewed out of the (high speed) printer.

The Advantages of a Yes-No World

One does not find the expression "digital computer" too often nowadays, because the word "digital" (which will be explained in a minute) is taken to be redundant. By vast majority vote, and for all purposes of this book, to be a computer is to be **digital.** By the same reasoning, you won't see the expression "electronic computer" much, either. Of these two characteristics, "electronic" and "digital," the digital aspect is much more central to the way computers operate, and will probably remain that way. In contrast, *electronic* computers are currently the most convenient to make, but the day of the electron may well fade into the morning of the photon, with electronics in computers relegated to the auxiliary status now occupied by mechanical devices. I will therefore spend some time justifying the fact that computers should be digital (giving you a clue at the same time why telephones, phonograph records, television, and practically all types of information storage and transmission will soon be digital as well), and mostly leave the electrons to figure out for themselves why they do what they do.

What is digital? What else could it be but something that has digits? What are digits? If you guessed that digits are *not* computer fingers, you're right. If you guessed that digits are the symbols 0123456789, you're almost right but not quite. The amazing truth is that digital *does* mean using digits, but the digits in this case are only "0" or "1." (Or yes and no, true and false, right and left, high and low, or whatever you like to think of as your ultimate dichotomy.)

That's digital, folks. Now the first question is *why*, and the next question is *how*. First of all, *why* would computing machines be built to store, transmit, and do all of their other operations on basically two types of quantities, call them 0-1, yes-no, or whatever? It sounds like the limit of unexpressiveness. Secondly, if you insist that everything be 0 or 1, *how* will you ever accomplish anything remotely interesting or useful? And how did the computer print $750 on my airline ticket then?

First questions first. The fundamental reasons for this digital world of yes-no are reliability, reproducibility, compatibility, portability, if you will. The very simplemindedness of today's logical devices accounts for their amazing proliferation. Because a watch, which tells you the time to the second, the date, the day of the week, and the month, is only internally shuffling around 0s and 1s (high and low voltages actually), it can be built by a glorified printing press rather than by a master watchmaker, use batteries and displays that were developed long before it was even thought of, and sell, along with hundreds of thousands of identical twins, for less than the price of dinner for two. The same story can be told about devices from remote control toys to hand-held calculators.

The question remains: why is it more reliable, reproducible, portable, etc., for devices to be fundamentally yes-no or digital? A homely example (perhaps from your childhood experience) will illustrate: you can make a toy telephone by poking a small hole in the bottom of each of two tin cans, and passing one end of a long string through the bottom of one can and the other end of the string through the bottom of the other can. If you knot the ends of the string so that they can't slip back out the bottoms of the cans, you can stretch the string tight, with the cans separated by the length of the string. If one person talks into one can, and another person holds the other can to his ear, with the string stretched tight, the speaker's voice will be carried over the string to the listener.

The string (or tin can) telephone is a classic *analog*, rather than *digital* device.

The vibrations of the air near the speaker, which the listener would hear directly if he were close enough, set the bottom of the speaker's tin can vibrating, and since the string is tight, the vibrations of the bottom of the can are translated into vibrations of the stretched string. The vibrations in the string are an **analog** of the vibrations in the air caused by the speaker. These analog vibrations go from the speaker's end of the string to the listener's end, where they produce vibrations in the bottom of the listener's tin can, and the bottom of this can sets the air in motion around the listener's ear. Now for the problem: If you keep getting more and more ambitious, and making longer and longer string telephones (assuming you can find enough open space to stretch the string out), they will eventually be useless, because the sound will be too faint for the listener to hear what the speaker is saying.

Now let's take this string telephone with the very long string and see if it can be converted to a digital device, and how it would work better. Even when the string is so long that the speaker's voice is *unintelligible* even if he shouts, the listener may still be able to tell when he's *shouting* or *not shouting*. Aha! A dichotomy! Alternatively, the speaker may become hoarse, and resort to tapping on his tin can with a stick. The amount of effort to produce a tap which is audible at the other end will be much less than shouting. If the only purpose of the telephone is to transmit a "yes," (no transmission at all then meaning "no," "0," "off," "down," "low," "no-ice-cream-truck-in-sight," or whatever the opposite of "yes" is for the situation) ...

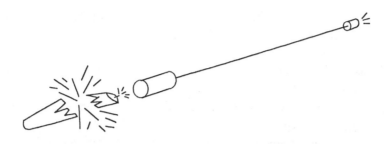

...the telephone will work quite well, as a digital device, long after its analog properties have failed.

We can make the example a little more realistic by supposing that the speaker wants to send letters of the alphabet to the listener. If the string between the cans is long, it may be impossible for the listener to distinguish the letters A-H-J-K, which all sound similar. The analog vibrations in the string are just not close enough (limping analogy) to the vibrations of the air near the speaker's mouth to be usable. If we somehow could **translate** letters of the alphabet to a language of taps (Morse code is such an effort), our string telephone could be used as a binary, yes-no device, and would function perfectly well. After all, as long as a tap gets transmitted from the speaker to the listener, it does its job perfectly well, whether it comes out sounding like "tap," "pat," or "splat."

Since we all know that there are no strings inside today's logical devices, it's worth stating the argument for digital devices in a more general setting: No matter how you want to process information (which is what computers and other logical devices are all about), the information will have to be stored and transmitted in the form of **signals.** It is impossible to store or transmit signals (even within the tiniest bowels of an integrated circuit) without some muddling or "degradation" which causes the signal to be changed in transit. The problem would be extreme in present day logical devices, which can perform millions of operations per second, where any signal is likely to be transmitted over and over again a mind boggling number of times. Any analog signal would be degraded beyond recognition at the end of such a process.

Binary signals are inherently superior to analog signals in two major ways:

They can always be sent at full power: For example, if you're just going to say "yes" over the string telephone, or else say nothing, you may as well shout "YES" at the top of your lungs, or even set off a firecracker in the can. The listener will have a much better chance of hearing something. Whatever sound is heard, the listener knows it means "yes."

• Degradation, which inevitably does occur, can be removed completely. In the telephone example, the listener on one line may be the speaker on another line. If she hears a "yes" or a tap, however faint, she can relay this signal at full strength to the next listener. On the analog line, where she hears something so faint that it could be either A or H or J or K, she can of course "amplify" this faint sound by shouting on to the next listener, but she may be shouting the wrong thing.

At this point, you may well believe that the digital or binary language has some important advantages. The next step is to show that, using this binary language, a computer can perform all the tasks you would want it to.

Did You Ever Play Binary Chairs?

Here is a variant of musical chairs which can be played by three players and will have you thinking digital in no time: Two chairs are placed at the end of a room, representing branches at the top of a tree.

The three players line up at the bottom of the tree, and the music starts.

Each player in turn goes from the bottom of the tree to the fork in the tree. Here, the player draws a card, which is equally likely to say "left" or "right." The player goes up either the left or the right

branch as the card indicates, and claims the chair on that branch at
the top of the tree. Any player he or she finds sitting in that chair
must give it up and go back to the bottom of the tree to start again.
When the music stops, the players sitting in the chairs at the top of
the tree each get the prize under their chair.

There is obviously not much to this game. If you wanted
to use it to sell soap on network television, you would have to do
something pretty spectacular to it. You could make the prize under
the right chair a yacht, or a vacation in Tahiti, to work up a little
interest. (Make the left chair less desirable, like a luxury car which
gets 3.7 miles per gallon of gas.) The participants, (properly coached)
could then frantically race up and down the tree, while the audience
shouted "right, right, right" each time one of them got to the fork.
(More moronic games than this have made it big.) At the end of the
game, one tearful loser would be somewhere between the bottom
and the middle of the tree (how about a year's supply of Tidyduds,
or whatever, for consolation), and the two winners would be at the
top. They could then turn in their tickets, "right" for the yacht and
"left" for the gas hog, presuming the prizes weren't actually under
the chairs in this case.

Rather than just make the prizes bigger, we could embellish
the original game by having more prizes at the top (and more players
running around). All we need to do is add more forks to the tree.
Suppose we make the tree be fifteen feet tall and have five forks, one
every three feet up. Now, every player has to draw five times to get
from the bottom of the tree to the top, and as you can see from the
picture below, we would be able to have *thirty-two* different prizes.
Assuming we still give the yacht away on the rightmost chair, the
audience could still yell out "right, right, right, right, right," so there
wouldn't be too much to learn. The yacht winner, (if indeed anyone
even got through the maze of branches to that spot on the top),
would be holding five tickets which say "right, right, right, right,
right."

Each of the thirty-two chairs at the top of the tree can
be matched up with a different prize. Rather than taxing your
imagination or covetousness with more yachts and cars, let's just
number the chairs (and the prizes) 0, 1, 2...31 from left to right.
You can still think of the possibility "31 = yacht," if that motivates
you.

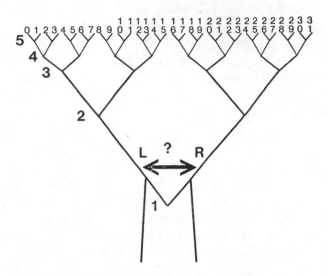

A Five-Level Binary Chairs Game

Now let me pose two questions, one fairly easy and one not too hard. If you know how to answer both questions, you will soon be able to see why the binary or digital language can specify just about anything you want it to. The first question is:

- If you draw tickets which say "left," then "right," then "left," then "left," then "right" (L–R–L–L–R), what chair will you claim at the top of the tree?

The easiest way to answer this question is just to play the game through mentally. You could even go back to the picture and trace your path through the tree with a pencil. There you are at the bottom of the tree. At the first fork you get "left," so go left to the next fork. Here you get "right," so go right, to the next fork. Here you get "left," so go left, to the next fork. Now you get "left" again; go left to the last fork. Finally, you get "right," and you're at the top in chair number ...

If you got it right, bravo for you. If not, you can try it with a pencil—just start from the bottom, and write "R" on each fork at which you turn right, "L" on each fork at which you turn left. If the letters you've written, from the bottom up, are "L—R—L—L—R,"

you wind up in chair number 9.

Now the question which is a little bit harder:

• If you want to end up in chair 23, what sequence of cards will you have to draw?

If you haven't got a clue as to how to answer this, just work *downwards* from chair 23 at the top, to the base of the tree. On each fork you climb down through, write down "L" if you're coming down through the left branch, and "R" if you're coming down through the right branch at that fork. When you get to the bottom, you can simply read (from bottom to top) the letters you've written: These are the cards you'll have to draw to get to chair 23. With a little perseverance, you should get:

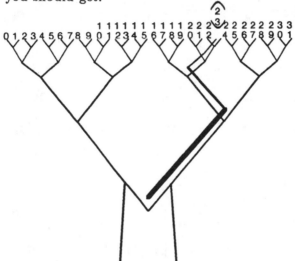

"Right, Left, Right, Right, Right."

The point of the two questions is this: If you know how to answer the first question above, you know that:

• Any *sequence* of five cards will get you to one particular chair at the top of the tree.

If you know how to answer the second question, you can see that:

• No matter what *chair* you want to reach at the top, there is a sequence of five cards which will get you there.

Since the number of chairs is reasonably small, let's write down the complete list of all possible ways the card drawings could come out, with L for "left" and R for "right."

Prize Catalog		
Prize Number	Tree Directions	Usual Binary Notation
0	LLLLL	00000
1	LLLLR	00001
2	LLLRL	00010
3	LLLRR	00011
4	LLRLL	00100
5	LLRLR	00101
6	LLRRL	00110
7	LLRRR	00111
8	LRLLL	01000
9	LRLLR	01001
10	LRLRL	01010
11	LRLRR	01011
12	LRRLL	01100
13	LRRLR	01101
14	LRRRL	01110
15	LRRRR	01111
16	RLLLL	10000
17	RLLLR	10001
18	RLLRL	10010
19	RLLRR	10011
20	RLRLL	10100
21	RLRLR	10101
22	RLRRL	10110
23	RLRRR	10111
24	RRLLL	11000
25	RRLLR	11001
26	RRLRL	11010
27	RRLRR	11011
28	RRRLL	11100
29	RRRLR	11101
30	RRRRL	11110
31	RRRRR	11111

The last column in the table above says the "usual binary" notation, which is nothing more than using "1" for "R" and "0" for "L." (The use of "1" and "0" is a very good choice for some reasons, like making arithmetic easier to think about, but any labels are strictly for the benefit of human observers. The machine itself typically gets its charge out of nonverbal volts.)

What this "binary tree" illustration shows very graphically is that you can get a lot of possibilities (thirty-two chairs at the top of the tree) specified *exactly and uniquely* by relatively short binary (i.e., two-choice-at-a-time) sequences. If you need a comparison, you can think of ordinary English words, which are 26-choice sequences. (In making up an English word, you have twenty-six choices for each of the word's letters. It makes sense that binary sequences used by computers are called **binary words,** or just "words" for short. The elements of the sequences, whether written as "L-R," "0-1," or whatever your favorite ying and yang are, are usually called "**bits.**" (It might be nicer conceptually if bits were simply called "letters," but that would cause confusion of its own.) Thus there are two-bit words, "00," "01," "10," "11," and six-bit words like "010010," and so on. Unlike human language, the binary language for a particular computer uses only words of a fixed length, and you will hear people talk about **eight-bit computers** or **sixteen-bit computers**, depending on what word-size the machine uses. (None of the human analogies like "two-bit author" or "four-letter word" are applicable.)

In the binary chairs example, we got thirty-two possibilities out of strings of only five cards, that is, five-bit words. By taking longer binary sequences, we can increase the number of choices at a tremendous rate. Consider making two copies of the tree in our example above, and placing them side by side. The number of possibilities (chairs at the top) would *double,* to sixty-four. If we call one of the new trees the "right tree" and the other the "left tree," we can join their bases together to make a new fork at the bottom of the whole structure. Players starting at this new bottom fork would only have to draw one more card than in the old game (six cards instead of five) to get to any point at the top of the new "super tree." The usefulness of this tree-grafting trick is that you can do it over and over again, *doubling* the number of possibilities every time you join the bases of two identical trees, but only making it necessary to draw *one more card* to get to any place on the top.

Great Trees from Little Acorns Grow

What does all of this forestry have to do with computing? Simply put, we have discovered that a huge number of possibilities can be specified by binary strings of fairly short length. Thus, we can use a language of binary words for communication within and between logical devices; and using reasonably short words, we can specify a very large number of different possible things for the device to do. Many early home computers were designed to talk to themselves in binary words of length 8, so that a single word in their language could specify one out of 256 different possibilities. Home computers using words of length 16 (65,536 possible words) and even longer will soon be common. Of course, as with English or any other language, words may be combined to specify something together. Just as the word "chairperson" represents something distinct from both a chair and a person, two binary words can be considered together to make a new meaning or possibility. Computers which can handle long word lengths, provided they are sensibly designed, are inherently faster and easier to program than computers with a more limited vocabulary. The circumlocution necessary in a small-word computer to express or accomplish anything complicated is not only time consuming when the program runs, but mentally burdensome to system designers.

All right then, you should now be convinced that the computer language, even composed as it is only of a bunch of "yes" and "no" pieces strung together, is flexible enough to say whatever you would want it to. In particular, any set of instructions or collection of facts which you could write down in English can be handled by the binary language, and consequently can be stored, searched for, and acted on automatically by a computing machine operating on its own binary home turf.

Let's do something specific, with a five-bit computer. Five-bit binary words give us thirty-two possible things to say with a single word, as we found out in the binary chairs example. The most reasonable definitions to give your thirty-two possible binary words depend on what kind of a message you want to get across. If you speak English, personally, a common thing to do is to use up twenty-six of the thirty-two possible five-bit binary words, *defining* each of these binary words to mean a different letter of the English alphabet. The six extra binary words left over can be used for punctuation remarks, like "end of word" (space mark), "question mark" (?), "end of sentence" (.), "pause" (,) "emphasis" (!), or "begin paragraph" (℗). For definiteness, imagine putting out all thirty-two characters (twenty-six letters and six punctuation marks), one to a chair at the top of the large "binary chairs" tree. It would be a good idea to put them in alphabetical order from left to right, so you know exactly where to find a letter when you need it. By doing this, the matchup between characters and binary words will be made—in case you've forgotten, the path to any character (chair), starting from the bottom of the tree, makes five turns through forks of the tree. If you want to get to chair 5, for example, your turns will be:LeftLeftRightLeftRight.

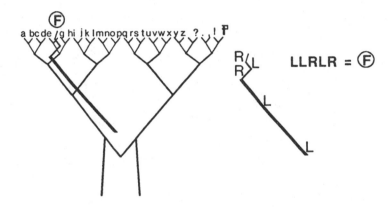

The matchup is between *the path* (written as LLRLR or 00101 to make it look like a word), and the *chair,* or *alphabetic character* where the path ends.

With all of the alphabet, as well as some punctuation so neatly specified, it is easy to get any complete English *message* expressed in the binary language: All you have to do is:

- take the letters and punctuation *characters* of the message in order, one at a time.
- write down (using 0 for left and 1 for right) the path from the bottom of the tree that leads to each character.

    Getting the English back from a binary message is even

easier, since you just:

- take the (five-bit) words of the message, one at a time.
- follow the path that they describe from the bottom of the tree to the top.
- write down whatever character you end up at.

With these definitions, it is entirely possible that you could find a portion of the memory of a five-bit computer filled with the binary information:

01110101001001111101000110000001100011011101010010011110111010011111110

Computer surgeons deal with this kind of gore routinely; in this book I will not. (So please don't faint or leave the room.) Nonetheless, such bewildering-looking and unexpressive chains of "0" and "1" are the stuffings of every computer cranium in the world, and you should at least give yourself a small pat on the back if you are now willing, undaunted, to pick apart this example with a few quick cuts of the scalpel and your binary atlas: First cut the chain up into words, just as you would an English sentence you might read. We have said that this is a five-bit computer, so it is simple to break the chain up into words—after every five characters, a new word starts. After the cutting, the pieces (words) are:

01110 10100 10011 11101 00011 00000 01100
01101 11010 10010 01111 01110 10011 11110

Now you can refer back to the tree above, and trace the path (0 for left turn, 1 for right turn) that goes with each one of these words. (For example, the first word (01110) gives the path LRRRL, leading up to the letter "O" at the top of the tree.) When the analysis is complete, the thought emerges:

01110(O) 10100(U) 10011(T) 11101(,) 00011(D) 00000(A)
01100(M) 01101(N) 11010( ) 10010(S) 01111(P) 01110(O)
10011(T) 11110(!)

Since guilt is not usually imputed to machines, we presume this phrase is stored in memory as part of a play, or perhaps as a message to be sent to the computer's **speech module,** when the neighbor's dog comes digging in the rose bushes (smelling just as sweetly for all the change of being called "10001 01110 10010 00100 10010").

Knowing that the binary language is rich enough to go far

beyond "yes" and "no" is part of the story, and perhaps a large part of the story, of why and how logical devices can operate. To complete the story, we need at least two more major pieces:

- How do logical devices **store and communicate** their binary information?
- How can these machines **transform** binary information to produce new binary information?

Storing and Communicating Information

You will probably be surprised to discover that the process of storing and communicating information, at least at the conceptual level, is quite simple. The simplicity is due in large part to our decision to stick to the binary, or digital, language. Since all information is ultimately going to be reduced to strings of 1s and 0s, any memory we might want to make can be made up of an orderly array of individual cells, and each cell needs only to be able to store a "1" or a "0."

Rather than jump right into the world of electrons, which is where most of the storing and transmission of data takes place right now (but the photon is coming on strong, thanks to Ma Bell and others), let's stick to something a little more tangible, like plumbing. There are many analogies, in fact, between plumbing and electricity—for example, you could say that *voltage* pushes **electrons** through a wire the same way that *water pressure* pushes **water** through a pipe. So, if you follow through my initial explanation, managing to keep your mental powder dry, we can restate the whole business of how to make a memory again later, simply converting all the plumbers into electricians. Initially, at least, you won't have anything more mysterious to deal with than garden hoses and buckets. (Unfortunately, I can't claim credit for discovering that plumbing can be used to transmit information. An advertising agency recently estimated the size of the television audience for one of its programs by measuring the drop in the water pressure of New York City when the program took a commercial break.)

Memories Are Made of This?

We are going to consider storage and communication here, and the two topics are closely related. That is, they must be closely matched in a logical device for this device to function well. An example is the technology of television, which is nice for communication, but up till now has done little but shuffle around pictures because of the lack of flexible and compatible memory devices. With the advent of videodisc and other random-access memory technology, television and other video devices have the potential to become integral parts of computing systems. (In a **random-access** system, you can retrieve any piece of information you want, without going through the retrieval of other pieces of information to get to it. This contrasts with **serial-access** devices, where to get one piece of information, you have to go through all the information in front of the piece you want. The early home videotape recorders have essentially serial access, i.e., you have to play through the tape in order to get to the scene you want. Videodisc technology makes it possible to go essentially immediately to any picture stored in memory, in much the same way that a phonograph needle can be picked up and put down on any track of the record, without playing intervening tracks. Even better, the search for the picture on a videodisc can be controlled by logic circuits, so that the picture will be found quickly and read without any noticeable degradation. Hi-fi recordings made by this technology will sound the same on the thousandth play as they did on the first.) Despite their interrelation, we will discuss memory first and communication later, but it is important to bear in mind the moral of the lost book in the library: If you can't get the information, it is useless.

Suppose you want to get your phone number stored by a logical device (i.e., a memory), so that you can send it to someone. What could the memory look like, and how would your phone number be stored in it? Logical memories are inherently as simple as the binary language they deal with. In fact, to store your phone number

. . .

**...you could make a logical memory from fifty
buckets set up in your backyard.**

If you think writing it on the kitchen blackboard makes a lot more
sense, hold on a minute. By the time the buckets get replaced by tiny
electron holders, we'll have a lot more of them in the memory, and
room to hold vastly more than your kitchen blackboard. Besides, we
want a better way of blasting this information all over the universe
than you can manage by copying it off the blackboard.

Let's say your phone number is, with area code, 202-555-
1212. A bucket, for our purposes, will only be used when it is
completely full of water or completely empty. (By now, you may
be expecting this kind of all-or-nothing attitude in Binaryville.) As
in the picture above, we can arrange our fifty buckets in ten rows of
five and we will have one row for each digit of your phone number.
Now, the question is, how to get each digit properly stored in the five
buckets assigned to it? If you look back to the quiz game example,
you will see that the numbers 0-9 were given the following binary
representations:

Prize Catalog		
Prize Number	Tree Directions	Usual Binary Notation
0	LLLLL	00000
1	LLLLR	00001
2	LLLRL	00010
3	LLLRR	00011
4	LLRLL	00100
5	LLRLR	00101
6	LLRRL	00110
7	LLRRR	00111
8	LRLLL	01000
9	LRLLR	01001

You may already suspect what we are going to do: Imagine for the moment that the individual *letters* "L" and "R" (or digits "0" and "1") in the above binary words correspond to individual *buckets* in a row, with "L" or "0" meaning "empty" and "R" or "1" meaning "full." For example, the list above shows that "5" is "LLRLR." The first digit in your phone number is a 2 (matched up in the table with LLLRL or 00010), which means it can be represented (in the first row of our bucket memory) by having the first, second, third, and last buckets empty, and the second to last bucket full. Looking left to right in this row, you would find: empty, empty, empty, full, empty, or 0,0,0,1,0, which is the binary code for "2." The other rows can be filled in by the same rules, so that the final version of your phone number, stored in backyard bucket memory, looks like:

(2) E E E F E
(0) E E E E E
(2) E E E F E
(5) E E F E F
(5) E E F E E
(5) E E F E E
(1) E E E E F
(2) E E E F E
(1) E E E E F
(2) E E E F E

Let's stay with the water works a while, and illustrate the next step—communication. What we will do now is to set up a system that:

- **Stores** any ten-digit number you give it.
- Whenever a command is given, it **transmits** the stored number to your next door neighbor.

Every step of the operation of this system will be clearly visible, and despite its Rube Goldberg flavor, it captures the essential workings of many modern transmission schemes, from teletypes to satellites. It just happens that for a powerful communication device like a satellite in orbit, it's easier to hit Chicago with electromagnetic radiation than with a bucket of water.

Before we do anything fancy, let's set up a hose between your yard and the next door neighbor's, with a funnel on your end and your end of the hose higher than hers. The idea is that you can dump water down the funnel, and it will run out in the neighbor's yard. Let's also suppose that your neighbor has a "bucket memory array" in her backyard which is identical to yours. The task is to make a device which is intelligent enough to retrieve the information (a ten-digit phone number) you have stored, transmit it (by means of the hose), and store it in the neighbor's memory array.

To make the idea clear, we can have you and the neighbor run through a "dress rehearsal" (galoshes everyone!) of what the device will eventually do. (I must tell you now that you both are going to play virtually mindless roles in this skit. In fact, it should be possible to train your pet dog to take your part, or a parakeet or an inchworm or anything you can enlist which is big enough to move the hose. The point is that *the mind is in the system* which will be emphasized by finally setting things up so that once the signal is given, the retrieval, transmission, and storage next door take place without further intervention.)

Now for the rehearsal: You and the neighbor will each need one additional bucket, which we can call the "start" bucket, and each have a stopwatch, or be good at counting "one thousand one, one thousand two, one thousand three," etc., to mark seconds. Your neighbor empties her "start" bucket and places the hose in it. She can now take a break and smoke or practice the violin until further notice.

On your side of the fence, we will suppose that your bucket

memory array has the phone number stored in it (in the form of binary code as above, e.g., if the third digit is "2," the buckets in the third row are empty-empty-empty-full-empty.) Your "start" bucket should be full. To bring the information out of the memory and transmit it to your neighbor, you go through the following ritual:

The Sender's Routine (algorithm)

STEP #0) Start your stopwatch at 0 seconds, then dump the "start" bucket into the hose. (This will fill up the neighbor's start bucket.) Put your start bucket back down, right side up.

STEP #1) Pick up the first bucket in the first row of the memory array (better have all the buckets close to your end of the hose), and begin to dump this bucket into the hose, as soon as the stopwatch says one minute has elapsed. (You may cleverly observe that this bucket is empty, and wonder why you are dumping it. I warned you the role was mindless.) Since the bucket you dumped was empty when you started, put it back in place upside down. (This habit of putting buckets back in their place upside down, if they originally were empty, will be generally followed. You will see its purpose.)

STEP #2) Pick up the second bucket in the first row of the memory array, and dump this bucket into the hose when the stopwatch says "one minute, fifteen seconds," i.e., fifteen seconds after you dumped the first bucket from the first row. Put the bucket back, upside down again since this one too was originally empty.

When you are finished with the first two steps, the first row of your bucket array, which originally stored the number 2, will look like this.

STEPS #3, #4...#50) Go through all the buckets in your memory array in the same fashion, i.e., third bucket first row, fourth bucket first row, fifth bucket first row; then to the next row—first bucket second row, second bucket second row...at last reaching the last bucket, which is the fifth bucket in the tenth row, dutifully dumping each bucket fifteen seconds after the previous one, and placing it back in the array, right side up if it was full, and upside down if originally empty.

STEP #51) Refill the start bucket and any buckets in the array which are not upside down. When finished, turn all the upside down buckets right side up.

The retrieval and transmission process, from your side of the fence, is complete. Your memory bank is in exactly the same configuration it was before the process started. In particular, if you go through all fifty-one steps again, exactly the same thing will happen, and the same *water pattern* will go through the hose. You may well wonder what your neighbor has been doing in the meanwhile, other than getting her lawn soaked. One way to find out is to read on immediately. If you care to stop now and try to figure out what would be necessary, I'm sure you could come up with a rough idea, at least so that when you see the answer, it will not seem mysterious.

The Receiver's Routine

When the receiver sees that the "start bucket" is filling up (she is expected to always have an eye on that bucket, which is why it serves as a starting signal), she starts her stopwatch at 0 and dumps all the buckets in her memory array, setting them back right side up. (This process "clears" the memory, and effectively erases any previous information it might have stored, such as her old boyfriend's number back in Davenport.) There may be a lot of clanging, as she dumps forty buckets in sixty seconds. She then takes the hose coming from your side of the fence, and puts it over the first bucket in the first row of her array when the stopwatch says "one minute." She holds it there for fifteen seconds, and then moves it to the second bucket in the first row. After fifteen seconds, she moves to the third bucket in the first row, and so on, until she reaches the last bucket in the last row. She then dumps her "start" bucket and goes back on break.

Due to the fact that the actions of the sender and the receiver are **synchronized,** the neighbor is holding the hose over a bucket in her array at exactly the time when you are dumping the bucket from that position in your array, and she ends up with full buckets in her array at *all the positions* and *only the positions* where you had full buckets in your array. Since the **configuration** of her backyard memory array is now exactly the same as yours, the transfer of **information** is complete.

What Have We Done?

By now you may understand the whole communication-by-bucket-brigade scheme perfectly well. (I fondly hope you do. If not, you might even consider play-acting the routines of the sender and receiver mentally, whether or not you want to go whole hog and actually try it with a friend, using paper cups and straws, actual buckets and hoses, or whatever.) Any ten digit number, (not just 2025551212) that is set up in the buckets can be transferred to the neighbor, provided she can carry a hose, read a stopwatch, and has about fifteen minutes to spare. So what? One way of looking at it is that your neighbor can now read off your phone number, if that's what you sent, and call you up for a luncheon date. If she had to guess your phone number by dialing numbers at random, one per second, it would take on average about five billion calls to reach you, even if she never dialed the same number twice. Even for a quick dialer, that's about 150 years at one call per second.

As we all know, modern logical devices don't involve buckets, water, and hoses—they are usually electronic. What these devices lack in obviousness, they more than make up for in usefulness. Electronic circuits, which are inherently no more complicated than the bucket routine just outlined, can easily be made today with densities of 10,000 elements per square centimeter, and support transmission rates on the order of one million bits per second. (Our backyard bucket example was a fifty-bit, i.e., fifty bucket, transmission.) Using electronics rather than aquatics, this information could be stored in about as much space as the period at the end of the last sentence, and the transmission could be carried out in the wink of an eye (Actually, about ten times faster than the fastest shutter speed on a good camera.)

Decisions, Decisions

It is a great step forward to understand that information can be communicated to machines to be stored and transmitted by them. The storage and transmission process can become a fine art in itself, as anyone who is interested in high fidelity recording can attest. Today's logical devices are nonetheless infinitely more interesting than the best high fidelity equipment of only a few years ago, and in fact will soon be the basis for most home high fidelity devices. The key to this superiority is the ability of logical devices to actively process and **transform** the information they communicate and store. Before the advent of logical devices, systems capable of making decisions, and communicating and recording permanently the outcomes of these decisions to be the basis of further processes, were composed of only one type of component—*homo sapiens*. We are no longer alone.

Logical devices are essentially machines capable of decisions. These decisions may be something as simple as deciding whether the square root of two is bigger than 57/50, or as complicated as finding a winning response to an opponent's chess move and deciding the most likely disease of a patient with a given set of symptoms.

How can such machines possibly be built? Certainly, those little electrons aren't smarter than humans? The answer is twofold:

- Logic in itself, the if-then state of affairs, is nothing too complicated. When you decide that 1 is bigger than 0, you are thinking logically, if not very deeply.

- If we make the outcomes of logical events storable and easily transportable (which is what the previous section of this chapter was about), simple logical **components** can be arranged and interconnected into interesting and much more complicated **systems**. The function of the entire system, considered together as a single logical device, can then be quite impressive.

To produce a reasonable understanding of how computers compute without going into large circuit diagrams, I will simply describe a few of the simplest and most fundamental logical devices. To illustrate how these devices can be put together as building blocks of a complicated system, we can then invent a few party games, where individuals play the roles of the elementary logical devices. The examples themselves are not complicated, but they will enable you to appreciate a recurring theme:

> A well organized structure can produce interesting and complicated operations, even though the individuals (basic elements) it is made of have very limited capabilities.

At the end of the chapter, we will take a quick look at one possible way that the elementary logical devices can be (and, in fact, currently are) manufactured out of silicon, metal, and so on, to operate electronically.

Building Blocks—The Simple Logic Elements

In order to get beyond the stage of shuffling information from one place to another, logical devices have been developed which are active **message processors** as well as message transmitters. By now, of course, you will not be at all surprised that these messages are going to be coded in a "0-1," "yes-no," "high-low," binary language. In the backyard bucket memory example above, you might think of the **hose** as a logical device, with perhaps the simplest imaginable operation—It takes a "1" (i.e., a full bucket) at its **input** from the funnel, and produces a "1" at its **output**. On the other hand, a "0" at its input results in a "0" at its output. (An empty bucket at the funnel end means no water out on the neighbor's side.) Such a logical device is hardly fascinating, but eminently useful. We will call this device a **path**. Paths are fundamental to both the internal workings and the external communication of logical devices. In modern logical devices, paths typically consist of electrically conductive material (often deposits of metallic film on the microscopic scale, and wires or metal pins on the human scale), but in some recent innovations, logical paths may be light pathways on a microscopic scale or optical fibers on a larger scale.

> **Logical paths** insure that the simple capabilities of the other elementary logic components can be coordinated.

Still Simple: NOT and AND

Believe it or not, we will only discuss two more types of elementary logic components here, beyond the simple path. With these simple building blocks, you will have the essential flavor of the workings of complicated logical devices, and see how the large devices are nothing more than orderly networks of the elementary components. The NOT element (you can pronounce it just like the word "not;" the capital letters are merely to avoid confusion) is the most basic logical component beyond the simple path. Whereas the path is the "yes man" who says "yes" if you say say "yes" and "no" if you say "no..."

> ...the **NOT** element is Mary-Mary-quite-contrary, who says "no" if you input "yes," and "yes" if you input "no."

In terms of input and output (which sounds more impressive), we can say that the output of a NOT element is the reverse of its input (if you want to be technical, call it the **complement** of the input). If NOT is Mary-quite-contrary, then AND is All-or-Nothing:

> The **AND** takes several inputs simultaneously, and only gives "high" as output if all the inputs are "high."

Any one of the inputs thus has "veto power"—if any input is "no" or "low" or "0," then the output is guaranteed to be "no-low-0." The AND type of decision making, although simple, is familiar and useful to all of us, since most of the things we decide to do will only be done if a variety of conditions are met. We will go on a picnic if:

A) The weather is nice.
B) The car is working.
C) Mom and Pop can be there.

Your picnic decision is thus an AND, where the inputs are A, B, and C above, and the output "picnic" is "yes" just when input A **and** input B **and** input C are "yes."

Truth Tables

The elementary logic components we have considered, paths, the NOT, and the AND, exhibit a characteristic feature of logical devices in general: These devices have a collection of **input channels,** each of which can receive a "0" or "1," and a collection of **output channels.** (The input channel for the hose is just the end that the water goes in, and the output channel is the end that the water goes out. The committee chairperson takes the opinions of the committee as inputs, and provides her opinion as an output. Our simple examples each have only one output channel.) Every possible pattern of 0s and 1s on the inputs of a logical device produces a definite pattern of 0s and 1s on the device's output. In the simplest case, where the device has only one output connection, this means that every possible pattern on the inputs is either a "yes" pattern, causing a "1" on the device's output whenever it appears, or a "no" pattern, which causes a "0" output. "Yes" patterns on the inputs always give "1" on the output; "no" patterns always give "0." Because of this fact, that every pattern on the inputs gives only one pattern on the outputs, the operation of any logical device can be neatly summarized by giving a so-called **truth table.** This table is simply a list of all possible patterns for the inputs of the device, each input pattern paired with the output for that input pattern. Here are the truth tables for the components we have discussed so far:

Logical Path	
Input	Output
0	0
1	1

NOT	
Input	Output
0	1
1	0

AND		
Input 1	Input 2	Output
0	0	0
0	1	0
1	0	0
1	1	1

Logic Symbols

Logical devices which have very many inputs and outputs cannot be described practically by making a list, one by one, of all the rows of their truth tables. Notice that devices like paths and NOTs with one input channel have two possible patterns of input, 0 or 1, two input channels means the four patterns 00, 01, 10, and 11, and so on, with the number of patterns doubling with each additional input, to the point where no one would print or read such enormous tables. The surprising and fortunate fact though, is that any logical device, no matter how many inputs and outputs it has, and whatever its truth table connecting inputs and outputs, can be constructed from the simple elements—paths, NOT, and AND—that have just been described. The situation is much the same as with ordinary arithmetic: There is no need to specifically learn how to multiply (3,235 x 2,172) or any such particular pair of numbers, provided you can do the elementary multiplications (1 x 1), (1 x 2), (2 x 2), (1 x 3)... (9 x 9), and know how to put the elementary multiplications together to find a larger product. Similarly, there is no need to write the enormous truth table of a complicated logical device. We can simply describe this device pictorially as an interconnected pattern of elementary devices, whose simple functions are well known.

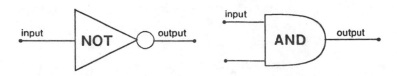

In *logic circuit diagrams*, the NOT and AND elements are represented by these symbols.

Paths connecting the outputs of some components to the inputs of others are simply drawn as lines between the components.

You will now have the chance, with an example, to become the designer of a very simple logical system. We will start with the description of what this new system should do, then write down its truth table, and finally draw the logic circuit diagram which shows how it can be constructed using only NOTs and ANDs, and paths between them.

The purpose of the example is not to make a design engineer out of you, unless that is your natural bent. Most people will not really deal with computers and computing at such a fundamental level. Nonetheless, if you understand this fundamental design process, you should feel that you are on solid ground understanding how it is that the more complicated devices you eventually deal with *really* can be constructed, with no magic involved. To use an analogy, most of us will be chefs in the world of computing, and will have little direct contact with the underlying chemistry. Nonetheless, since cooking is fundamentally a chemical process, the chef who knows chemistry will certainly understand his art in simpler and less ritualistic terms, and may even be apt to produce some worthwhile innovations due to this understanding. In this design exercise, we will build an OR device. (Just like "or," but a logical device.)

Building an OR Device

The OR device is very similar to the AND in that it represents a decision process with which we are all familiar. The OR device has one output, which is "1" or "true" if *any* of its inputs is "1" or "true." Imagine these devices as committee chairpersons in a feasibility study. The AND is Mr. Pessimist, who polls all of his members (inputs), and says, "No, the plan won't work," unless *all* of the members say "yes." In this context, the OR is Ms. Optimist, who will say "yes," if any of the inputs is "yes." If you wake up in the middle of the night, you may suspect that a burglar is at work if:

1) You hear noises on the roof OR

2) Someone is tampering with the door OR

3) The sound of breaking glass is coming from the kitchen.

Your decision to call the police is thus an OR decision based on three possible inputs, and if you want to make an electronic burglar alarm, you can bet that it will have to incorporate a logical device which has this OR decision capability. For definiteness, let's look at an OR component with three inputs. There could be as many inputs as you like for a particular OR device, just as the optimist and the pessimist could head committees of any size. The truth table for a three-input OR device is given below, and if you take a minute, you can probably write it down before looking:

OR			
Input 1	Input 2	Input 3	**Output**
0	0	0	0
0	0	1	1
0	1	0	1
0	1	1	1
1	0	0	1
1	0	1	1
1	1	0	1
1	1	1	1

All right, we have an OR component specified. Now how can we make it from paths, ANDs and NOTs? We can describe the way an AND device works as follows: **"If any input is *no* the output is *no*."**

Stated this way, we get a clue that AND and OR are very similar, if we give the OR's description as: **"If any input is *yes*, the output is *yes*."**

I'll write the descriptions under each other, for emphasis:

Comparing AND and OR									
AND function:	If	any	input	is	*no*	the	output	is	*no*
OR function:	If	any	input	is	*yes*	the	output	is	*yes*

The solution is now clear—we can make an OR component by somehow changing "no" to "yes" in an AND component. Of course, the NOT fills the bill perfectly for doing this, since it is designed to reverse things. So, to make an OR...

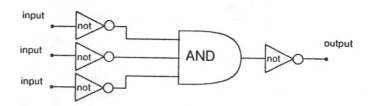

...we take an AND component and put NOTs before all its inputs and after its output.

Suppose one of the signals coming into an input is "yes;" the NOT we have put on that input will make it a "no." Now, this input to the AND is a "no," so the ANDs output will be "no." But then, the NOT on the output of the AND changes this "no" to a "yes." Also, if none of the initial inputs is "yes," then all of the (reversed) inputs to the AND will be "yes," triggering the AND to say "yes." This "yes" is reversed by the final NOT to make the final output "no." With one AND and four NOTs, we have indeed made an OR device.

Logical Party Games—Post Office Revisited

You now have all the tools at your disposal to design the logic circuit for any device you could imagine. The one thing you do not know is how the logical devices (NOT, AND, and path) can ac-

tually be constructed out of physical materials to operate electronically. (We do have some aquatic technology from the backyard
bucket example, but that's hardly practical.) These physical details
will be discussed at the end of the chapter. For the time being, we
can think in terms of organizing party games, where each player is
a NOT or an AND element, and players are connected by "paths"
made of string. Each player will then have one or more input strings,
and one output string. We will represent:

- "high" or "1" by a taut string.
- "0" or "low" by a slack string.

      In this scheme, the NOT player pulls on his output string
if his input string is loose, and lets his output string go slack if his
input string is taut. The AND player pulls her output string if all
of her input strings are taut, and leaves the output slack if any of
the input strings are slack.

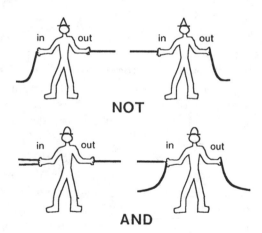

The party game versions of NOT and AND.

As party game organizers, our task will be to connect the input
and output strings of a gathering of players of this sort together so
that something amusing happens. If you can organize such party
games, then you could make perfectly believable electronic versions,
with batteries, pushbuttons, and flashing lights. The players would
be replaced by those little cockroach-looking silicon chips, and the
strings by wires. (In keeping with the party atmosphere, you should
know that most electronic "chips" you have seen would be called
DIPS, for "dual inline package," by the cognoscenti.)

As with most party planning, it's best to start simple here, with something that only involves a few guests. A nice simple game would be the "memory cell" game, where the players are interrelated to be a logical memory cell. We all know that computers have memories, and there could hardly be anything more basic to construct. To make a **memory**, we need to have a device with (hopefully many) different states, which can be put into any one of its states by a command from the outside, and will stay in that state until it is reset. A modern logical memory, like the backyard bucket memory used earlier in this chapter, is nothing more than a network of **memory cells.** A very useful memory cell, called a **latch**, can be designed with two inputs and one output:

- The **output** of the latch cell shows what the cell is currently "remembering," either a 1 or a 0.
- The cell's **command** input, by changing from 0 to 1, signals the cell to forget what it has previously stored.
- The cell's **data** input tells what new data (1 or 0) to store, when the command input signals it to forget old data.

As long as the command input is "0," the cell is "latched," and remembers its information unchanged. In terms of the backyard bucket example, the latch memory cell is just like a single bucket. Without such basic memory cells, nothing would ever get remembered. Once the basic cell can be constructed, larger memories can rapidly be built up.

It would be good to convince yourself at the start that neither the NOT nor the AND players, by themselves, could be a memory cell: Presume that when you do nothing to an input string it goes slack. Then the undisturbed NOT player's output is always taut. If you come along and pull his string, the output will go slack, but only as long as you maintain the input. Similarly, the normally slack output of an AND can be made taut, but only as long as you keep the inputs taut. That just won't do for a memory, which must change according to what you input, and *stay* that way until further notice while you go away and do something else.

One NOT will not work, but two NOTs will (something positive from two negatives). Basically, we connect the NOTs output back to its input, with the second NOT used to keep the system from vacillating. Imagine NOT, the Mary-quite-contrary, in an echo chamber. She initially says "yes," hears the echo "yes" and says "no," hears the echo "no" and says "yes" and so on until something breaks the cycle. However, if Mary were on the telephone to another Mary-contrary, she could say "yes," (and receive "no" from the other Mary) forever until interrupted. If the first Mary could be convinced to begin the conversation any way we wished, the process would provide a memory cell: We could check back at any later time, and they would still be at it, with the first Mary constantly repeating the word ("yes" or "no") she began the conversation with. Here is the logical version of the two-Mary's loop:

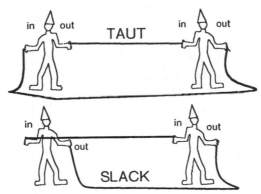

If two NOTs are looped together, the output of the first NOT will remain steady in either the taut or the slack state.

In the party game, you might well be content with the two-NOT loop as a memory cell, but you would have to go around manually and set it up in whatever state you wished to store. In order to make the process more automatic, we introduce a new player, the NOR. The NOR says "yes" just when *all* of her inputs are "no." The NOR is fundamental enough that you may prefer to think of it as a single player (logic element), and logic circuit designers often depict it with a single symbol:

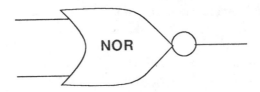

The logical NOR symbol.

Like every other logic function though, the NOR can just as well be built from NOTs and ANDs. In fact, if you look back a few pages to where we built up an OR element from NOTs and ANDs you can see that a NOR could be built easily as well, simply by leaving out the final NOT on the output:

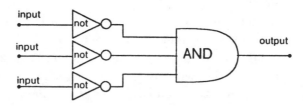

A logical NOR made from AND and NOT

Our immediate interest in the NOR is that it gives us a way to automatically interrupt the two-NOT-loop so that it can be changed automatically by *sending a signal,* rather than by some extraordinary intervention. The resulting memory cell is a true logical device, able to be **controlled** by the same binary language it **stores.**

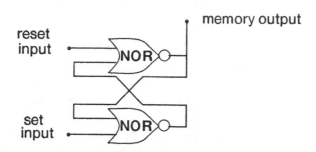

Replacing the NOTs in the two-NOT loop with NORs provides us with "*set*" and "*reset*" inputs.

A "yes" signal on the *set* input will put the memory cell in the yes state, and a yes signal on the *reset* input will put the memory cell in the no state, where it will stay until further notice. The simple automatic cell above is called a **set-reset** or **SR flip-flop.** It is not quite as flexible as the latch memory cell we have set out to design, but can easily be souped up with a few more components:

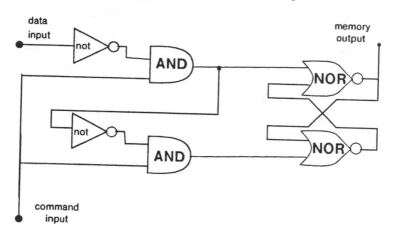

With additional elements added, the set-reset flip flop becomes a "latch" memory cell as described above.

I would not advise you to be carried away at this point with your knowledge of logic circuits; building the world's next supercomputer may be a bit beyond your reach. Nonetheless, you should feel that you understand the basics:

- Information is coded a yes-no binary language.
- Communication is by means of high-low signals over paths.
- Decisions are made by interconnecting NOTs and ANDs.
- Storage is handled by arrays of memory cells.

In fact, if your interest and talent should lead you to become a logic designer, you might not need to know very much more about binary coding and communication and memory devices than you do now. The major effort would be in acquiring skill at organizing logical structures, starting from NOTs, ANDs and basic structures like ORs, NORs and others built up from them, into sophisticated and efficient devices.

A Quick Visit to Siliconsville

Early in this chapter, it was promised that you would eventually understand why a computer could be affected by a cosmic ray, but not by its frustrated operator's shouting. If you have been following along, you should know now that the operator won't have any effect by shouting: "May you chase your tail till your circuits burn," or any other appropriate curse, unless he can transfer his tail-chasing program to the computer's innards, all properly broken down into binary form and stored in memory cells. Unlike shouting, cosmic rays *can* be disruptive to a computer's functioning because they can travel, like x-rays, through the computer's exterior and cause an **electrical change** within. The change is minute, and would have no noticeable affect on humans or on the early room-sized computers. Unfortunately, modern logical devices are constructed from microscopic components such as memory cells, whose states can be altered completely by a microscopic electrical change. (The party-game logic components described above would not be affected if a fly happened to enter the room and sit on a string. If the components were scaled down to be a thousand times smaller, the fly would be a major hazard, changing "no" to "yes" wherever he landed and stretched a string.) The **detection** and automatic **correction** of such externally caused errors is a central issue in both computing theory and in the practical design of machines.

The Metal-Oxide-Silicon (MOS) Technology

The logical revolution is underway because of the sophistication of the **microelectronic** technology it is based on. Without this base, which makes it possible to automatically fabricate logical devices to **microscopic** dimensions, computers would be merely clockwork curiosities and expensive tools for the privileged few. No cursory discussion of the microelectronic circuits used to make logical devices can do justice to the variety of the subject and the creativity of many workers in solving thorny design problems. Nonetheless, it is true that any logic function can be built up by combining the **NOT** and **AND** components, and so the following brief tour of NOT and AND in Siliconsville should give you some real insight.

The building blocks of present day microelectronics are silicon-based **semiconductors**. The key idea in understanding semiconductors is the notion of **electron mobility**. In order to produce electric current, the electrons involved have to be mobile enough to respond to the pressures (voltages) imposed. If you are stuck at a cocktail party talking to a bore, the pressure certainly exists for you to move away. Nonetheless, because of crowding, politeness, or other considerations, you may not be mobile enough to do so. The molecular structure of **silicon** provides a lattice of positions for electrons. This lattice could be compared to an egg carton, but with its individual wells (positions) for *electrons* instead of *eggs*. An extra egg would have no well to rest in, and tend to be very mobile. In pure silicon, there are no extra electron "eggs" to be mobile, and electric pressures and currents are not easily transmitted from one location to another on the lattice. An impurity such as phosphorus can be introduced into the silicon lattice in small amounts without breaking up the crystal structure, but since phosphorus has one more available electron than silicon the electrical properties change substantially: the extra electrons from the phosphorus rattle around like eggs without wells. The resulting hybrid crystal becomes a **semiconductor**.

The hybrid silicon-phosphorus crystal would not be very interesting simply as an electrical conductor. Ordinary metals like copper and tin transmit electricity much better. The more useful characteristic of a semiconductor crystal is that its mobile electrons can be pushed away from a region of the crystal if an external electric field is present. At a very fundamental level, this is a NOT in the making: A conductor **X** is positioned so that an electrical effect in **X** will push away the mobile electrons from a region of the nearby silicon-phosphorus crystal **Y**.

This strategic positioning of crystals next to each other makes it possible to *stop* an electrical event which needs **Y** as a conductor by *starting* an electrical event in **X**, and a logical NOT can be constructed. You might imagine two adjoining rooms **X** and **Y** in which music clubs meet. A full-volume meeting of the rock-and-roll group in room **X** may flush out all of the classical music fans from the adjoining room **Y**, and prevent any further information transfer inside that room. The technical name for such an interacting juxtaposition of conductors is a **transistor**. Rather than using a single region **X** to chase away the electrons from **Y**, we can just as easily use two or three or possibly more separate blocking regions **X1**, **X2**, and so on. Then **Y**'s event can happen only when neither **X1** *nor* **X2** are active: This is the MOS version of the logic element NOR. The NOR element will do just as well as AND, as a basic logical building block with which to construct any imaginable logic function. In fact, AND can be constructed from NOR and NOT:

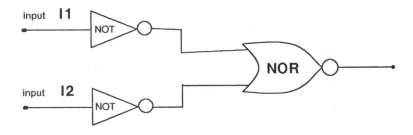

A NOR element, combined with NOTs to make an AND. The output, on the right, is "yes" just when inputs I1 *and* I2, on the left, are "yes."

The idea of the transistor junctions described above is simple enough: You can stop the flow of current in a path of crystalline silicon-phosphorus by chasing away the mobile electrons from a section of the path, much as a dam keeps fish from travelling along a river. The way the chasing is arranged, in actual microelectronic devices, is even simpler: In the MOS technology, a transistor is made by crossing one path, insulated by a thin layer of oxide, over the top of another. An electric charge on the top path will push away all the mobile electrons under it, preventing any current in the bottom path. In schematic form, here is...

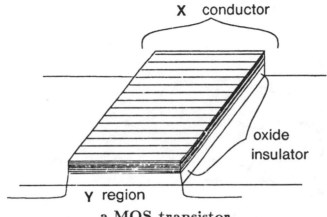

...a MOS transistor.

The paths themselves in MOS circuits are "stenciled" on top of a wafer of silicon, using masks with microscopic cutouts to outline the paths on the wafer. Successive layers of paths, with insulation "sprayed" over each layer after it is finished, are built up into a sandwich of Metal, Oxide, and Silicon, or MOS, for short. The more precisely the stencil masks can be drawn, the more transistors and resulting logic elements can be packed, in a one shot "spray paint" fashion for each of the three layers, on the surface of the wafer.

Despite the briefness of our Siliconsville tour, the essence of the landscape should be clear. (You can find a readable and detailed itinerary in the *Scientific American* issue "Microelectronics," available as a separate offering from the publisher. A complete reference is in the bibliography.) Tens or hundreds of thousands of simpleminded components like NOTs and ANDs, etched and interconnected by MOS technology on a thumbnail sized piece of silicon, comprise a sophisticated **microprocessor**. The microprocessors themselves can be "printed" almost as rapidly as old fashioned books, and sold competitively for less. With the microprocessor as a base, powerful and affordable personal computer systems are now a reality.

4

The Sensation/Action Paradigm

When does the brain wake up? We are all familiar with biological brains of various sorts, from the human type in all its variety down to that of the earthworm. These brains have little of their original appeal once they have been isolated from their natural environments. A large part of the problem is that they no longer maintain themselves properly, once removed from their sources of nutrients, waste disposal, etc. With human-made logical devices, things are a little simpler—no nutrients to be broken down, just a direct power source of some type, and typically no waste disposal necessary at all. Nonetheless, the unplugged computer and the *in vitro* brain are uninteresting and non-functional.

All right, let's plug the computer in. The *in vivo* brain and the switched-on computer have definitely more going on. Active and self-sustaining, they are now capable of varied and interesting processes. The brain may be composing a Third Symphony. The computer may be finding a pattern in the stock market or in 25,000 archeological fragments. But something is still missing: How did the brain ever discover music as a concept, or develop the symbols and patterns with which it thinks about music? How did the computer ever find the archeological fragments? Beyond the capability to maintain itself and carry out internal processes, a fully functioning brain or logical device must have external contact.

This chapter is about making contact—about the interface between a mind and its environment. By bridging this interface, a mind becomes capable of both changing and being changed by the world around it. The chapter is not about what has traditionally been called **input/output**, or i/o for short. Focusing on input/output usually means trying to improve the ease with which *humans* can communicate with a computer, and vice versa. Input and output are undeniably important, and you can find out more about them in Chapter Ten. In this chapter, though, we will concentrate on more novel and radical developments in the computer/environment interface, where humans are just one component of that environment.

The radical developments which will come about in this interface all center around the *elimination of human intermediaries*. More and more, computers will be built to actively **seek** information from their environment, rather than having it pre-processed and spoonfed to them. Just as radically, the flow from device to environment will be enhanced. First, the **display** capability of devices will improve drastically (My, how the smack of typewriter or print-hammer on paper has an antique ring to it nowadays!). In addition though, perhaps more drastically and certainly more dangerously, logical devices will routinely have the capability to *directly and physically change* the world around them. It is only a small step beyond to make these devices relatively self-reliant for energy and mobility. You need not look to vintage science fiction or the latest intergalactic fantasy movie to get an idea of what your personal robots of the very near future will be like. Scan the last five years' offerings of computerized toys, and chart the progress of these devices' decreasing power demands, increasing mobility, and ever wider range of remote control and communication features.

Human Interface—The Window is Widening

For the vast majority of logical devices constructed until now, the communication interface has been severely limited. With the first computers, one had to literally reach in and rearrange the innards in order to change the computer's idea of the state of the world, and retrieving the results of computations might involve a long and painful process such as observing and translating positions of internal switches. Imagine having to perform brain surgery to communicate!

Slowly but surely, the interface has developed. Fifteen years ago, the communication process could easily have been: Information goes to punched cards which are fed to computer which produces punched cards which are fed to an interpreter-printer which translates them and prints them, one at a time, on paper. The input side of the interface at that point was much faster than manually setting switches, about as fast as typing. The output side was faster than typing, but you could read faster than the lineprinter could print, and once it presented you with 2,000 pages of output, you were on your own as far as wading through it.

At present, the punched card is well past its peak of usefulness, and has disappeared entirely from the more modern installations. A modern child is quite likely to never see a punched card, and also quite likely to interact with a computer for the first time when the computer speaks to her. Synthetic voices are not only built into several children's toys, but programs are also available which are capable of translating text into computer speech, and will soon be as widely marketed as the toys. Such technologies, and others like them, will not only make computers easier to use, but enable large groups of people (in this case children and the visually handicapped) to participate to an unprecedented degree.

The human interface with present personal computers, for example, can be based on a powerful combination of input and output devices:

- a **display terminal** similar to a television, but able to show words, pictures, or other images with great clarity and full color, and at high rates of speed, without the unnecessary use of paper.

- **interactive editing programs** which enable the user to rapidly and automatically find, examine, modify, and store any desired portion of a large file or document (such as a program, in particular), jumping quickly from one place to another rather than paging interminably through intervening material.

- **high speed mass-storage** devices such as magnetic or optical discs. These devices make it possible, for example, to have the complete instruction manual for a computer system stored right along with your individual data and programs. Did you forget how to use a particular command, or do you wonder what commands might help you implement an idea you have? Simply key in a request, and the relevant portion of the manual will be displayed for you.

You can sit down at such a computer and call on a variety of programs, or search for programs in memory, run these programs using data which you have gathered or which have been transferred automatically from some other person or program, and systematically scan the output for key features or entire sections. Often the whole process requires only a few keystrokes from the user for direction, and thousands of lines of output may be scanned over in seconds to locate a key phrase or section.

For wealthy clients such as movie studios or rocket designers, computers are now available which support data flow to the user and from the environment at rates 100 or 1,000 times faster than "ordinary" computers. One can design automobiles or sculptures or music in a truly interactive arrangement with such a computer, where the effects of any changes are instantly seen. (Imagine the inhibiting effect on even the greatest painters if they had been required to separate their viewing from their painting; for example, if paint had to be applied in total darkness, then viewed at some later time! It is a tribute to the great orchestral composers of the past that they have flourished effectively under such a restriction.) In a few years' time, high speed interactive systems will be within the reach of small groups and individuals. Rather than patching together small pieces of output information, as we now do when computing, we will soon be presented with panoramic views, and be able to find patterns in the large scale as well as the small.

Computer Nerves and Logical Muscle Evolve

Side by side with the improvements in the computer-as-tool will be developments in the computer-as-organism. This logical brain-tool we have constructed is literally going to wake up and be a mover and shaker. The emphasis of this chapter is on the **sensation/action paradigm**, a framework of dynamic contact with the environment, and internal feedback processes, in which a brain, whether human, animal, or silicon " wakes up." As you will see, the sensation devices for computers can not only parallel the human senses, but go much beyond, enabling the computer not only to see, hear, touch, taste, and smell, but also be in direct contact with phenomena previously inaccessible to humans. Action mechanisms as well are in a rapid stage of development. In many cases, logical devices can simply be given control of existing machines, such as looms, saws, welders, or trucks. In other cases, hands, arms, or locomotion devices are tailor-made. The end product of this sensation/action development is a "new wave" of computers able to support their own independent existence, carrying out tasks with a high degree of autonomy, and exploring areas beyond the capability of humans to give immediate guidance. The coupling of human minds to computer action devices, with all the **electronic telepathy** computers are capable of, will provide an innovation as significant as the invention of the wheel. The new territories mapped out for us by these emerging electronic explorers, within the world around us and even beyond into the cosmos, will change our views and ways of thinking. The magnitude of the revelation is impossible to guess. The endeavor parallels the voyages of Marco Polo and Columbus.

Speed and the Sensation/Action Paradigm

Perhaps you have read at one time or another that a computer (or just as importantly a program written to solve some problem on a computer) has just made a significant improvement in speed. It's nice to know, for example, that you can get a mathematical problem solved now in minutes which might have taken days only a few years ago. Such an improvement though, is one of quantity rather than quality.

By contrast, speed at the sensation/action interface is making qualitative changes in the evolution of computers and the human use of them. A closed loop in which perception affects action affects perception...is possible in more and more processes. Computers qualitatively begin to look less like plants and more like animals. Speed is an essential element in making sensation/adaption processes possible for computers. These processes simply cannot happen at slower speeds. (The turtle-tracker can babysit with only a look every fifteen seconds. The birdwatcher had better be considerably quicker, if he wishes any sort of a sustained view.)

In fact, the sensation/action paradigm is only fully realizable when the sensation side has enough speed to process its input without piling up a backlog. Sensation inherently happens in "real time," rather than being a process where data is acquired to be mulled over at leisure. On the action side, increasing speed brings about devices which have the capability to alter their own states and that of their physical environment directly, on a time scale which makes the external events they perceive seem to change smoothly and predictably. Only when this level of speed is achieved, do logical devices begin to function as true perceiving, attending, conscious objects. Stimuli can actually be searched for and kept in contact.

If you bide your time a bit, you will very soon see more and more personal computers appearing based on a combination of high processor speed (ten million basic machine cycles per second and more) and large word (simultaneous processing of thirty-two bits and more) size. Such machines represent a quantum leap in power from the first generation of "home computers" which were based on eight bit words and might perform as few as two million basic operations per second. Small wonder, then, that these new machines will be capable of widely expanded use and qualitatively different levels of interaction both with their human users and with the world around them.

Personal Architecture

The majority of people in today's modern (pre-modern?) societies have little to say in the structure of the immediate environment they call "home." Whether it's an apartment, condominium, or a classic single-family detached house, your personal housebeast is a sluggish pet. Most of the improvements you can make are superficial, almost all of them disappointingly static. (Imagine being asked by a builder: "Now for your new home, would you like the front door to be closed or open?") Based on the implementation of logical devices capable of sensing and acting, individuals can begin to create a home environment for themselves which can be as changeable as the needs of the occupants, economical through efficient use of resources, and safe through constant monitoring to avert dangerous conditions before they can develop. An unparalleled range of choices and capabilities for "personal architecture" is beginning to appear. It will be as difficult in the near future to imagine a home without logic as it now is to imagine a home without electricity.

The extension and enhancement of this range of choices in the future will go hand in hand with the development of the sensation/action capabilities of logical devices. In the factories, computer muscle has already developed to the point where it will lift logs and build ships. When the muscle appears in the home, cooking meals, arranging furniture, cleaning, managing energy production and use, watching for burglars and pets, and more, the revolution embodied in our entrance to the logical age will be vividly "brought home."

To avoid any air of futurism in this discussion, we can first consider just a few of the devices available today whose operation combines the ability to sense and act, based on logical principles. These devices are less than the tip of an iceberg, but they are already impressive in relation to old fashioned technologies. We will then take a look to the near horizon beyond these devices, to see how an intelligent contact with, and control of, our home environments is emerging. Beyond the near horizon, the possibilities are even greater. The principles of sensation and action outlined in the rest of this chapter are likely to literally shape the world over the coming decades.

Aware and Active Devices of Today

One of the first "new-wave" logical devices you might have encountered, or soon will, is a programmable microwave oven. In contrast to your pocket calculator, say, this is a computer which is capable all by itself of making something happen in the real world. In addition, it has the capability of changing its actions according to its own (somewhat limited) perception of how the job is going. That is, you do not have to know in advance how long it will take to cook a turkey, but only the internal temperature (85° C. or so) that the bird should reach, regardless of its size, in order to be done. You may also decide to cook the turkey for a fixed amount of time, if you wish. The oven will keep track of this time for you, and if you are leaving at eight o'clock in the morning and want the bird to be finished at six o'clock sharp, the oven is easily programmed to turn itself on in the afternoon at just the right time to be finished by six. A key word is "programmable." You can change all the characteristics of the oven's operation by entering information on its keyboard.

Another device which you are already familiar with is the logical clock. This type of clock has replaced mechanical devices not only in microwave ovens, but in digital watches, digital alarm clocks, and whole-house light and appliance controllers. These clocks offer more than increased accuracy at low cost:

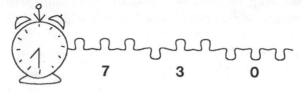

The encoding of time information into logical form enables this data to be stored and communicated automatically between many remote devices.

In the "old days," it was of course possible to make an alarm clock by having the mechanical hands of an ordinary clock press a lever or trip a switch. Rotary electromechanical switches can turn a device on and off at *several* selected times. But controlling and coordinating every electrical device in a house by such mechanical means would involve a labyrinth of wires and levers. With logical-device technology, a central logic unit can keep time and direct arbitrarily complicated patterns simultaneously for all of the electrical devices it controls. The commands are sent to the remote devices without the need for mechanical links of any kind, and with no additional wires beyond the household wiring already used to power the devices.

A final example of computer sensation/action in the here-and-now can be found in many automobiles: A large number of automobile ignition systems are presently logic-controlled, so that such things as fuel and air feeding rates and spark plug timing are controlled by a computer, reacting dynamically to changes in engine conditions, and simultaneously monitoring combustion byproducts, unused fuel, pollutants, and so on.

The Home Awakening

If we look beyond the immediate present, the prospects for computer sensation/action devices are everywhere. Let's look for a moment at the kind of things you might implement in your own home of the near future. A **heat sensor**, as we have already seen, can be used to make an oven into a programmable action device— if the computer knows the temperature without your telling it, it can act independently of your direct supervision. An even more basic use of heat sensing would be to help you drastically reduce your winter heating bill. With currently available technology, it is possible to make an extremely efficient "track-heating" system. The track-heating device would consist of an infrared heat lamp, or a more highly directional infrared source, mounted in a track fixture similar to that used for track lighting. Logical actuators (action devices) enable the lamp to position itself anywhere on the track, and point in any desired direction, as well as turn itself on and off automatically. Infrared sensing devices would enable the track heaters to "see" the people in the room, and track their movements, so that any heater which was turned on would always be pointed directly at someone. With such an arrangement, it would be possible to keep all the people in a room warm, without unnecessarily heating the rest of the room area. If you still had an old fashioned, central heating unit, you would only need the thermostat set high enough to keep the water pipes from freezing. The potential savings range from big to huge, depending on the climate. Track heating is just one possible energy saving scheme of the many you will see appearing. Logic is getting cheap as rapidly as fuel is getting expensive.

There is of course a lot of heat to be had for free from the sun, even on a cold day. The trick is to point your absorbing device, or "heat collector" at the sun when it's shining, and insulate the heat collector when there is no sunshine available. A combination of heat sensors and position actuators, similar to the track heating arrangement, will keep a **solar collector** pointed in the best direction to soak up the sun. Other arrangements with shutters, curtains, shades, etc., can let heat into a house automatically when it's available from the environment, and *keep* it in when the environment is cold, whether the "solar collector" of interest is a hot water reservoir or an ordinary room.

The classic military use of infrared detectors is "people sensing," and this use, unfortunately, has a practical place in the home environment as well.

A home security system based on a central computer and logical sensation/action devices can easily replace a Byzantine (and impressively expensive) menagerie of mechanical and electronic gadgets of the "dumb" variety.

Many of the components of the system will simply be parts of other devices ("off-duty" track-heating elements for example), and together they will sample a whole spectrum of heat, light, sound, and movement. Unusual occurrences that indicate dangers, from a fire condition developing or from a would-be burglar, or whatever, can be detected in time to deal with the situation. Action devices will give the system some real muscle and effectiveness. After all, the dedicated intruder may be less impressed by an alarm bell going off than he is by a shot of tear gas, and you can probably count on your neighbors to arrive and help you (automatically telephoned by mutual agreement) more quickly than the police can. Even without drastic measures, prevention and deterrence will be the main effects of such systems. Unless the burgling class suddenly takes an interest in electrical engineering and/or CIA techniques, people's homes should once again be castles of security. This benefit alone, given the current near-epidemic of vulnerability to crime, could motivate extensive use of home computers. Given an effective alternative, does anyone want to own something as dangerous and indiscriminate as a firearm?

On the less paranoid side of things, there is a lot more potential improvement to a home than reducing the bills and keeping it safe. The entire environment created in a home can be much more dynamic and variable. Windows, doors, and even walls can be made to appear under appropriate conditions, and otherwise unobtrusively fade into the background. The relation between form and function is the meat of architecture. At present, we are robbed of many decisions about the form of things in our personal space. Many restrictive and unwieldy forms are thrust upon us by devices we choose only for their function. Given a choice, we might keep the chairs and tables, rugs and paintings, refrigerators, and furnaces of our current home, or we might prefer to have their function, while reserving the current space they occupy for something more attractive. Few of us would continue to waste the large boxes of space given to refrigerators, stoves, televisions, and stairways and/or elevators.

Your refrigerator, for example, would work very nicely as a completely heat-tight bin under the floor, insulated to the hilt. Rather than squandering your cooling efforts as well as your space by opening up this entire enclosure fifty times a day, you could remove and replace things through a small airlock/dumbwaiter arrangement. A sensor and a home computer, utilizing only the current bar-code system implemented by supermarkets, could not only retrieve a particular item, but give a complete rundown on the refrigerator's contents, or answer a specific question, such as, "What do I have to buy if I want to make enchiladas tonight?" The "dumbwaiter" would in fact be quite bright, since it would weigh and measure the size of the things it carried in or out, and assign them to the right size bin in the hidden refrigerator, reading the bar code and relaying to the central computer the contents, weight, and storage location of this bin, for subsequent retrieval. (If you *like* the idea of wondering where the salami went, or wondering what's behind the pickle crock in your present refrigerator, you can still capture this excitement. Just ask the computer to give you a hint, rather than fetch the salami.) You could even just guess bin numbers, until the computer sees you have the right answer. More practically...

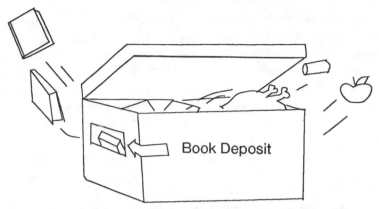

...you could ask the computer to determine, by comparing your larder contents with the ingredient lists of your cookbooks (also stored in memory), what you could have for dinner without a shopping trip.

Alternatively, you could give it your menu plans for the next few days, and have it make up a shopping list of things you need to buy.

Once you start clearing out all the prefab boxes, there will be a lot of space to redesign on your own. Your home computer will be an indispensable assistant. A phone call to a computerized furniture store will enable you to explore many possibilities, transferring whatever data you wish from their catalog directly to your home files. You can then have your computer produce a drawing of your living room or kitchen, and "try out" various shapes and styles of furniture, by putting them in the picture using the information from the store. Patterns and colors of rugs, curtains, and so on, can all similarly be tried out.

Artifacts—Creativity and Productivity

As anyone who has ever made pottery, sewn clothes, hung a door, or carved a cabinet will attest, there is an incomparable satisfaction to designing and making things "from scratch." The computer offers significant help for the design process. Tailor-made plans, for everything from sewing to carpentry, can automatically be produced by adding a small bit of information (aha, substitution again!) to patterns, i.e., programs, stored in the computer. Changes are automatically allowed for in everything from parts and supplies lists to dimensions and materials. When you add to this the real-world action capabilities we are going to explore in this chapter, the computer becomes not only a designer's assistant, but a worktool of unprecedented precision. In the future, the do-it-yourselfer can be whatever mixture of artist, craftsperson, or inventor she or he wants to and has the talent to be on a particular occasion. The artifacts, from furniture to garden irrigation systems to sculptures to home alcohol production facilities, will not only be gratifyingly unique and personalized, but capable of using new and efficient technologies as a starting point.

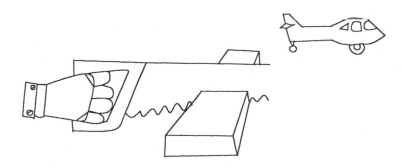

Far from being restricted to words, numbers, and other such mindwork, the personal computer promises to be an invaluable assistant in our handiwork as well.

As just one example, suppose you wish to make children's toys. In a storybook with pictures of a thousand things, there may be one or two that catch your child's eye and imagination. If you go to the store though, you will not find the winged bus or the airplane made from bananas that you are looking for. No matter: Just trace it out for the computer, and have a program work up a rough model using three-dimensional blocks. Working alternately from several views, you can call for additional material, smoothing and reshaping with simple keystrokes. Symmetry and other esthetics can be programmed in as well. When you are satisfied with your model, the computer can produce instructions for the finished product. Perhaps the instructions will go straight to a cutting device on the workbench to make a wooden figure, or perhaps the small blocks and pegs of a puzzle. Perhaps you wish to do most of the work, carving, painting, and finishing yourself. Even if the finished product could be bought in the store, there would be no substitute for the pleasure of this process. Toys, books, puzzles, and games could be made by everyone, in the same way that writing is now no longer the exclusive province of calligraphers.

The "useful" arts such as sewing will also get a big boost from personal computers. You can get an inkling of this from the appearance of computer-controlled sewing machines for home use. (Cams and gears seem to be on the wane everywhere, don't they.) Computers are already cutting fabric for clothing manufacturers. When you think about it, making clothes is an ideal area for the use of computers. For any garment, you have a basic pattern, which should be modified to suit the individual wearer. Rather than going to the store and buying some rough approximation to the desired result—printed on an awkward sheet of paper—and then making the necessary alterations by dint of rough guess or long experience, you should expect much more from your sewing store of the future. You go to the store with your measurements in explicit detail, perhaps on a cassette tape (only you and the computer will know). You put this tape in a machine at the store, and then begin to look at the various offerings for this season, pictured as they would look *on you*. You may try several views if you like, and various options suggested by the designer for tailoring, fabrics, and/or accessories. When you have come up with just the right thing, you can order by pushing a button or two. Just pick up the fabric, all of the pieces cut perfectly for your specifications, as you leave. You will have used up, and be charged for, a minimal amount of material. If you wish to buy the material elsewhere, just take your cassette tape to another yard goods store, with the information of the pattern stored on it. You may do as much or as little of the assembly and final sewing as you care to, depending on your tastes, budget, and the occasion. For the creative, patterns may even be altered substantially, starting from the designer's original idea.

If you wish to make things at home for profit rather than pleasure, a computer assistant will also give you a wide range of options. If you start from existing plans, you may wish to make size changes, modifications, and substitutions. The computer can keep track of these changes and the way they affect the materials needed, strength of the object, and appearance, giving pictorial feedback at any point. (Automobile designs have been developed using such computer feedback for many years now to squeeze weight out of cars and improve mileage.) Using the computer, one gains all the facilities of an elaborate "modeling workshop" where materials may be combined and designs tested, with a skilled "assistant" maintaining updated drawings and plans. Once the final design has been developed "on paper" ("in logic" would be more accurate), the object might be produced directly at home, or marketed as a set of instructions for machines in an **automated factory**. The automaker's slogan, "Can we build one for you?", takes on the impact of a substantial offer. An automated factory would be capable of bringing together materials for processing and returning a final product partially or completely fabricated. One would merely have to give instructions to the factory in a standard format, a task ideally suited to the computer. The information transfer involved in a typical process is not great—much less than in the familiar process of dropping off your negatives and getting color prints returned, perhaps the next day.

Old Modalities—The Classic Five Senses

In discussing the development of computer sensation, it is natural to start from the five human senses—sight, hearing, touch, smell, and taste— with which everyone is familiar. For each of these senses, we will be able to identify:

- **stimulus phenomena,** which are events in the external world relevant to the particular sense.
- **sensors,** which are parts of the body which are in direct contact with the external world, and are physically changed by the stimulus phenomena.
- **transducers,** which translate the physical changes of the sensors into signals which the brain can process.

In order to develop computer sensation we devise new sensors and transducers for the computer, enabling it to mimic the human senses of sight, hearing, touch, smell, and taste. Beyond that, one can tap other aspects of the environment to be totally new stimulus phenomena. Computer sensors and transducers can then be developed to make the computer "tune in" and become aware of these new phenomena.

Sight

The sense of **sight** in humans depends on light as the stimulus phenomenon. It is now known that the range of physical phenomena which humans sense as light represents only a portion (in fact the middle segment) of a very large spectrum of electromagnetic radiation. The colors of the rainbow show how the stimulus phenomenon of light varies over a range of colors, from reds and yellows at one end to greens and blues at the other. If our eyes were more sensitive, we would be able to look across the rainbow of colors, and instead of stopping at the red on one end and the blue on the other, we would continue to see more colors beyond. These colors are as real as the reds and blues, although we are not tuned in to them.

A little **infrared** vision capability, for example, would enable you or your computer to see people at night without lights, and cut down on your heating bills just by looking at the outside of the house and seeing where the energy leaks were. By developing **ultraviolet** vision at the other end of the spectrum, beyond the blue, we will be able to detect events with x-ray vision, or even gamma-ray vision. Computer sensors for such super-eyes already exist.

The human **sight sensor** is of course the eye, or perhaps more specifically the retina. Light energy changes the physical structure of chemicals (primarily the "visual purple" rhodopsin and iodopsin) in the retina. In the eye, two types of receptors (rods and cones) are found. These receptors differ with respect to both brightness and color sensitivity. The specialization of cells, and their strategic distribution in a pattern over the retina, make the human eye superior as a sensor to the finest color television cameras available today.

The **transducers** for sight are the cells of the retina, which, along with the optic nerve, translate the physical (chemical) changes, caused by light striking the retina, into nerve impulses which are carried as electro-chemical signals to the brain. The code for these signals, as well as the interpretive process which takes place in the brain, is only roughly understood. Cracking this "code," especially with respect to feature and pattern recognition, would provide a major breakthrough for understanding these processes in general.

Hearing

Our sense of hearing depends on waves in the air around us, pressure vibrations which are transmitted to the eardrum and bones of the inner ear to set them in motion. Unlike light, which can travel through empty space, the stimulus phenomena which produce our sense of sound must occur in a material medium. In a classic experiment, you put an electric bell in a glass container. You can see the clapper of the bell moving, and hear the bell through the glass. The air is gradually pumped out of the container, and the sound of the bell fades into silence, although the clapper can still be seen striking. No medium—no message here.

The **sound sensor** for humans is essentially the eardrum, with an intricate array of pivoting small bones, which are set in motion by sound waves in the air. As an intermediate step, the sound waves in the air are transformed by this array into vibrations of the fluid of the inner ear where they are detected by hair cells of the organ of Corti. These hair cells appear to be specialized, and "tuned" to respond only to certain frequencies. (If you hold down the "sustain" pedal on a piano, and sing a note, you will still hear the note, resonating from the piano, when you stop singing it. If you damp only the string for the note you are singing, the resonance will disappear.)

As a **transducer,** the inner ear converts the physical vibrations of its components into nerve impulses to be sent to the brain. There is evidence that the sensitivity of the ear to various frequencies changes dynamically under control of the brain, (enabling the human listener to easily follow the sound of the trumpet player in the midst of an entire orchestra of sound, for example.) Such perceptiveness and selectivity are only beginning to be realized in transducers coupled to computer programs.

Touch, Smell, and Taste

What people may refer to as a "sense of touch" encompasses a wide variety of sensitivities. Suffice it to say that humans are able to detect, through sensors involving the skin and muscles, the shape, weight, texture, and temperature of objects with which the body comes in physical contact. Impulses usually are coded and sent to the brain, but special-purpose detectors may have their own processors, enabling them to bypass the cerebral cortex altogether. Such bypass systems are usually called **reflex arcs.**

The sense of smell requires airborne chemicals as stimulus phenomena to interact with sensors in the nasal cavity. The nasal receptors of various types form an array of sensors, each type sensitive to a different kind of chemical structure in stimulus phenomena. The combined output of the various types of sensors is transmitted and integrated by the brain, enabling rapid recognition of complex scents.

Taste, like smell, is triggered by the chemical properties of stimuli, and involves primarily sensors located on the tongue. The notable fact about the sense of taste is that only four types of taste receptors (sweet, sour, bitter, and salt) are used, and yet a wide variety of taste perception is possible through the combination of the outputs of these receptors, and the simultaneous perception of smell.

New Modalities of Sense

Beyond the construction of sensors and processors for sight, sound, touch, smell, and taste, the development of logical devices will bring new senses into play. Initially, at least, these senses will rely primarily on **electromagnetic** stimulus phenomena. We are familiar already with radar, in uses from spotting planes to catching speeders to clocking the pitcher's fastball in the World Series. A computer attached to a radar device is merely "seeing" in a portion of the electromagnetic spectrum which is invisible to humans.

In the electromagnetic domain, computers attached to appropriate sensors are presently able to:

- detect and track moving objects with radar.

- sense the proximity of metallic objects.
- see temperature differences in objects without touching them.
- detect astronomical objects and events.

These capabilities can be used for guiding missiles, automobiles, or household robots. (The current uses reflect sad priorities.) Crop conditions, energy use, and forest fires can all be remotely monitored. The galaxy can be mapped with clarity in previously undetectable dimensions.

Outside the electromagnetic domain, transducers for computers are bringing other sensations within reach: **Ultrasound**, or sound at frequencies higher than humans can hear, is already in use. A thin column of ultrasound will penetrate tissue and be reflected from the boundaries between organs inside. A probe emits this sound column and picks up the reflections, obtaining only a small bit of information about the body's internal structure. The early applications involved looking only at a small area, such as the brain midline, or heart valves. The data obtained required further analysis and calculation by the user, and the technique only worked at all in cases where the location of the structure and its typical behavior were already approximately known. But, nowadays, the ultrasound probe has become more nearly an integrated computer "eye," so that the information is assimilated automatically (no punched cards needed, thank you) with transformation and integration of the stimulus performed simultaneously. As the probe is moved in systematic brush strokes over the patient, an image appears simultaneously, pieced together on a bedside television screen—a functioning heart, its problems clearly delineated, or perhaps a fetus silently waiting. Ultrasound probes connected to home computers could play a large role in a new era of medical self-help.

Chromatography and **spectroscopy** can be used to detect the chemical composition of samples, with precision down to parts per billion. Chemical analysis of this type can find the "fingerprint" of gunpowder on the arm of a suspect's coat, or detect minute quantities of marker elements planted to trace a plant's metabolism, the activity of individual parts of a human brain, or a protein's structure. **Motion** and **direction** sensors guide satellites and airplanes in feedback loops which make the inhumanly complex job manageable. (There are usually two persons in the cockpit of a modern airliner, and enough switches for at least ten hands.)

To all these new modes of perception, we can add the fact that all of the newly acquired information is inherently transportable. Television and radio have been with us long enough that hearing a live performance of the London Philharmonic, ensconced in a New York easy chair, is routine. For many people, the television coverage of the bashes and grunts of a football game, even the sweat and grimaces of the injured, makes the stadium spectator's view dim by comparison. Computers will be no less **telemetrically** aware. The new senses become wider, more powerful, and more immediate as time progresses. It is difficult to imagine the possible range of uses—scientific, technological, medical, or recreational. We have had millions of years to explore the world of the five senses. The new world is vast and uncharted.

Action Capabilities—Our Minds Move the World

By now I hope you have a good idea of how the computer can be given eyes, ears, and sensation of various sorts. But what about the action side of the sensation/action interface? Let's look at how the computer can be given muscle to **do** things, as well as sense things, on its own. After all, there are thousands of things, running the gamut from managing automobile operation to constructing buildings and dams, that we *theoretically* know how to make or make better, but *physically and technically* are not able to improve. By looking at the most popular computer applications of the early eighties, you might come to the conclusion that computers, confined to an ivory tower environment of pure thought and abstract display, will gradually become irrelevant in the face of the nitty-gritty material needs of modern societies. Nothing could be farther from the truth. Computers will soon be digging ditches (for a variety of reasons), with about the same demand for human supervision as the combines which now reap acre after acre of farmland, while the operator in the cab watches *I Love Lucy* on television.

The two parts of action are energy and control. That is, in order to carry out some physical action, you must provide energy, in a controlled fashion, to the world around you. Control and energy are independent and complementary to each other. If you are paralyzed by a clinical dose of curare, your mind will function perfectly, and your capability to **control** actions will be unaffected. (For example, you could dictate a letter using a code based on your eye blinks or your brain alpha waves, and tell your wife/husband where to move the sofa, just as well as you ever could.) Nonetheless, since you would not have direct access to the energy transfer capability of your muscles, you would not be capable of direct action. On the other hand, you would be little better off if you had the **energy capability** of your muscles, without any control of them. Like the gorilla on the golf course, you would drive 500 yards from the tee— and 500 yards again when you got to the green.

Computers and other logical devices, as you are well aware by now, excel at the **control aspect.** If you like golf, your computer could calculate, for any possible lie on the course and any set of wind and grass conditions, the best choice of club and the optimal direction and speed of your swing to get the ball up to the pin. This calculation does not, however, swing the club or otherwise move the ball. In fact, the batteries which run your calculator for weeks would never survive for more than a few seconds if you attempted to press them into service to run a club-swinging motor. You can now see the nature of our task, if we want to make a logical device capable of direct action in the physical, large scale world: We will have to provide a link between the computer's **low energy** existence and the much **higher levels of energy** needed to take physical action.

The process of linking up a low energy **control signal** to a higher energy level effect may be either a straightforward **switching** or a wider-range **amplification.** The linking process is so commonplace as to pass virtually unnoticed. A typical American home has probably a hundred switches and a score of amplifiers. Since most of us do not care to expend the energy required to do laundry by hand, we have washing machines, which enable us to supply a low energy control signal (if you don't have the strength to push the washing machine buttons, you've definitely reached a personal energy crisis), which **switches on** the much more energetic process of thumping and scrubbing clothes. If you play a phonograph record, chances are that you use an **amplifier** to boost up the low energy signal coming from the movements of the needle on the record, so that the amplified signal can drive a speaker. Other switching and amplification examples abound, and you will probably be more aware of them from now on.

The distinction between switching and amplification is just

a **digital** versus **analog** distinction of the type we have encountered before.

- If your application is of the yes-no variety, e.g., "turn on the alarm and the coffee pot at 7:45 sharp," what you need is a **switch**.

- If you want a smooth transition from low energies to high ones, such as "move the paper cone in my hi-fi speaker forward when the needle in the record player moves up, by exactly one hundred times the distance," then you need an **amplifier**.

Switches—How to Turn It On

Let's look briefly and not too technically at how **switching** works, and then consider amplification. As usual, these ideas do not require you to understand electricity. Let's suppose that your source of energy is a water wheel. There may be a lot of energy available to be picked up from this wheel; for example, to grind flour by moving a much larger stone than you would care to move by hand. Presuming that the water will be in motion all the time, how can you arrange it so that the wheel will only go around some of the time, that is, arrange a **switch** to turn the wheel on and off? There are many possible ways to make such a switch. One way would be to construct a sliding trough above the water wheel:

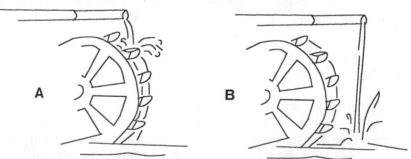

If the trough is retracted (A), water flows over and turns the wheel. If the trough is extended (B), the water misses the wheel, which does not turn.

When water power is more plentiful than other forms of energy, as it has been historically in many places and currently is in others, mills and mechanical switches of this general sort can be useful. It is much easier to slide the trough "switch" than grind the grain yourself.

The most common kind of switch for modern people is, of course, an electrical one. Rather than providing a changeable section in a water pathway as the trough-switch does, an **electrical switch** provides a removable section in the path of an electrical current. The most basic electrical switch can be made simply by taking an electrical conductor (a wire, a metal strip, etc.,) and cutting it. When the cut ends of the wire are touched together, current can flow through from one piece to the other, and when they are separated, it cannot. Any arrangement where you can easily make and break an electrical connection is essentially a switch. (By this token, any wall outlet is a switch, since you can turn any appliance on and off simply by plugging it in or unplugging it at the outlet.) Switches become interesting when they are arranged to do their job automatically.

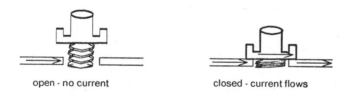

open - no current   closed - current flows

A switch which you can find in thousands of applications is the pushbutton switch.

The pushbutton switch shown in the picture is ordinarily held open by the spring, so that no current flows. When you push the button down, the top metal piece makes a connection between the input wire, on the left, and the output wire, on the right. (Most washing machines will shut off if you open the top door, and if you look around the door opening, chances are you will find the pushbutton switch which arranges this.) Pushbutton switches can be fairly large, such as the ones you will find on the doors of your car or refrigerator to turn on lights, or they can be made extremely small. A very small pushbutton switch will need very little pressure to be pushed shut, and might even be designed to be opened and closed by moving a **magnet** near it.

The variety of such mechanical switches, and the ingenuity

which has been used to arrange them, is a fascinating but anti-quated subject, much akin to the study of mechanical clockwork mechanisms in this day of the crystal and solid state watch. None-theless, mechanical switches are easily made and obvious enough in their operation to be useful in teaching about or experimenting with circuits. For example, if you still have doubts about the logic elements AND and OR which we discussed earlier, it would be salutary to make yourself an AND element and an OR element using push-button switches: If you connect two pushbutton switches in a row, a so-called "series" connection, you have made a logical AND element. That is, current is able to get through only if *both* buttons are pushed. If you connect two pushbutton switches side by side in a "parallel" connection, you have made an OR element. Current can get through if *either* or both of the buttons is pushed.

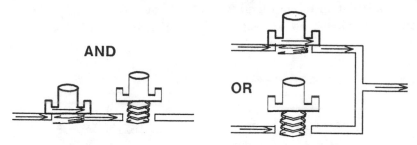

Pushbutton versions of AND and OR

If the typical 20th-century computer were a mechanical masterpiece of clockwork rather than a maze of patches and paths etched in silicon, old fashioned mechanical switches like gears and pushbut-tons would be perfectly satisfactory. The computer could control large scale events via gears and levers reaching out from its in-ternal mechanics to engage bigger gears or poke the buttons of switches. The translation of low energy to high energy would be from small mechanical changes in the computer to large scale mechani-cal or electrical events in the environment. Since computers are overwhelmingly electronic, and increasingly microscopic, we do not usually need mechanical gears and switches.

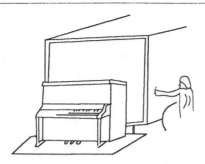

**Electronic switches must be capable of trans-
lating a** *small electrical* **change into a** *large physical*
change.

(Often, the small electrical change is translated to a bigger electrical
change several times before the final electrical cascade produces its
large scale effect.)

Before the days of silicon technology, the most popular
switch to translate a small electrical change into a big one was the
solenoid. A solenoid consists of an electromagnet connected to
something like a small (or very small) pushbutton switch. When
current activates the magnet, it attracts a piece of metal which
pushes the switch. If the electromagnet and the pushbutton switch
are very small, only a very small amount of current through the
magnet's coil will be needed to activate the switch, which will enable a much larger current to flow in the main circuit. The action interface for modern computers could conceivably be based on
solenoids, but solenoids have some serious drawbacks. First, their
electromagnets are relatively expensive to make and hard to design
to extremely small dimensions, and secondly, the mechanical parts
of a pushbutton switch are subject to wear, bad alignment, etc..
Not surprisingly, completely electronic counterparts to the solenoid,
without any moving parts, have been developed with silicon **solid
state** technology.

Presently, the two chief "silicon solenoids" are the **silicon
controlled rectifier (SCR)** and the **thyristor.** Conceptually,
these devices behave in the same way that a solenoid does. That
is, they enable a small electrical effect to open or close a much
larger electrical circuit. Their advantage is that they contain no
mechanically constructed electromagnet, no moving parts to wear
or become misaligned, and can be cheaply fabricated and scaled
down to minute dimensions. Chances are, the first "robot arm" you

install on your home computer, for drawing and cutting patterns for sewing or stained glass or woodwork perhaps, will have switches made of silicon controlled rectifiers and thyristors, and no solenoids at all. Several of the early home computers offer household current controllers based on SCR technology as optional accessories, but their expense hardly seems justified to turn on and off any single appliance. (The electric alarm clock, you will recall, has already been invented.) Newer computer accessories, enabling you to tap directly into your household wiring and transmit control messages to any device plugged in anywhere else in the home, are much more practical. The internal operation of thyristors and silicon controlled rectifiers is only peripheral to the discussion here, but is based on the same principles as solid state amplifiers, which we will discuss next.

Amplifiers—Electrical Pantographs

**When Archimedes was doing PR for the lever
a few thousand years ago, he envisioned it as
being used with a human on the long end.**

The human has to move his end of the lever perhaps a foot in order to get the other end of the lever, near the big rock, to move an inch. That's fine with the human, because he spreads out the work of moving the rock one inch over twelve inches of his pulling, and so only has to pull with one twelfth the amount of force necessary to lift up the rock directly. If, however, the lever is used backwards, with the human on the short end, it becomes a motion amplifier.

**If the human moves the short end of the lever
an inch, the long end moves a foot.**

The lever as a motion amplifier is not much use, since you can
only move it up and down. By interconnecting several such levers,
though, you can make an artist's **pantograph**, which amplifies motion in the up-and-down and side-to-side directions simultaneously.

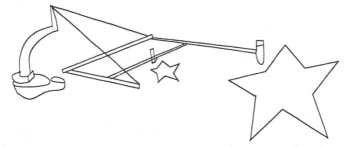

**With a pantograph, you can draw or trace a
small figure at the "short end," and an exact
replica, but of larger dimensions, will be traced
out at the "long end."**

An amplifier does for an **electrical voltage** or current exactly the
same thing that a pantograph does for motion—it changes the scale
from small to large, but keeps the proportions the same. Your stereo
amplifier might have an amplification factor of twenty, in which case
a half of a volt in will produce ten volts out, and one volt in will
produce twenty volts out, etc. (Contrast this amplifying operation
to the switching action of a solenoid, which gives you *nothing* in its
main circuit until you put in enough current to trip the magnet, and

at that point gives you the *whole shot* of whatever the circuit can provide.)

Input and Output Transducers

As you know from our previous discussion, a logical device deals with the world in terms of a binary alphabet. The sensors for a computer are devices which convert some kind of external event into this language. If the computer is electronic, which most computers you will deal with are, the sensor has to convert the stimulus phenomenon into a pattern of high and low voltages. Translating some external event into voltage patterns is not mysterious or difficult. If you can turn on a flashlight or a light switch, you know how to transfer a voltage to somewhere you need it (from the batteries in the flashlight to the bulb). It's not any more involved than turning on a faucet to get the water where you want it. The more sophisticated thing is to get the translation done automatically. If we were really interested in aquatic technology, now would be the time to discuss automatic sprinklers. Since it's electrons rather than water we want to push around, let's look at a few of the many devices by which potential stimulus phenomena like temperature, sound, motion, or electromagnetic radiation can be automatically translated into patterns of electron pushing.

Before we actually do a little hardware review, there is a point to be made about analog versus digital signals. The typical stimulus we want to sense or detect (let's say temperature to be specific), is usually a continuous, gradually variable quantity. (Temperature varies smoothly from hot to cold, so if it is 40° F. now and 42° F. ten minutes later, we know that it was 41° F. sometime in between.) This continuously variable, **analog** nature of temperature as a stimulus means that when we devise a mechanism to make temperature affect electrons, the resulting electronic effect will itself probably be a continuously variable analog change. As we all know by now, logical devices of any sort must deal with **binary**, high/low, all-or-none signals. The upshot is that if we want an **electronic logical** device to be able to sense and comprehend something like temperature, the process has two stages.

- First, the temperature (analog) effect is made to produce an electrical effect (also analog) by a suitably constructed

transducer.

• As a second step, the **analog** electrical effect is translated into a **digital** electrical effect (i.e., a pattern of high and low voltages), which the computing device can deal with directly.

All of our discussion about sensors for real computers will concentrate on the first step in the sensing process, the conversion of a continuously varying stimulus signal into an analog continuously varying output signal (voltage). (The second step, converting a voltage into a pattern of all-or-nothing voltages on the "input buckets" of some electronic logical device, is *independent* of the particular sensor being used, and so we will discuss that separately, after the various types of sensors are reviewed.) If you are put off by thinking about voltages, just imagine voltage as water pressure, pushing electrons like little bubbles through wires which are like pipes.

The two stages of getting sense knowledge into a computer can be illustrated by hauling out the garden hose again, in case you're feeling nervous about electrons, or the analog/digital distinction makes you feel schizophrenic. I will give the specifications of a hypothetical aquatic computer, and show you how a sensor can be built for it. Here are the specifications of the "aquacomputer:" The input for this device is a row of four funnels, with hoses attached at the bottoms.

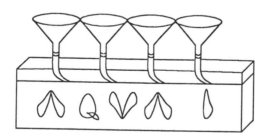

The device will check the input funnels once an hour, allowing water to flow out of the hoses for two minutes. For the rest of the hour the hoses are stopped up.

This aquacomputer is a typical logical device, and in order for it to work properly, each funnel must be either empty or completely full at the beginning of each hour. (Believe it or not, if you translate hoses to wires and water pressure to voltage, and make the time scale in millionths of a second rather than hours, the aquacomputer could be a reasonable representative of an **electronic** logical device. Of course, you have to use your imagination to think of all the interesting things which will happen to the water pattern after it is sent out from the aquacomputer's inputs, much as you find the description of a human eye fascinating knowing there is a brain for it somewhere.)

Our example will be to devise a *wind sensor* for the aquacomputer. (Actual electronic computers can be used to track wind speed and direction on board yachts, and have helped win victories in international competition.) Our simple wind detector will be a large sail attached on one side of a mast.

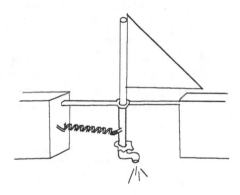

The mast is free to pivot around in a circle. The bottom of the mast is attached to a water faucet.

When no wind is blowing, the spring shown on the mast holds the faucet almost shut, and when the wind blows, the sail turns the mast around, which turns the faucet open. The stronger the wind, the more the sail is able to open the faucet, working against the spring.

At this point, we have completed Step 1 of the sensing

process. The **analog** stimulus *phenomenon*—wind strength has been converted into an **analog** *aquatic* signal—the amount of water coming from the faucet. The sail, mast, and faucet make up a sensor, and by means of this device, we have the relationship: more wind—more water, less wind—less water. This relationship is an analog one. We could run a hose from the faucet, and anchor the other end of the hose on the sidewalk, directed upwards at an angle by a nozzle so that the water from the hose arcs out and splashes down on the sidewalk some distance away.

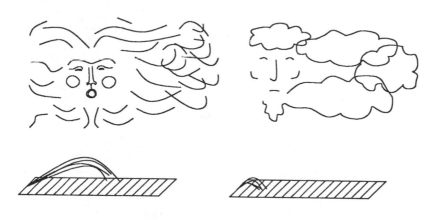

The *analogy* we have created is that the more wind there is in the sail the more the faucet will be open, and the farther away the water will squirt to the ground.

*As the wind blows, so the water flows...*In fact, we could mark the sidewalk with chalk, at various distances where the water can hit, and give these marks descriptive labels ranging from "calm" to "breezy" to "hurricane."

Now on to Step 2. How do we get the **analog** water signal translated into a **digital** signal at the input of the aquacomputer? Let me remind you that there are sixteen possible patterns we can make with the four input funnels of the aquacomputer, where each pattern is an arrangement of completely full and completely empty funnels. Here is a list:

The Sixteen Bucket Patterns				
Pattern Number	Bucket No. 1	Bucket No. 2	Bucket No. 3	Bucket No. 4
0	empty	empty	empty	empty
1	empty	empty	empty	full
2	empty	empty	full	empty
3	empty	empty	full	full
4	empty	full	empty	empty
5	empty	full	empty	full
6	empty	full	full	empty
7	empty	full	full	full
8	full	empty	empty	empty
9	full	empty	empty	full
10	full	empty	full	empty
11	full	empty	full	full
12	full	full	empty	empty
13	full	full	empty	full
14	full	full	full	empty
15	full	full	full	full

All right, let's pick sixteen different wind conditions, since that is the most information we can handle with the four buckets. (That is, if we pick more than sixteen wind conditions for the aquacomputer to sense, it will be confused, since there will then be not enough bucket patterns to give one to each condition. When some bucket patterns are shared by more than one wind condition, the aquacomputer must treat both conditions identically, since they appear the same at its bucket inputs.) Due to the analog part of the sensor which we have set up already, picking sixteen wind conditions corresponds to making sixteen chalk marks on the sidewalk. Wind condition #12, say, is *defined* to be the condition that causes the water from the hose to reach chalk mark #12.

From this point on, it's fairly simple. The possible patterns of the aquacomputer buckets have also been numbered 0–15 in the above table. (The numbering is a standard one, if you take "empty" to be "0" and "full" to be "1," as we have discussed in the previous chapter on the binary language.) We now just want to arrange it so that when wind condition #12 occurs, the bucket pattern #12 is placed at the input of the computer, and so on for all the possible wind conditions and the corresponding numbered bucket patterns.

A simple solution is to hang buckets over each of the chalk marks, to catch the water which would ordinarily fall at that chalk mark. Now run hoses from the bottom of each of these catcher buckets so that they empty into the buckets on the aquacomputer input that we want filled. For example, bucket pattern #12 is:

#1 #2 #3 #4

full-full-empty-empty

so the bucket which we hang over chalk mark #12 should have two hoses coming out the bottom, which pour into buckets #1 and #2 of the computer input and fill them up. Similarly...

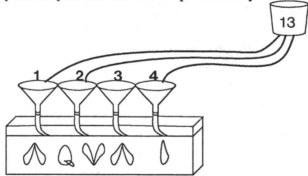

...the bucket over chalk mark #13 should have hoses emptying into the aquacomputer's buckets #1, #2, and #4.

And so on for all the chalk marks (i.e., wind conditions).

Well, so much for the aquacomputer. I hope that you can use it as an example of the basic concepts of building a sensor for a logical device. It's the kind of thing you could rig up for a science fair project, with a multiple speed electric fan as a wind source, and paper cups and drinking straws to replace the buckets and hoses. If you are clever, you can find other ways of doing this, particularly to cut down on the number of hoses (straws) used. Better yet, try to imagine sensing something else besides wind, so that it will feed into the aquacomputer inputs. There is nothing like a little hands-on to make all the mystery vanish, if by now there is still any left for you.

For the sake of realism, we must now leave the water works to see the electronic sensors used by ordinary computers.

Versatile Sensors for Computers

Light Sensors

Several types of sensors are currently in use to make a computer or other logical device sensitive to "light." (The meaning of the word "light" here is taken to be all kinds of electromagnetic radiation, from infrared to visible light to ultraviolet.) We ordinarily think of seeing light which comes to us from other sources, such as the sun or electric lights. Computers, too, can be arranged to see in this fashion. In addition, though, computers have the action capability to generate the "light" they need. With low frequency electromagnetic radiation (in the **microwave** region below infrared), the most common thing is that a sensor detects the *reflections* of radiation it has sent out as a probe. A **radar** (**RA**dio **D**etection **A**nd **R**anging) installation is like a man with a miner's lamp on his head, who sends light out in whatever direction he turns to look. A better analogy for radar would be the blindfolded person throwing tennis balls. He can tell how far away things are by how long it takes the tennis ball to hit them after he throws it, and he can even distinguish, say, between a brick wall and his neighbor's picture window. The radar installation merely replaces the tennis balls with short pulses of microwave radiation, and typically bounces these pulses off planes or unsuspecting sports cars, rather than picture windows.

A number of different types of light-sensing technologies can be used. The color television tube is the most well known light sensor, and is by far the most versatile for sensing visible light. A wide variety of other sensors also exist, specialized to react to microwave, infrared and ultraviolet light as well as visible. These other sensors can be classified as emitters, conductors, and diodes.

The color television camera is the end result of decades of interest, financial incentive, and consequent invention for detecting and transporting realistic visual images. (Network television programming may make you wonder if the effort was not misplaced.

Cheer up. As you can tell from the falling price tags, more and more television cameras will be escaping from big business into the hands of real people.) The basic idea of a color television camera is that the information in a picture can be broken down into a mosaic, and if we give the tiles of this mosaic, keeping them in order, to someone else, then she can put the mosaic back together. That is, an arbitrarily large photograph can be mailed in arbitrarily small envelopes, provided you have enough envelopes.

Let's be a little more specific. The word "camera," as in "bicameral congress" and all that, means "room." An old fashioned picture camera consists of a dark room with a small hole poked in the wall to the outside. The light coming through the hole makes an image of the scene outside on the wall of the room opposite the hole. Imagine now the following game. You are inside this room, looking at a splendid view of the Rockies, let's say. A friend is on the telephone from Kansas City, and you must describe the scene to her so that she can make a pencil sketch. To make things more difficult, your friend is not really an artist. In fact, all she has are eight lead pencils, from a #0 (really dark black) to a #7 (hardly makes a visible mark). If you tell her which one to use, she's pretty good at using it to make an "x" on the paper wherever you tell her. Can you help Kansas City get even a rough idea of what the Rockies look like, there in the clear morning air with the sun shining on their snow-capped peaks?

Yes, of course you can, if you use the television camera's strategy. Let's suppose that the walls in your room are tiled with small tiles, perhaps 100 rows from top to bottom, with 100 tiles in each row.

- The first thing you do is get your friend to make a picture of a blank tiled wall, or use graph paper with 100 rows of 100 squares each, whichever she'd rather.

- Now find the brightest spot on your picture-wall and circle it on the wall. Mark this circle #7. Now find the darkest spot, circle it, and mark this circle #0. Find a spot that is half as bright as #7, circle and mark this #4, and so forth, so that you end up with circles numbered 0–7 on the wall, and the spots inside the circles range in brightness in even steps from darkest to brightest.

- Now, just start from the tile in the upper left hand corner of the wall, and give your friend on the telephone the number of the circled point which is closest in brightness to the tile you're looking at. (The upper left hand tile probably is a piece of the sky, or one of those snow-capped peaks, so it's going to be #6 or #7 in brightness.)

- Go to the second tile in the top row and read out its brightness in the same way, and so on, from left to right. When you finish the top row, start at the leftmost tile of the second row from the top. When you finish this row, go to the third row from the top, and so forth, all the way to the bottom row.

If your friend uses the pencil numbered according to your directions, and fills her squares in left to right, top to bottom, in exactly the same order you are reading them, her end result will be a fairly creditable picture of the Rockies. If you use a lot of very small tiles, the picture will look much like a newspaper photograph. (If you find this routine strongly reminiscent of the backyard bucket memory rehearsal in Chapter Three, you are definitely catching on.)

You will be piling up quite a phone bill by relaying the picture this way, and will undoubtedly be bored by the time you read out the last tile, since there are 10,000 tiles in 100 rows of 100 tiles each. A television camera, being a typical electronic device, doesn't get bored, and is very, very fast. In fact, it will easily send pictures of the Rockies, or whatever else you put in front of it, at the rate of twenty entire pictures (not tiles!) per second, for months on end, if you like. Rather than having a tiled wall, the inside of a television camera has a coated surface much like the retina of the human eye. The locations on this retina are scanned in rapid fire succession, left to right, top to bottom, and the more light there is at any point, the higher the voltage sent out when that point is scanned. The output of the device is thus a rapid sequence of high and low electron-pushing voltages, in the same way that your telephone message was a sequence of high and low numbers between 0 and 7. At any instant, the voltage, or number sent, corresponds to the brightness of the scene at the point currently being scanned. Obviously, the television camera is only useful because a corresponding picture device, based for example on a **cathode ray tube**, can reassemble and display the picture just as fast as the camera sends out the voltages. The entire breakdown, shipping, and reassembly process is done automatically and reliably, without breaking of pencil leads or gnashing of teeth, geared or otherwise.

Color cameras carry out this whole process in triplicate simultaneously, through three filters and three retinas. Imagine your friend in Kansas City has eight red pencils (from light to dark as before), eight of blue, and eight of yellow. She could produce a full color picture by the tile method above, but for each tile, you would have to tell her not just the overall brightness, but the relative brightness of red, blue, and yellow. Combinations of these "primary colors" would produce the entire range of hues in the picture.

Lest you think that the only light sensor you can (or in fact should) consider hooking up to a computer is a television camera, it should be emphasized that the television camera, especially in the color broadcast version, is a complex and sophisticated beast, built upon an elementary (**photosensitive**) type of light sensor. The elementary sensors themselves will probably be of more interest in cooking up something yourself. We will describe several types of elementary sensors, and you can let the color television camera be your inspiration as to the potential for use.

An **emitter**-type sensor is constructed using a material whose electrons can be knocked off by radiation of the type we wish to detect. Most materials used in this fashion respond in the ultraviolet range, but materials (e.g., potassium or cesium oxide) exist which are sensitive to visible light. The liberated electrons can be made to flow through the device, and the **analogy** established is that *more radiation* produces *more flow* (current) of electrons. Useful emitters are **photomultipliers**, which are capable of detecting the most minute quantity of light; **phototubes**, which have less sensitivity but also produce less background noise; and **photocells**, which are capable (and as we all hope, will become more capable) of being used to provide **power** as well as **signal** voltages from a strong light source. Other sensors used are **photoresistive** devices; their resistance to electrons flowing through them decreases as light strikes them. The more light, the smaller the device's resistance. **Photodiodes** and **phototransistors** are based on the silicon transistor technology, and behave much like phototubes. An important use of the transistor-type devices is to **isolate** the internal logic circuits a sensor leads to from the potentially dangerous source of its input. For example, a direct electrical connection of a photocell to your home computer might not be wise, if a current surge or some other disaster in the photocell circuit could reach the delicate innards of the computer and wreck something. An isolation stage could be employed, where the signal from the photocell would be converted to light pulses, which would be detected by a photoresistive device on the computer. No direct electrical connection between the photocell and the computer would then exist.

Sound Sensors

Electronic sound-sensing for the most part today is based on either **crystal** or **magnetic** devices. (If a crystal is deformed, however slightly, a voltage can be detected between its opposite sides. If an electrical conductor is moved in a magnetic field, a voltage will be induced in the conductor.) A sensor is made by placing the crystal or the conductor in contact with the sound medium (usually air or liquid). The sound *vibrations* in the medium set up analogous vibrations in the crystal or conductor, which are reflected in analog *variations in the voltage* produced. The strength of the voltage produced by the sensor, and the frequencies of vibrations to which it will be most sensitive, are determined by the physical characteristics of the crystal or conductor (usually a coil of wire) used.

People who are old enough will remember the crystal microphones of early tape recorders, which were sensitive generally, but unfortunately *very sensitive* to high frequencies. Your tape recorded memories of special events with these devices probably sound like there is a lot of wrapping paper being removed in the background, whether or not there is. Today's "dynamic microphones" are based on the moving coil principle, and have been tuned up to a frequency response which more nearly resembles that of the human ear. Other detectors are tuned to ultrasound, which is used in imaging objects from the size of human organs down to the microscopic level.

Temperature Sensors

One of the most versatile sensors for temperature is the **thermocouple,** which is made by cutting a piece of wire and joining it, at both ends, to both ends of another piece of wire cut from a different kind of metal. The result looks like a bracelet, with two junctions where the ends of the dissimilar pieces of wire are joined together. Because one type of metal is more congenial to electrons than the other (that is, their energy states are lower there), the electrons tend to move across the junctions to this more congenial environment. The higher the temperature, the more mobile the electrons are, and the greater the rate at which they can move across the junctions. To use this device as a temperature sensor, one of the junctions is kept at a constant **reference** temperature, and the other is used as a **probe**. When the temperature in the probe is higher than in the reference junction, electrons in the less congenial metal flow from the reference junction toward the probe junction, since it is easier there for them to get across. The hotter the probe junction (the greater the **temperature** difference between it and the reference junction), the greater the push (**voltage**) sending electrons toward the hot junction.

The thermocouple device produces an **analogy** between temperature changes in the probe junction and corresponding voltage changes in the metal on one side of the device. Thermocouples are widely used because of their sturdiness and large number of possible configurations. By varying the choice of metals used, they can be made to work in a temperature range from -250° C. to 2000° C. Thermocouples arranged together in a series can be made into a thermopile, which is sensitive enough to produce a voltage under the influence of starlight or a warm body within a hundred feet or so. Such sensitivity may suggest romance to you, but the practical uses tend to be toward detecting stars and intruders of various sorts.

Position Sensors

The classical hardware for position-sensing involves a movable coil in an electrical transformer of some sort. The position of the coil determines the amount of voltage it will transmit. Our wind sensor for the aquacomputer would undoubtedly be replaced by an electrical **servo** mechanism of this type, in a real application. Small changes in position can also be detected by the **piezoelectric** phenomenon described in the section on sound sensors.

With these vintage servo devices, you can certainly make a marketable rooftop antenna rotor. If cost is not particularly important, you can implement enough functions on a space probe to make sure its solar panels and everything else move around to the right place when you ask them to, from a few million miles away. It is high time though, that the impact of miniaturizaton and solid state fabrication make a mark on these devices as well. For example, using **fiber optics**, one could sense the position of a mechanical arm, or rod, or whatever, simply by depositing reflective metal patterns directly on the arm itself, so that optic fibers would reflect light back in a pattern determined by which part of the mechanism was in position under them. The pattern could be deposited using photographic techniques, and the accuracy of the device could easily be in millimeters, or perhaps in microns. The television camera, in combination with digital signal-processing techniques, can potentially be used to monitor the positions of a large number of devices simultaneously.

Taste/Chemical Sensors

The chemical composition of a solution can be sensed and translated into an electrical event in several ways. **Absorption** methods use an infrared probe to see the "color" of the solution in infrared light, much the same way that humans differentiate chablis from burgundy in visible light. When the chemical properties of the solution affect its ability to be **ionized** and transmit electrical current, the amount of current which can be produced provides the translation of chemical changes to electrical changes. Other devices use high energy light to stimulate the sample, and then record the **luminescence** when the light is removed. (If you have seen a watch dial which glows in the dark, you have used the same technique. You may also use it in the future to monitor and automatically adjust "chemical solutions" in your home, ranging from the dishwater and the laundry bleach to the chicken soup.)

Actuators—Computer Muscle

An **actuator**, or action device, is a means by which energy can be transferred from the computer to its environment. The most common type of actuator presently in use is the **electric motor**. From kitchen food processors to record player turntables to vacuum cleaners and washing machines and furnaces, we are all accustomed to throwing a switch and having an electric motor do the work. For all their seeming complexity, electric motors are based on one simple fact: When electric current flows through a conductor, the conductor becomes a magnet.

Like any other magnet, the **electromagnet** attracts metal and either attracts or repels other magnets (including other electromagnets), depending upon how the magnets are lined up. All of the wires, windings contacts, etc., you find if you open up a typical electric motor merely serve to keep the magnetic forces directed in such a way as to drive the shaft around and around continuously. The situation is much the same as getting a mule to chase a carrot—you simply hold the carrot out in front of him. If you want the mule to go round and round and turn a mill wheel, say, you have to devise a mechanism to keep the mule pointed in the right direction. With the mule, the situation is simple: You hang a bar out over his head and have a carrot hanging down by a string from the end of the bar. The mule keeps walking after the carrot, which always stays in front of him. If the mule is attached to the mill wheel by a pole, he then just goes round and round.

Logic circuits can switch electromagnets on and off in extremely rapid succession, and thus make electric motors by the carrot and mule principle: Imagine a mule surrounded by a ring of television screens, with a logic circuit turning on the screen just ahead of the mule as he goes around. There would be no problem keeping up with a jackrabbit or a greyhound instead of the mule, and if we use electromagnets instead of televisions, a metal "mule" can be kept spinning at many thousands of revolutions per minute.

Once you discover that turning on a current in a wire makes it a magnet, and reversing the current turns the magnet around, you can make many other useful actuators besides motors. To mimic the muscles of the human body, **position actuators** can also be developed. Your legs, for example, can work like a motor if you are riding a bicycle, but their great usefulness, and certainly that of your hands, arms, fingers, etc., is not that they can produce continuous power, like a motor, but that they can move (and move objects) to any position within their range, and stop or hold the object in place. Logical devices can also perform this function, by changing the magnetic field gradually in a series of conductors, to coax a metal object (or another magnet) from one position to another, and then hold it there. If you have an electronic rotor for your television antenna, you are already familiar with electronic positioning. When you change the position knob in your living room, the magnetic field around the antenna base on the roof is changed, and the antenna lines up to a new position. In fact, the rooftop antenna rotor is probably the most common position actuator found in people's homes today, unless you consider stereo speakers (as you well might). It is a sure bet, though, that antenna rotors, if not speakers, will soon be far outnumbered by robot arms.

Another effect caused by a current in a wire, which is cruder than the magnetic effect so useful in motors in position actuators, is that an electric current in a conductor produces **heat**. This effect underlies common heating devices from electric furnaces to toasters and hair dryers. Most heating applications with which we are familiar hardly need sophisticated control mechanisms, but nonetheless the switching and timing capabilities of computers can be effectively utilized. The "prehistoric" temperature regulation devices in most homes, from radiator valves to old fashioned "one temperature all the time" thermostats, can all be profitably replaced. By selecting different temperatures for different times of day end using outside heat when it is available, all automatically, a substantial energy savings can be realized. A more sophisticated use of electric heating is in providing precise **temperature control** for chemical processes. With the possible exception of photography buffs who do their own color prints, most people are not familiar with such applications. Manufacturing and industrial requirements for precise temperature control are common though, and since chemistry underlies processes from cooking to food production, important home uses of computers for precise temperature control will undoubtedly begin to appear.

In heating, as well as in myriad other areas, the "wave" of the future is light. It would be more precise to say that "electromagnetic radiation" is the wave of the future, since much more of the spectrum will be used than the small portion we humans see as light. Versatile and efficient ovens using **microwave** (below infrared) radiation are already commonplace. The most spectacular computer action device of the near future will be the **laser**. For precise energy delivery in chemical processes, etching and engraving or cutting and welding, or for high speed communications applications, reading and writing millions or billions of bits of information per minute, the laser is unsurpassed. The expense of lasers has until now confined them largely to factories and laboratories. Their first large scale impact on homes will be in videodisc players. Other communication applications such as high speed, high quality graphics are now moving from the development stage to production and widespread availability. A videodisc player may represent, at face value, perhaps two and a half hours of movie sound and pictures. In terms of information though, those pictures and sound are represented by roughly ten billion bits. That amount of memory capability (equivalent to roughly two thousand volumes of English text) will soon be put to vastly more uses than saving pictures and high fidelity sound. Books and entire libraries of text (and computer programs!) will be able to be cheaply produced and distributed on an unheard of scale. The laser as a tool may develop more slowly than the laser as a pen, but the home market of do-it-yourselfers and creative craftspeople will not only support but eventually demand its unequalled flexibility, and make it economically self-supporting.

Analog to Digital and Back

At this point, we will just give a brief outline of how voltages and other analog electrical effects can be converted to the binary language, and how binary signals can be transformed and recombined into smooth electrical changes. Practically speaking, it should be emphasized that **analog-to-digital (A/D)** converters can be obtained "off the shelf" to meet various specifications, so that if you are planning a programmable kitchen assistant, let's say, your best bet would be to check the available modules, and simply buy one ready-made. If you own a personal computer, chances are that some variety of ready-made A/D converters are available to interface with it directly. From this perspective...

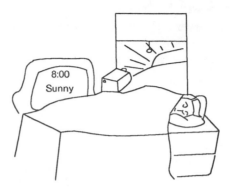

...your choice of a personal computer should take into account how easily you can get analog/digital converters to wake it up to the real world.

Let's suppose you have an A/D chip. A typical setup would be that the chip has two inputs, which are to be connected by wires to a sensor of some type, so that the voltage from the sensor reaches the two **input** pins on the chip. The **output** of the chip consists of a row of pins, which are to be connected directly to your computer. At any given instant, the voltage on each output pin is either high (logical "yes") or low (logical "no"). All the output pins taken together spell out, in a binary word, the code for the analog voltage on the input connections. (In the aquacomputer wind sensor example, the collection of catcher buckets formed an A/D converter, translating the analog aquatic variations of the hose stream moving up and down the sidewalk into the binary pattern of full and empty funnels at the aquacomputer.) Similar decoding strategies work for electronics as well as with aquatics, based not on well-positioned buckets but on their electronic counterpart, **comparators**.

Although scores of conversion strategies exist, we will discuss only one approach, **parallel conversion**, as an example here. The parallel conversion method is a "brute force" approach requiring a relatively large amount of circuitry. Nonetheless, the circuitry is very regular in form, ideally suited to manufacture by large scale integration methods such as the MOS process discussed at the end of Chapter Three. In addition, parallel conversion is the hands-down speed winner for A/D conversion, making it possible to catch and process high speed data such as video transmission "on the fly." As a result, parallel conversion devices for high fidelity video and audio signal-processing are already available at moderate cost. The description of parallel conversion here should help you to understand other strategies you may encounter elsewhere.

Imagine that you are going to design an analog/digital converting chip, rather than just buy one off the shelf. Let's suppose that the voltage from your analog sensor device (maybe that infrared warm-body detector in your burglar alarm) will be in the range of 0–15 volts, depending on whether it is picking up signals from a mouse (1 volt) or a 6' 5" hulk (13 volts) creeping through your front door. If you didn't have a computer, you could attach the sensor to a pen recording device, which moves a pen back and forth on a moving strip of paper as the voltage from the sensor changes. If you turned the recorder on at night, it would make an analog drawing of the night's voltages on its strip of graph paper. You could peruse this drawing along with your morning paper, if you wished, and be able to tell how many times the cat went in and out, what time Harvey left for work, and any other events involving warm bodies and your front door.

**Any warm body in the vicinity of the door will
cause a voltage change.**

The key component in the *automatic* conversion of this chartful of voltage information into digital form is a device called a **comparator.** It has two inputs, for a pair of analog voltages, and one logical output. If we call the inputs A and B, the device works as follows:

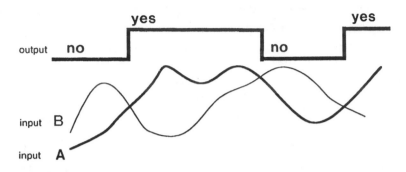

When the input voltage from A is higher than the input voltage from B a logical "1" (high voltage) appears at the output. Otherwise, the output is logical "0" (low voltage).

A comparator can be very useful by itself. For example, if your cat Max will produce three volts on the infrared detector when he stands at the door, you can make a simple burglar alarm with just a comparator. If you connect the "B" input of the comparator to a three-volt reference (such as two flashlight batteries in series), and the "A" input to the infrared detector's output, the comparator will signal when anything causing more than 3 volts i.e., something bigger than Max, is at the front door. That is, the output of the comparator will be "1" just when the infrared energy detected is more than what Max produces. You can use this comparator output to drive **switches** to turn on lights, sound alarms, call the police, launch tear gas cannisters, or whatever seems appropriate for your nervousness level. An advantage of connecting the comparator to a computer, rather than using its output directly, is that you can put in the computer's memory that Harvey will be leaving for work between six and six-fifteen A.M., so hold the tear gas.

The **parallel conversion** analog scheme uses a large bank of comparators, with each one assigned to a different voltage level (that is, with this voltage level connected to one of its inputs as a reference, while its other input is "free" to follow the incoming analog signal.) This "places" the comparator at a certain *voltage level*, in the same way that the catcher buckets for the aquacomputer were positioned at various *distances* along the sidewalk. The analog voltage input from whatever sensor you are using is applied to all the "free" ends of the comparators simultaneously, and our desired translation from smoothly varying **analog** voltage signal into a **logical** pattern is automatically accomplished: No matter what voltage appears at the input of the converter, the result at the **outputs** of the comparators will be a **binary** pattern of 1s and 0s. For example, if you want to break the infrared sensor's voltage up into sixteen ranges (above 0 volts, above 1 volt,...above 14 volts, above 15 volts), your A/D converter will need sixteen comparators. No matter what voltage comes in, the result out will be simply 1s and 0s: all of the comparators referenced below the incoming voltage will output "1," and the remaining comparators will output "0."

Although your infrared signal converter might have *sixteen* yes-no comparators working within it, its logical output can be signalled to your computer using only *four* yes-no signals. The reason is that only sixteen *patterns* of yes-or-no can appear on the comparators' outputs in response to *any* voltage input. It is not possible, for example, to obtain a pattern where the first comparator gives "yes," the second gives "no," and then the third one gives "yes" again. All the comparators up to some level must have "1" on the output, and beyond this level all must be "0," and there are only sixteen places where the first "0" could start. You will recall (or you can cheat and look back to the aquacomputer-with-wind-detector example,) that there are indeed sixteen patterns you can make, using only four logical output pins.

As a typical situation, suppose the incoming analog voltage is 12.372 volts. The comparator outputs will have the following pattern: All comparators referenced to 0,1,2,...12 volts will have "1" or "high" on the output, while the three comparators referenced to 13,14, and 15 volts will have "0" or "low" on the output. As a final step, this logical pattern, which is based on the 1s and 0s of *sixteen* comparator outputs, is condensed, using standard logical AND and OR components within the device itself, to a unique **four-bit** pattern and placed on the *four* final A/D outputs. Such a sixteen-level A/D converter is more commonly called a **four-bit** converter.

More accurate parallel converters, like sixteen-bit (65,536 levels) devices, can require tens of thousands of internal components. Fortunately, such circuits can be laid out in a very regular pattern, drawn by a computer and photographically miniaturized. Complete circuits for this level of conversion accuracy and greater have already been designed and are currently available as single chips. The large costs of developing such chips is easily justified by an enormous number of uses such as encoding television and audio signals. Digital technology will give home recording and playing a range of capabilities previously unavailable even to studios. In addition, the "record wear" problem will be eliminated. The ten thousandth play of an audio or visual recording will be indistinguishable from the first.

The recording/reproduction process, either audio or video, is perhaps the most important early example of the reconversion of digital signals back to the analog form they came from. (You may be happy to store your coffee in waterless crystals, but you would not drink it in that form.) The-digital-to-analog reconstitution, whether to drive the paper cone in a stereo speaker or the electron gun in a television receiver or to position a robot arm, is conceptually simple: Every possible **binary word** is assigned a **voltage** value, and when the binary word appears at the device's input, a **switching circuit** of some type switches that value onto the output.

In the most basic scheme, the voltage value which goes with each binary word is fixed once and for all, perhaps by summing up fixed values for each digit which is "1" in that word. (The value we give to an ordinary decimal number like 7,145 could be explained, going from right to left in the number, as 5 plus (ten times 4) plus (ten times ten times 1) plus (ten times ten times ten times 7). Binary codes can be evaluated in the same fashion, using *two* rather than the *ten* appropriate for decimal arithmetic. Thus, a simple decoder might translate the binary word 01101, going from right to left, into a voltage equal to 1 plus (two times 0) plus (two times two times 1) plus (two times two times two times 1) plus (two times two times two times two times 0), or thirteen volts.) More sophisticated digital-to-analog devices can be constructed which *change* the voltage switched in by any given binary word, to adapt to changing contexts. Such devices, whether "expanding" the resolution of low-volume audio passages or compressing telephone transmissions, use logical processing at a much higher level than simple decoding and switching, and comprise an entire technology of **digital filters.**

> As the use of logic circuits for information storage and control becomes widespread, the importance of digital-to-analog conversion will increase correspondingly, to mesh the logical gears with the physical.

Orchestrating Many Devices Together

Beyond the construction of action devices and the significant impact these devices will enable computers to have on our physical environment, the logical age promises to bring about widespread change in the way machines are thought about, designed, and used. Concepts such as flow of control and communication, portability, and ease of diagnosis, modification, and repair are central to good computer programs. These same ideas will be applied with great success beyond programs to the physical devices these programs can automatically control.

Making Machines—The Logical Way

If you look at a complicated machine such as a typewriter, what you will find is a collection of coordinated smaller mechanisms, each of them doing a particular function. For example, if you have a typewriter with a moving print-head, then when a key is pressed, the machine must:

- Move the ink ribbon in front of the print-head.
- Strike the desired image, through the ribbon, onto the paper.
- Advance the print-head to the next position.
- Advance the inking ribbon.

In present day mechanical devices, each of the actions above is controlled by a separate mechanism, and the mechanisms are coordinated by complicated mechanical linkages of pulleys, eccentric cams, levers, etc. All of the mechanical linkage is necessary simply because, in the vast majority of pre-logical machines, the individual mechanisms have no intelligence. Wherever it is necessary for two actions to be coordinated, a **mechanical linkage** has to be provided to ensure that coordination.

It is a tribute to the mechanical ingenuity and production skills of advanced societies that complicated machines ever leave the designing table and enter the assembly line. Nonetheless...

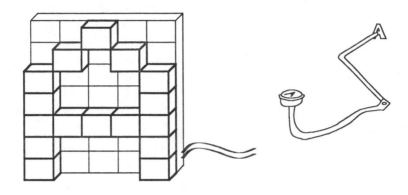

...more and more mechanical control linkages in machines of all sorts are disappearing, with self-adapting and programmable logical devices taking their place.

Present day devices composed of mechanically linked parts, rather than communicating logical subsystems, present serious drawbacks in both their design and use:

- There is little compatibility of mechanisms between devices. You cannot routinely, for example, use your automobile engine to provide electric power for your house, as you might want to if you were good at producing alcohol. Similarly, the pump in your washing machine is absolutely useless to you if the nearly identical pump in your dishwasher breaks down.

- The dissimilarity of mechanisms doing nearly the same function means that for repairs you must find different people for different devices, or if you take enough interest to learn how to maintain one of your own home devices, the knowledge will typically be nearly worthless in maintaining any different, even though similar, mechanism. If you find a skilled and conscientious auto mechanic for your family Stratocruiser auto, he is unable to help you with your television or your washing machine, and may not even work on your other auto, which happens to be not a Stratocruiser but a Slickmobile.

- Changing and/or customizing the operation of a manufactured device is typically either impossible or a major undertaking. Typewriters with exchangeable print elements have been introduced, so that you can select type styles or alphabets. These typewriters are still fairly expensive. Washing machines are attempting to provide more flexible and economical options (with a disconcerting increase in the complexity of the control panels.) But don't think about changing the compression ratio of your car to compensate for factors such as climate, altitude, or the car's condition, unless you want to rebuild the engine.

- Once you buy a device, you are typically a hostage to the manufacturer for major spare parts, as well as for repairs. Since practically everything beyond the level of nuts and bolts is special to each manufacturer and/or application, it is rarely profitable for a competitor to gear up and produce alternative spare parts or repair service. Even in such large volume fields as auto parts, a willing competitor may not be able to produce an exact substitute for the original manufacturer's part. Rather than "take a chance," we end up buying parts and repairs at a monopoly premium.

- A large amount of lead time and fabrication start-up cost are associated with the introduction of any new product. If you invent a better mousetrap, you may be able to manufacture it in your garage, but if you invent a better washing machine, you will probably have to have a technical staff just to produce a working model.

But what is the alternative? If you have become accustomed, through reading this chapter or otherwise, to the idea that logical devices are capable of action, it may occur to you: The same planning and maintenance principles which apply to programs can be used in the design and construction of machines. A well designed machine should consist of intelligent submechanisms linked together by a communication network. The construction of submechanisms should reflect only the **tasks** they do and the **constraints** (power, space, heat dissipation, etc.) that they operate under, so that any particular submechanism can be incorporated into a vast range of possible applications.

In sharp contrast to the graven-in-stone design of old style mechanical devices, the machine of the near future will consist of an orchestra of intelligent submechanisms, linked together by a communication network. Aspects of this construction are beginning to appear already in computer hardware such as printers and disc controllers, as well as in advanced scientific laboratory instruments. The internal communication network may be implemented by electrical wires, optical fibers, or even free radio or optical transmissions bounced around the room. The heart of the communication network will be a logical message processor and controller, which will not only direct the messages from individual devices to each other, but actively process information about the state of the machine to generate command information. Changing the operating parameters of the machine will merely involve changing the program of the central message processor. Repairs and troubleshooting can be carried out with diagnostic signals sent out from the processor to individual parts. By monitoring subassemblies while they are in operation, many breakdowns will be able to be predicted and preventive action taken. Point by point, the drawbacks outlined above will be remedied:

- A standardized communication interface will enable any device to substitute for another with the same function and environmental restrictions. If you need a lifting force of two grams or two kilograms, there will be no need to custom design both the lifter and its linkage. You will buy the lifter "off the shelf" and perhaps plug its optical fiber control line into a central communication control unit. The central unit will determine when the lifter should lift, and within a certain range, the amount of force to be applied. A single device might work for all applications in the range of 2–200 grams, specified by the control signals it receives. Complicated and expensive components could be interchanged between devices to increase their usefulness. (You seldom need to heat and air-condition your home at the same time.)

- The repair process will be common to all devices which have a similar function. The same communication network which controls the device in ordinary operation can be used to exercise the device and check its operation over the range of conditions under which it must operate. Troubleshooting and isolation of defects can be accomplished without the perils of old fashioned "exploratory surgery."

- Modification of an existing device is as simple as changing the program in its central communication unit. If you want to change your furnace over from burning wood to burning used motor oil or high sulfur coal, the rate of fuel consumption, amount of air flow, and temperature of combustion must all be varied. If the valves, vents, etc., which control these parameters of the furnace are logical devices, and the furnace also incorporates sensors for temperature and pollutants, the changeover will be easy, or possibly even automatic. The flexibility of machinery in general should become a desirable and achievable goal. You would not expect to use a single mechanical punch to process both cookie dough and steel, but a logically controlled laser cutter could perform both functions rapidly and efficiently.

- The force of competition can be brought into play to produce ever cheaper devices. The sheer number of people who wear wrist-watches is the key fact explaining that a computer watch incorporating a wide variety of functions can currently can be bought for less than a magazine subscription.

- Innovative ideas can quickly be brought to completion in working mechanisms, assembled from available components in novel combinations and with creative central programs. The high school "whiz kid" who makes something novel and useful will no longer be such a rarity. After all, computer concepts and programming experience are ever more common at the high school level.

Keeping the Furnace in Touch with the Windows

The advantages of using intelligent **communicating subsystems** rather than mechanically linked "dumb" devices extend not only to the construction of "machines," but to any situation where a large number of devices can be orchestrated to provide a coherent and efficient environment. An excellent example is in the development of a "personal architecture" for people's homes, as discussed above. The communication link is already "built in" most homes in the form of the electric wires connecting together all wall outlets, switches, lights, and so on. Without any rewiring, **messages** can be sent over this existing system, to and from any appliance or device hooked into it for **power**. (The centralized **remote switching systems** now widely available use this principle, as did earlier "wireless" intercom systems.)

Using the built-in communication capacity of your house, every electrical device in the house can potentially be coordinated, monitored, and effectively utilized. The central message and logic center will of course be the home computer. Just as electrical power is now standardized throughout the country (110 volts, 60 hertz), and standards have been established for the safe and uniform operation of electrical devices, it is high time for standardization to be initiated for the **logical interfacing** of electrical devices. An individual would then be sure that any electrical device purchased, from a toaster to electric window shutters to fans, furnaces and ventilators, could be automatically brought under logical and central control through messages transmitted and received on the same house wiring which supplies its electrical power. All home computers would have the capability of transmitting and receiving information on the household wiring in the standard form. In fact, Home Bus Standards Association has already been established to promote such uniformity.

With a consistent and standard interface, you could have an electric thermometer for every room in your house, which simply plugs into an available wall outlet. The heating and air conditioning vents could similarly be plugged in. The central computer's program is simple: For heating, shut off the vents in any room where the electric thermometer for that individual room shows a higher temperature than required (for that hour of the day!), and otherwise open it. If all vents in the house are closed, shut off the furnace. If the 110-volt communication were standardized, as for example FM stereo broadcasting is, the sheer market size would produce competitors falling all over themselves to make these thermostat/vent combinations, providing an immediate energy saving **retrofit** for conventional homes, and selling for less than a day's worth of fuel oil.

Often, of course, it is insulation and isolation which a person wants in his own environment, rather than excessive links to the outside. The availability of logical devices could provide safety and security in a much more extensive fashion than is currently possible. In case of external power failures or central logic failures, devices would revert to "safe" modes, with backup power supplies for the most essential functions. Electronic "passwords" could ensure that sensitive functions or devices would be restricted. Such features would enable cohabitants of the same electrical system, be it a house, apartment complex, or college dormitory, to maintain private control devices from stereos to thermostats without unwanted fiddling, snooping, or other intrusion.

5

Games, Hypergames, and Metagames

One of the most immediately appealing (and lucrative) applications of computers is to the development and support of games. Even in research environments (especially in research environments?), one finds in fact a keen interest in developing and playing games, from chess to target practice to Star Trek. Student computer centers at universities all over the country host students playing games with names like "Galaxy," and "Adventure." Some of the games are regular social events, with several players at different terminals interacting simultaneously to hunt, zap, and even occasionally help one another as part of the action. Creative students contribute by adding new games to the available repertoire.

As we all have observed, the commercial market for home computers and home computer products has been initially flooded with games. This emphasis is not likely to disappear. In fact, research projects currently underway at Bell Laboratories and elsewhere may eventually result in nationwide game **networks** being set up, which you can tap into for slightly more than the price of a local call. Whether you use these networks to play intergalactic shoot-em-up with the best hotshots in the nation, or simply would welcome the opportunity for joining or kibitzing in a bridge game at any hour of the day or night, you can expect more in games from computer power than you might have thought possible.

In this chapter, we investigate some of the possibilities for use of computers in games. At the simplest level, illustrations are given of the computer's ability to support attractive interactive displays—once you've played Monopoly on a live screen, that dead cardboard is going to seem rather dull! Along with this display capability is the prospect of relieving game players of complicated bookkeeping functions. (There are many games which would be much more fun to play if they weren't so miserable to keep score in.) At more advanced levels, the computer itself can be used to create **hypergames** and **metagames**. In hypergames, the computer is used to create new materials and environments for an existing game either in realistic or abstract/fantastic settings. In metagames, a superstructure is developed within which games can be directed, combined, and created.

Moving Images—Games Become Alive

"Give 'em the old razzle-dazzle," the song says. We humans are captivated by color and motion, and more by color-in-motion, pattern, and variety. Color television screens across the world are attentively watched round the clock, whether they convey vital information, fascinating drama, or sitcom drivel. To modernize the Bard:

> ## The Display's the Thing

Games, and especially interactive, come-alive hookups for them to color television, are being intensively developed by a host of manufacturers. The board game, for all its popularity, is undergoing a radical change. The dull, dead cardboard and sluggish markers are being replaced by moving figures on a live television screen. Let's look at what an intelligent, interactive display can do for games from the simplest to the most complicated. Whether your favorite game is Monopoly or Clue or chess or bridge, you will find a wealth of possibilities, even with the simplest of "color computers." Whether you jump in now and buy one of these for practice, or wait a year or two for the next generation(s) of machines, your eyes are going to be opened.

The simplest games to describe are the "pinball" variety, which involve skill and reflexes to a great degree, and usually little or no mental effort. These games are bought and played with great relish, and will undoubtedly be a staple product of manufacturers for years to come. A popular, non-electronic game a few years back was "air hockey." In this game, two players stand at opposite ends of a table, each defending a goal. Each player has a paddle, which can be used either to stop the puck from entering the goal, or to drive the puck toward the opposing goal. The attraction of the game is that the puck rides on a cushion of air, with very little friction, so that the speed of play is terrific. Drawbacks were that you needed to devote a fair amount of space to the hockey table, the puck seemed to fly off it a lot, people bashed their fingers, and the whole thing could degenerate into a game of muscles rather than skill.

An electronic hockey ("pong," "paddle," or whatever it might have been called) appeared on the home scene not long after tabletop air hockey. Without even realizing it, this was many people's first experience with computers and computer displays of any sort. A few connections to your television set, and *voilà!*, the goals and the players appear (admittedly, only crudely drawn, and in black and white) on the television screen. Each player has a knob, (or a lever or a "joystick" or something) to move his players around on the screen, and the puck bounces around more than fast enough to keep you busy. As an electronic display (and game), these foot-in-the-door devices can only be called primitive. They nonetheless were better in many respects than a much more expensive tabletop air hockey, and were bought and enjoyed by millions. Recently, a tournament sponsored by the Atari computer company to promote one of its sophisticated "pinball-"type games drew more than 10,000 contestants from across the country.

The latest versions of plug-in-and-go television games are in full color, allow extensive use of strategies and options for play, and are mainly limited in their effectiveness by the poor quality of **graphic display** devices in the early eighties. As microelectronic techniques become more advanced and production facilities more abundant, cheap special-purpose graphics chips can be expected to appear. Coupled with other technological advances, among them the laser picture recording system, these developments guarantee that cheap and realistic display features will become commonplace. Game displays will soon seem less like stick diagrams and schematics, and more like computer-controlled movies.

How would a computer-controlled movie work? There are many possibilities for using a computer to produce animated pictures, and practitioners of the art are found everywhere from movie studios to space laboratories. Whatever the technique, the underlying principle of computer movies is to take a basic graphic display device and use a computer to feed it pictures in rapid sequence. The most common kind of graphic display you will find in early personal computers is a so-called **pixel** (for **picture element**) display.

> In a *pixel* display, the computer divides the face
> of a television picture tube into a large number
> of small squares. Pictures are made by filling
> in the squares like the tiles of a mosaic.

With the early personal computers, you typically have only a fairly small number of different kinds of tiles to put in the mosaic (maybe eight shades of grey, from black to white for making a black and white picture, or perhaps 64 colors of tiles to make a color picture.) In its crudest form, the pixel method produces very artificial looking images. As the size of the tiles is decreased though, reasonably lifelike pictures can be reproduced. For a picture the size of an ordinary television screen, acceptable color and quality (similar to newspaper pictures) can be obtained with a mosaic made up of one thousand rows and one thousand columns, (a million tiles in all) and with two thousand rows and columns or more, the picture begins to be nearer to the quality of a photograph. As of the early eighties, high resolution (1000x1000 or better) color displays are not widely available for inexpensive personal computers, but are being developed rapidly.

Interactive Movies

In order to make a movie with a pixel or "raster scan" display, a home computer would have to be able to display a new mosaic roughly twenty times a second, in the same way that your home movie projector flashes the individual frames of a movie one after another. (If the pictures could not be displayed this quickly, they would be much less appealing. Five pictures per second would appear to be five discrete images displayed in succession, rather than providing the illusion of a continuously changing scene. One picture per second would not sustain the continuous feedback and illusion of contact and control which enlivens interactive games from pinball to space war.) The technical difficulty with the pixel method is that, with a high resolution display of a million tiles, a movie based on twenty pictures per second would require the computer to rewrite twenty million tiles per second. That task is too demanding for early home computers, which typically can do their fastest individual operation no more than four million times per second. Faster personal computers will undoubtedly appear, perhaps able to do 100 million basic operations per second in ten years, as large computers are able to do now. Nonetheless, a "brute force" implementation of computer movies by the pixel method would still demand a substantial portion of the computer's total processing power just to maintain the display.

If they become cheap enough, high speed computers might possibly be put to such "non-intellectual," or so called **dedicated uses** as being the controllers of animation displays. One such "dedicated use" is already common—think of how shocked the computer expert of the sixties would have been to find a "full fledged" computer dedicated entirely to running a single data terminal, transforming it from basically a typewriter into an "intelligent" device. Nonetheless, such full fledged **microprocessors** are now the size of a matchbox, and cheap enough that it is practical to have one inside each of the many kinds of "intelligent" data terminals available in the early eighties. One can even find computer systems for home use, where one computer does all of the "thinking," and another, equally powerful device (perhaps an identical twin) simply sits inside the data terminal, passing, routing, storing, and displaying the information the terminal receives and sends.

In addition to such "dedicated computer" strategies, it is likely that interactive computer "movies" and animation techniques will become available even before such high speed home computers are common. Special-purpose hardware for creating and updating television pictures is being developed actively along several approaches. For example, the ordinary pixel display could be replaced by a "smart" mosaic in which tiles change themselves automatically, based on predictive techniques (using their current and recent past states and that of other tiles nearby.) Such an array would in effect be a large mosaic of interconnected microcomputers. Recent manufacturing techniques known as Very Large Scale Integration (VLSI) make it possible to put large arrays of this type in very small packages. The only input required to this "intelligent mosaic" would be a correction signal to adjust those (few) tiles in the picture whose behavior deviates significantly *from the prediction.*

Another alternative to pixel display can be based on the concept of **transformations.** That is, the display device is constructed especially for drawing a limited number of basic patterns such as geometric figures, or perhaps simply designed to rapidly fetch and display any specified frame from videodisc storage. A controlling computer then determines what item from the display device's portfolio to fetch up and how to transform it, to approximate any picture you wish on the screen. Typical transformations would be:

- moving a figure from one part of the screen to another.
- rotating a figure to a new orientation.
- fading out or fading in an image.
- shrinking or enlarging an image.

For example, a rough animation of "horse rides into the sunset" in this language would be to apply the transformation **(rotate right–rotate left–move toward vanishing point–shrink)** repeatedly. The human psyche would interpret the resulting wobbling, shrinking, drifting, image as a horse trotting into the sunset.

The transformation method is successful because the transformation commands have little **information** content. (Contrast how long it would take to instruct someone to paint a copy of the Mona Lisa, versus how long it takes to give instructions for moving the copy to a new spot on your wall.) Moving an image on a television screen may require no more than changing the timing of the basic video signal. Using shaded geometric figures as the basic portfolio, Hal Alles and his co-workers at Bell Laboratories have already implemented the interactive processing and display of realistic images, within the framework of telephone transmission. In this framework, rapidly changing scenes such as spaceships in battle are simultaneously and interactively presented to the "pilots" in a game, while the data transmission across the telephone lines linking the players is a mere trickle of transformation commands. A wide variety of such "social games" will be played in the near future by home computer owners.

Once you have a computer which can *display* movies, you might very well be interested in how to *create* them from your own ideas and material. Cartoonists have long used the "key frame" method for producing animation. An expert cartoonist is utilized to draw only the "key" frames (perhaps one out of every ten or fewer) of an animation sequence. Less skilled assistants then produce the intermediate sequence of drawings between key frames, by copying the main features and changing them in steps to make a smooth transition from one "key frame" to the next. Computers are ideally suited to this "cartoonist's apprentice" role. Once a pair of "key frames" is given, the computer can use its repertoire of transformations to determine the transformation which takes one key frame into the next. Intermediate frames can then be generated automatically by dividing up the transformation into as many steps as desired. This theme occurs again and again...

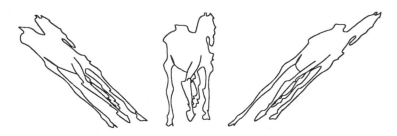

...the human sets the pattern; the computer implements it using repetition and programmed variation.

You can imagine the excitement of an animated sketchpad—at your disposal you have perhaps five thousand realistic images, which can be brought separately or in combination to the screen. Your repertoire of transformations includes changes in the position of the images, viewing angle, lighting and size. You can rearrange and revise each new scene until it is ready to be the next "key frame." Not only will the background and other static elements be transferred automatically from one key frame to the next, as cartoonists manage to do now by drawing on clear plastic over a fixed background, but sequences based on recurring transformations can be programmed to progress automatically as well, such as " cowboy rides into the sunset," or "boy A kisses girl B." You will only have to add artistic details, such as required if cowboy A must get rid of a wad of tobacco before kissing girl B. At your signal, the frame is stored, or the entire animation sequence is played back, with the intermediate scenes interleaved to make a lifelike presentation.

Even simple games, and undoubtedly many of your old favorites, can be livened up considerably by replacing cardboard playing boards, wooden pieces, etc., with livelier components. A perennial favorite is the game Battleship, which *could* be played with only two sheets of paper. The papers are divided up by grids into small squares, so that each square has a horizontal and vertical label. For example, the upper left hand corner square might be labeled A–1 and the lower right hand square H–8, etc.

The Battleship Game							
	A	*B*	*C*	*D*	*E*	*F*	*G*	*H*
1	A1	B1	C1	D1	E1	F1	G1	H1
2	A2	B2	C2	D2	E2	F2	G2	H2
3	A3	B3	C3	D3	E3	F3	G3	H3
4	A4	B4	C4	D4	E4	F4	G4	H4
5	A5	B5	C5	D5	E5	F5	G5	H5
6	A6	B6	C6	D6	E6	F6	G6	H6
7	A7	B7	C7	D7	E7	F7	G7	H7
8	A8	B8	C8	D8	E8	F8	G8	H8

At the beginning of the Battleship game, each player places "ships" on his paper, so that they occupy several adjacent squares. Players take turns guessing, one square at a time. If Player 1 guesses all of the squares which are occupied by one of Player 2's ships, the ship is sunk. Play continues until all of one player's ships have been sunk, and the other player wins. With a "live" display, rather than those dull pieces of paper, players could make their guesses by using a keyboard, or perhaps simply by "pointing" with a light pen or other device on their screen. After each guess, the television screen flashes a new picture on the screen. Perhaps it is just the wide, wide ocean. Perhaps though, a frigate or a PT boat appears. You then have only seconds to fire as the ship takes evasive maneuvers—BLAMO, a real Fourth of July explosion takes place on the screen.

Another perennial favorite among the board games is the "Monopoly-type," where players progress around a board which recreates some environment such as "real estate" in the original game. Players' fortunes are decided to some extent by chance, as they roll the dice to progress from one position on the board to another. Strategy also comes into play, as players decide on what risks to take and which to avoid. Of course, such a game is not restricted to dealing with real estate. Popular variations have been set in contexts ranging from managing race relations to becoming a semiconductor tycoon. Let's look for a moment how a Monopoly-type game can be improved by using an "electronic board." For starters, that business of going round and round a board with about 80 squares on it is really pretty dull, and largely necessitated by the fact that incorporating much more variety (800 or 8,000 squares, say) would either produce an enormous piece of cardboard, or require a lot of fine print, and some tiny markers which you would need tweezers to move around.

With an "electric board" devised by having a computer control your color television screen, it would be no problem to have one square for every county, say, in the United States. Your "moves" could be by auto, which would take you easily within counties or to neighboring counties. For these kinds of moves, the "electronic board" would show you the local county geography, or even the simulation of driving along a road in the desert or by the ocean, as appropriate. If you needed larger range travel, across the country, say, the board could obligingly "zoom out" and show you features on the scale of hundreds of miles rather than miles. Chance mechanisms could be graphically displayed, and automatically introduced into the game. Rather than "drawing a card" to see your next turn of luck, you might see your gas gauge appearing on the screen, perilously near empty, as the words "gasoline leak" flash across the screen. Your car can graphically have a flat, or your plane lose an engine or pick up a tail wind, changing your intended destination. Once you arrive at any given spot, the geographic display on the screen can become more detailed, or disappear temporarily as the screen displays your options. Would you like to go prospecting for oil? Invest in a used car lot? Buy a seed company or a railroad? Which of the competing players have been in town lately, and what are they up to? You can switch back and forth between display of this information, local geography, and updates on significant aspects of your current status in the game, including finances, income and risk prospects, and so on.

The "electric board" for games of the future will be in many respects like a helicopter hovering over a large "countryside" full of information. If you put several players "in the air" at the same time, you have the prospects of many types of games. What could the countryside look like? It could be a detailed map of the world (electronically stored maps exist already, and the condition that an expensive computer is needed to access and display them is only a temporary stumbling block of the early eighties.) The "countryside" over which you hover might not be geographical at all, but perhaps a collection of paintings unlike anything you have ever seen. (A videodisc storage system, of the kind already in production, can hold 50,000 pictures.) As different players "take the controls" of the helicopter window in turn, the game progresses. Perhaps it is an art collection or auction game. Perhaps a guessing game, with the paintings displayed in partially blacked-out fashion. Can you reconstruct a small piece of a Rembrandt? Guess the painter of a picture from only a few scraps of the canvas? Guess the dominant color, the date of composition...? The possibilities are limited only by your own imagination. These "countrysides" are what computer scientists call **databases**. Things are becoming exciting for non-experts because more and more, large databases are being electronically produced, which means that they can potentially be accessed by anyone who has a computer. Whether you're into maps, markets, or Mondrian, the "big guys" out there are taming the frontier—getting data into electronically manageable form. The computer is your personal helicopter, and even if you never become an aviation mechanic, now is the time to learn the rudiments of flying.

Lively displays will enhance more "cerebral" games as well. The function of a good display is to change our perception of events into a form where we can capitalize on our unique human processing capabilities, such as pattern recognition and other heuristics. Rather than sitting on one side of a chess board, trying vainly to think twelve moves ahead, imagine yourself as the president of an unruly assemblage of delegates. The queen speaks up: "If you don't do something, I can be captured in three moves." "Well," you reply, "check around with the rest of the pieces and see if any of them can help you." While the queen is bustling around, you hear a petition from the "file lobbyist" urging you to take control of the king's bishop file, the center lobbyist warning that your center is weak, etc. This very humanlike scenario can be accomplished simply by means of improving the "display" presented by an ordinary chessboard. In addition, threatened pieces could tremble, and potential bad moves be indicated by squares on the board turned into gaping pits. One could then get to know the "personalities" of the different pieces in more human terms, as well as learn, from playing experience, the good "rules of order" for the assembly, and correct priorities to produce a winning game. Who knows but that some such perception might be the secret behind the skill of the best players? During the game, every piece and every square on the chessboard can be given both an offensive and defensive "strength" dependent on its position and that of the other pieces. If this strength is displayed visually, for example by having green for offensive strength and red for defensive strength, the amount of strength indicated by the brightness of the color, it would be possible to switch back and forth between colors, try out different potential moves for effect, and pick up offensive and defensive patterns. Other scenarios (perception modes) are possible, and are capable of changing your entire experience of the game, if not the quality of your play. A whole new literature and a real theory of the game could be developed, expressed in the language of these previously inexpressible patterns.

"Livelier displays" for games also free players from a host of boring bookkeeping functions. The Monopoly board, for example, can have your current assets displayed along with the board's geography or alternating with it, the mortgage value of your real estate holdings, and other financial data. Prediction information such as the average income you can expect in the next five turns from players landing on your properties can also be displayed. A backgammon board could easily have superimposed over every "blot" (single piece) its chances of being hit on the next roll, as well as other information such as the estimated advantage of one player's position over the other's. Games from Scrabble to blackjack to bridge can have all scoring and tallying done instantly as each play is made, and displayed in a variety of forms. Solitaire games are especially worthy of improvement. With computer speech modules, the program could supply you with some running commentary, including information, prediction, nagging, and encouragement as you wish.

Hypergames—Old Games in New Dimensions

Computers not only bring excitement to the display of existing games, but they also allow a fresh view toward games themselves. Existing games and rules are no longer seen as rigid and fixed, but merely as prototypes or structures upon which whole evolutionary families of games can be built. Starting from an existing game, we can develop both its materials and the environment, making them more complex and dynamically interrelated. The new games which result are **hypergames,** relative to their primitive ancestors. Some evolutions which you develop will be eminently successful, much like the humans and other varieties of hyper-lemurs which abound today. Other paths may fade out quickly, but even your dinosaur hyperlizards or Edsel hypercarriages will provide interest and amusement of their own. If the original game has already been put in the form of a computer program, interesting hypergames often can be built up...

...**using only the simple substitution techniques described in Chapter Two.**

No exhaustive catalog of techniques for producing hypergames can be given, much as one cannot make a list of possible birds, beasts, and plants which could (or in fact will) evolve from the leaves on our current evolutionary tree. The *process* of developing hypergames, nonetheless, can be simply described as explication and expansion.

The targets of this explication are not only the visible, physical materials of the game, but in addition the theoretical elements of strategy and chance, and the interactions possible between elements and/or states of the game at different times. Thus, the game of bridge may become **hyperbridge** because it is played with **hypercards** (such as cards which may change when played and/or combined with other cards, or when played at different times), or it may become hyperbridge because new possibilities for strategy and chance have been allowed in the play of the game. In bridge, for example, possibilities could be extended by allowing the players to bid for partially predictable hands, in addition to the usual contract mechanism of bidding for trump suit and order of play. The "play of the cards" might be extended to involve something more physically and/or mentally challenging than extracting a card from the hand and placing it face up on a table. In that case, a "well played" deuce of clubs might even on a rare occasion beat a poorly played trump ace of spades. Beyond giving this general scheme for creating hypergames, the best way to describe the process is by examples.

The Materials Evolve: Hypercards

What kinds of hypergames can be produced by letting the materials of the game evolve? Consider ordinary playing cards, the basis of hundreds of games. What can we do with them if they become hypercards? Perhaps the major way in which cards are used is to establish an order of precedence, much like the chickens' barnyard pecking order. Thus, an ace beats a king beats a queen beats a jack, etc. With hypercards though, things needn't be so cut-and-dried. The rank of the cards might indicate their strength, or potential. In an otherwise unembellished contest, an ace *should* beat a king, and more probably beat a queen, but the outcome is not determined until the battle is over.

A good hypercard, well in keeping with its historical trappings, might be a player in a jousting tournament.

The ace is a proven champion, his lance only wavering ever so slightly as he rides to the tilt. The king is a little less steady, and so on down to the deuce, who has all he can do to keep the lance from dragging on the ground. The rules of the joust are simple: The players ride toward each other, with their shields in place and their lances aimed as best they can manage. The rules of the contest, suitably engraved in stone, might be: "Whosoever shall come closest to the center of his opponent's shield, him shall he unhorse." So, as you now sit with your hand of hypercards in a card game, you are the leader of a motley band of jousters. Since your ace aims his lance the steadiest, you might play him first. Suppose your opponent plays a deuce—the poor fellow doesn't have a prayer. Nonetheless, the cards are played. Instantly, the television screen shows the split image: Over your steady lance, you see the shield of the deuce approaching; your aim is almost dead center. On his side of the screen, your opponent looks over his wobbly lance and sees the ace's approaching shield. Valiantly he works the computer controls, attempting again and again to bring his wavering aim back into line. With a crash of metal and wood, the jousters meet. The deuce's lance hits the outside of the ace's shield and is deflected. The ace hits near the center, and the deuce is unhorsed.

If your opponent had played a stronger jouster than the deuce, perhaps a jack, the contest would have been suspenseful. Riveted to your controls, you both would follow your jousters to the collision, trying right up to the point of impact to aim closest to the center. Usually, the ace would beat a jack. Perhaps often, he would not. If there are several players, the play of each hand would produce a jousting tournament, rather than a single tilt. The hypercard-as-jouster is, of course, only one possible theme. You may prefer other variations, injecting the hypercards into football, Wild West, demolition derby, or other arenas which strike your fancy.

In addition to their role in establishing rankings, cards are also used for "constructing" things in games. For example, in rummy or poker, one attempts by drawing and other plays to "make" certain hands, such as three of a kind or a "full house." Hypercards could add additional interest to this role as well. As an example, we can use the game of poker as a starting point and, with hypercards, turn it into a cattle drive along the frontier trail. In ordinary poker, a hand of five cards has a rank, ranging from the highest "straight flush," consisting of ace, king, queen, jack, and ten of the same suit, down to the lowest combination, which is a collection 2-3-4-5-7 with cards of different suits. Depending on the type of poker, a player's final hand of five cards may have come about in a variety of ways, either from the cards originally dealt, or as an improvement of this original hand, accomplished by discarding from a larger hand or exchanging cards. (Poker players distinguish exchanges made with the dealer from self-improvement methods such as finding better cards in one's boot or shirtsleeve.) While the improvement of the original hand admittedly offers some excitement, and often some risk, the final hand you make does nothing but sit there and wait to be compared against the competition. It does not offer you a challenge to do something with it.

With suitably "beefed-up" hypercards, that hand of five cards can represent five little dogies to be driven along the trail. The farther you can get them down the trail, the better you do, so that in a solitaire game you might try to drive them 100 miles in two minutes (Mach III dogies?), or in a competition you would try to be the first one to reach Kansas City or Dodge.

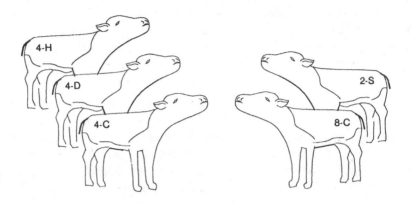

Hypercard dogies—This three-of-a-kind hand will "git along" in a hurry.

In order to preserve the poker nature of the game, the hypercards should be constructed so that good poker hands correspond to easily manageable "herds," and poor hands correspond to unruly ones. This can be accomplished by giving some social structure to the hypercards, in addition to their individual characteristics. Rank of the cards might be expressed as speed, so that an ace-dogie moves faster than a king-dogie which moves faster than a queen-dogie, etc. Social arrangements are incorporated so that dogies try to find similar dogies: A three-of-hearts dogie, which might be depicted as a smallish (for the three, which is a small number) red-brown (to stand for hearts) calf, would be happier (i.e., "git along" faster) when other calves of the same size (threes of other suits) or red-brown (other size hearts) calves were nearby.

As a player in cowboy hyperpoker, your challenge would be to round up your handful of dogies and get them on the trail in a good configuration to move along quickly. Of course, they would tend to stray and balk along the way, so skillful wrangling would still be needed after the drive started to get the best speed. By dint of artful nudging, prodding, and perhaps a careful selection of routes, your "two-pair" herd of dogies might beat a "three-of-a-kind" herd into Dodge City, even though the odds would be somewhat against it. You would just have to bust your braceros trying, take all the possible shortcuts, and hope the competition gets snowed on.

Randomness and Luck, Computer Style

Another use of cards is to inject randomness and/or lack of information into a game. (Since the cards are shuffled before each hand of a game such as poker, you will not be a very successful player unless you have a strategy for playing which covers any possible hand you might get.) In addition to this randomness, there is lack of information—you must *guess*, based on the cards in your hand and the bidding and play of the other players, what cards remain in the hands of the other players at any point in the game. In games which do not use cards, randomization is often produced by rolling dice, tossing coins, spinning spinners, and so on.

The element of uncertainty, whether you call it luck, chance, or randomization, adds spice to most popular games. Computer programs can incorporate randomness as a versatile and integral part of many games, bringing Lady Luck into the picture in a much more versatile, adaptable, and interesting fashion. The basic computer strategy is as simple as dividing a spinner into several regions; randomness can be produced with virtually any computer and programming language. Familiar methods of producing randomness, such as dice and cards, can not only be imitated, but modified and customized to create **hyperdice** and **hypercards**. Entirely new effects can be produced to change the character of a game and its balance of luck and skill.

Before looking at the computerized version of randomness, we can examine the familiar processes of tossing coins and rolling dice. Intuitively, we feel that when a die is rolled, it is:

- Impossible to predict exactly the number which will be uppermost when the die stops.
- Equally likely that any number 1, 2, 3, 4, 5, 6 will come up.

We also have experience with randomness where all of the possible outcomes are not equally likely, such as lotteries where a person's chance of winning can be increased by buying more tickets. Even with ordinary dice, all outcomes may not be equally likely: If someone tosses two dice simultaneously, and only tells you the total showing on both dice, the possible outcomes are the totals 2, 3, 4, 5, 6, 7, 8, 9, 10, 11, 12. These outcomes are not all equally likely (7 is the best bet), but it is still impossible to exactly predict before the dice are rolled which of the possible outcomes (totals) will in fact occur. Computer randomness, however we produce it, should incorporate these characteristics.

The computer brand of randomness is a function (of course). When you apply this function, usually by giving its name as input to some program, what you get back is a "random" number. Imagine a genie named Random who lives in a box and has a coin. Every time someone needs a little chance in their life, they just yell out "Random!" The genie dutifully flips his coin and responds "heads!" or "tails!" If you like hamburgers and chicken equally well, you might use such a genie to decide what to have for dinner. Perhaps you could train him (certainly if he were a computer function instead of a genie you could—simply by substitution of some words in the program) to directly shout "chicken!" or "hamburgers!" rather than "heads!" or "tails!", avoiding any further discussion.

The most common kind of randomness function you will find for a computer does not give back just one of two possibilities, but one particular outcome (number) out of possible thousands or millions. For example, if you are using the BASIC programming language, you can say " RND(1)" (for RaNDom) to the machine. What you get back is a decimal fraction somewhere between 0 and 1, like maybe .276423. The assumptions are that:

- Any fraction between 0 and 1 which your computer can write is equally likely to come up, and that if you say "RND(1)" again, you will get another number chosen randomly from all the possibilities: .000000, .000001, .000002, .000003...up to .999999 . (That makes a million possibilities, for example, if your computer only handles decimal numbers with 6 or fewer digits.)
- There will be no connection at all between numbers you get from one use of rnd(1) to the next.

The function rnd used in BASIC, and similar functions in other languages, are referred to as **random number generators.**

A random number generator behaves in the same way our genie Random would, if we gave him a spinner to spin inside the box, and had him call out the position on the spinner when it stopped, rather than just "heads!" or "tails!"

Imagine "0" marked at the top of the spinner, with a million little tic marks all around
the circumference (either a large spinner or a
sharp eyed genie needed) numbered .000001 to
.999999.

The genie just spins the spinner and then calls out the number closest
to where the tip of the spinner stops.

As an example, here is a three-line program written in
BASIC which will get you ten random numbers in a row: (By the
way, capitalization is ignored in BASIC. Some early computers had
only upper case letters, but nowadays lower case is usually available,
and is easier to type.)

```
1 for i = 1 to 10
2 print i;rnd(1)
3 next i
```

If you give this program to any computer which understands BASIC, what you will get back will be something like the
following display:

1	.771027
2	.781830
3	.751740
4	.473969
5	.181555
6	.203217
7	.515900
8	.266449
9	.955597
10	.335541

Without knowing BASIC, you can easily guess what would happen if the number "10" in the first line of the program were replaced by "20" or "30" or "10,000"—you would get 20 or 30 or 10,000 random numbers instead of 10, as shown. The large number of possible outcomes from a typical random number generator makes it easy to produce many kinds of randomness, for a variety of games and effects.

A simple example to start with is the classic coin toss. A coin toss is used at the beginning of many games to assign positions for the players, and so on. If we want to use a computer's random number generator as a coin, we could just call out "heads!" if the number comes up less than .5, and "tails!" if it comes up greater than .5.

The spinner can be divided in half for "heads" and "tails," using the numbers less than .5 for "heads" and the numbers greater than .5 for "tails."

Making the random number generator into a "coin" is no more difficult than painting a spinner in two different colors. In fact, we only need to add a few lines to the elementary BASIC program listed above to accomplish the whole spinner-to-coin transformation. After all, the program itself can check whether the number from rnd(1) is less than 1/2 and print "heads" in that case, otherwise "tails." Here is the modified basic program, along with reminders (**REM**) at the end of each line, telling what that line of the program does. Line 2 of the program is a **branching point**, because the program can go in two directions (executing line 3 or line 4), depending on the **decision** (is the number from rnd(1) less than .5?) made at this line.

1 for i=1 to 10: rem (sets up a "loop" of 10 repetitions)
2 if rnd(1) <.5 then 4: REM (go to line 4 if rnd less than .5)
3 print i; "tails": goto 5: rem (print "tails" and omit line 4)
4 print i;"heads": rem (print "heads")
5 next i: rem (continue the repetition process)

Notice that in this program, the number from rnd(1) never is printed—it is only used to determine whether the program will go from line 2 to line 3, or skip line 3 and go to line 4 instead. To the casual user, the program behaves exactly like a coin being tossed. If you copy it into your computer, you will get something like the following output when you run it:

```
 1 heads
 2 heads
 3 heads
 4 tails
 5 tails
 6 tails
 7 heads
 8 tails
 9 heads
10 tails
```

By simple substitution, you could just as easily have this program give out "chicken" vs. "hamburger" if the situation warranted it, or red vs. black, or home vs. visitors. You would only need to replace the words "heads" and "tails" in the program. Conceptually, you can always think of using a spinner, and deciding how you should paint it to do what you want. Once you have the spinner laid out properly into regions, whether it's two regions labeled "heads" and "tails" for a coin, or six regions labeled "one," "two," "three," "four," "five," "six," for dice, or fifty-two regions for a deck of cards, the rest is simple. Every *region* on your labeled spinner corresponds to a *range of numbers* (between 0 and 1) on the circumference of the spinner. Just arrange the computer program so that the label from this region will be printed, whenever the number from rnd(1) comes back in the appropriate range.

Here is a BASIC program that uses the number from rnd(1) to act like dice rolling. Conceptually, we have a spinner divided up so that the numbers less than 1/6 are labeled "1," the numbers between 1/6 and 2/6 are labeled "two," and so on. The program starts by saving the "spinner" number from rnd(1) as a variable called **v** (this is the phrase **v=rnd(1)** in line 10). This saved number **v** is then checked against all of the boundaries 1/6, 2/6...5/6 of the spinner (lines 20–70), until the right region is found. When the right region is found, the program jumps to one of the lines (1001–1006) in the printing section and prints the appropriate label. (In case you want to pretend that you have a spinner, and check that the program is working correctly, it prints the number from rnd(1), after the label "one," "two," or whatever it finds.)

```
5 rem A BASIC program for dice rolls
10 for i=1 to 10:v=rnd(1)
15 REM check-the-number section *****
20 if v<1/6 then goto 1001
30 if v<1/3 then goto 1002
40 if v<1/2 then goto 1003
50 if v<2/3 then goto 1004
60 if v<5/6 then goto 1005
70 goto 1006
1000 REM printing section *****
1001 print i;"one";v:goto 5000
1002 print i;"two";v:goto 5000
1003 print i;"three";v:goto 5000
1004 print i;"four";v:goto 5000
1005 print i;"five";v:goto 5000
1006 print i;"six";v:goto 5000
2000 REM go back and repeat
5000 next i
```

If you run the program above, you get something like this:

```
 1 five .771027
 2 five .78183
 3 five .100174
 4 three .473969
 5 one .078155
 6 two .203217
 7 four .5159
 8 two .266449
 9 six .955597
10 three .335541
```

Whether or not you are beginning to understand BASIC by this point, your substitution instincts should enable you to modify the programs given to produce many kinds of randomness. For example, the last program could give you a deck of cards, if you changed the *six* lines 20...70 into *fifty-two* lines:

```
20 if v<1/52 then goto 1001
30 if v<2/52 then goto 1002
40 if v<3/52 then goto 1003
. . .
520 if v<51/52 then goto 1051
530 goto 1052
. . .
```

The lines in the printing section would also be changed appropriately to something such as:

```
1001 print i;"two of clubs":  goto 5000
1002 print i;"two of diamonds": goto 5000
1003 print i;"two of hearts":  goto 5000
1004 print i;"two of spades":  goto 5000
. . .
1049 print i;"ace of clubs":  goto 5000
1050 print i;"ace of diamonds": goto 5000
1051 print i;"ace of hearts":  goto 5000
1052 print i;"ace of spades":  goto 5000
. . .
```

Even from this brief introduction, you can see the possibilities emerging for hypercoins, hyperdice, and so on. You only have to imagine an "intelligent" spinner. This spinner, in the form of programs using random number generators like rnd(1), can rearrange and relabel its own regions dynamically during the progress of a game. You could have a hypercoin, for example, which gives any probability you wish to tails turning up. (With a spinner, you can get "tails" to have twenty percent chance say, rather than fifty percent, simply by coloring twenty percent, rather than fifty percent of the spinner's circumference for "tails." With a computer to automatically prompt you and rearrange the spinner as necessary, the following interaction might take place. (A BASIC program to support the interaction is listed afterwards.)

> **Program:** What chance of tails?
> **Player:** .8
> **Program:** 1 tails
> **Program:** 2 tails
> **Program:** 3 tails
> **Program:** 4 heads
> **Program:** 5 tails
> **Program:** 6 tails
> **Program:** 7 tails
> **Program:** 8 tails
> **Program:** 9 heads
> **Program:** 10 tails
>
> **Program:** What chance of tails?
> **Player:** .2
> **Program:** 1 heads
> **Program:** 2 heads
> **Program:** 3 tails
> **Program:** 4 tails
> **Program:** 5 tails
> **Program:** 6 heads
> **Program:** 7 heads
> **Program:** 8 heads
> **Program:** 9 tails
> **Program:** 10 heads

The Hypercoin Program in BASIC

```
05 input "What chance of tails";x:REM (new chance of tails)
10 for i=1 to 10:REM (sets up a "loop" of 10 repetitions)
```

```
20 if rnd(1) < x then 40:REM (go to line 40 if rnd less than x)

30 print i; "heads": goto 50:REM  (print "heads"; omit line 4)
40 print i;"tails":REM  (print "tails")
50 next i:REM  (go back and repeat from line 10)
60 goto 5:REM  (restart; a whole new run from line 5)
```

Because randomness is such a characteristic feature of our experience of things from the weather to stock prices, the attempt to incorporate it into computer programs goes far beyond games. In this book, you will see the random number generator reappear prominently in the chapter on Modeling and Simulation. Other potential uses of randomness, from network switching to sensory sampling, will become apparent to you if you dig a little deeper on your own into any particular subject. For now, let's return to the immediate topic, which is hypergames.

Liar's Hyperdice

Perhaps the most popular form of hyperdice, before the age of the computer, were those used by crooked players. "Loaded" dice can be constructed by inserting an off-balance weight inside. The crook's idea of hyperdice is to replace the usual dice in the game with two sets, one fair and one loaded. You roll with the fair set, he rolls with the crooked set; he gets a lot of doubles, or sevens, or whatever he has loaded the dice for, and you typically lose, until you wise up. This type of hyperdice is not a very interesting evolution, although it is profitable enough not to be an endangered species. It does bring out the point that if one allows hyperdice, the chance that any particular number comes up may be *different for different numbers 1, 2, 3...6,* and may perhaps *change* (as it does when the crook surreptitiously switches the dice) from one roll to the next.

Let's see what hyperdice might do for the game of **Liar's Dice,** a perennial favorite at bars and elsewhere. Liar's Dice can be played by two or more people, and is played using a variety of rules, but we will use here a fairly simple version for two players:

1) Both players have five dice. At the beginning of the game, an amount is bet and all players roll their dice, but do not show the results to any other players until the game is ended.

2) The five dice each player has are used to make a poker hand, according to the correspondence 1 = ace, 6 = king, 5 = queen, 4 = jack, 3 = ten, 2 = nine. These "hands" rank just as in poker, with the highest hand being "five aces, or 1-1-1-1-1," and the lowest being 1-2-3-4-6. Of course there are no "suits," and hence no flushes.

3) One player chosen in advance starts the game by naming a hand, (such as "full-house, fours over twos," claiming to have a hand which is at least as good as the "full house" 4-4-4-2-2).

4) The other player can either challenge the first player's claim, or claim a higher hand herself. If she wishes to claim a higher hand, she may take another roll of some or all of her dice, after which she can no longer challenge the first player but *must* claim a higher hand.

5) Players proceed alternately, and at each turn, the player must challenge the last player's claimed hand, or claim a higher hand. Each player is allowed only three chances to re-roll during the game.

6) The game ends whenever the first challenge is made. If the challenged player does not have a hand as good as claimed, the challenger wins the bet, otherwise the challenger loses.

One way of looking at Liar's Dice is that each player has a fixed "budget" of dice-rolling (rolling the dice is allowed on three additional turns after the first), as well as a fixed "stake" in the game (the initial bet).

> Whenever any aspect of a game is *fixed or constant,* we can produce a **hypergame** by making that aspect *variable* and *changeable* by **chance or strategy.**

Applying this idea to the Liar's Dice game, we might want to allow the players to use their budget of "three rolls" in an infinite variety of ways, rather than simply deciding, at each turn, to roll or not. Why not let them have *half* of a roll, or a *quarter* of a roll, or whatever fraction they would like on a particular turn, until their three-roll budget is used up? In addition, players can be allowed to "load" the dice when it is their turn, provided they are willing to pay for the privilege by increasing their stake, or bet, in the game.

Hyperdice can be *fractionally* rolled as well as being susceptible to "bribes" in the form of further bets.

Here is a possible dialog between a computer program which uses hyperdice and one player in the Liar's Dice hypergame:

———

Player: How do I stand?

Program: Your hand is 2-2-4-4-6. Your opponent claims a full house, 5-5-5-2-2. You have 1.75 rolls left, and your stake in the game is $.55 .

Player: I'll spend 1/2 roll on the 2's.

Program: OK, you now have 1.25 rolls left. Rolling the 2's ... Result: 6 and 1. You now have 1-4-4-6-6.

Player: Roll the "1". Give me a 90% chance for "5".

Program: You will have to ante up for that. You have 1.15 rolls left, and a 90% chance for 5 is worth 12.62/5 = 2.53 rolls, so your deficit is 1.38 rolls. At the going rate, that will cost you $.35.

Player: I'll take it.

Program: You have 0 rolls left. Your stake in the game is $.90 . Rolling the dice. You got a 6! Your new hand is 4-4-6-6-6.

Player: OK, I'll claim the full house 6-6-6-4-4.

———

All of the features in the above game are accomplished by the program, by automatically "loading" the dice in an appropriate fashion. For example, if you want to spend 1/2 of a (five-dice roll), the dice are loaded so that each one has a 1/2 chance of not moving and 1/2 chance of being rolled as usual. If you want to have ninety percent chance of getting a particular number, the program calculates automatically that that would require 12.62 ordinary (one-dice) rolls on the average, and charges you for that amount. The dialog and the rules of the above game are merely meant to be suggestive. Your imagination is the only limit.

Hypercards can be "loaded" theoretically in much the same way that dice are physically loaded. Imagine the cards as being shuffled around in a hat and then dealt out, rather than flipped together in the usual fashion. You might make the high cards heavier than the others, so that they would tend to settle at the bottom of the hat. With this setup, the dealer would have some control over what kind of cards are drawn, by choosing to pick the cards from the top or from the bottom of the hat. (If the difference in the weight of the cards is small, there is little control, otherwise there may be a great deal.)

Metagames

In an ordinary game, the choices a player can make are usually called "moves." The term covers everything from a chess player's castling to a basketball player's hip fake. To describe the idea of metagames, we can say that as a metagame player, your choices go beyond simple moves— you may select larger scale options, such as games, players, strategies, or viewpoints. The spirit of metagames is to create a superstructure of strategy and interaction above and beyond a basic game or collection of games as they progress.

If the basic game is basketball, for example, there are only ten players directly involved at any one time. The classic metagame player in basketball is the coach, who chooses players and strategies rather than hook shots or layups. In a good game, the coach's role interacts dynamically with that of the ordinary players to enhance the game substantially. The fans at home and in the stands are also metagame players, to the extent that they have various options, ranging from simple cheering to prediction and friendly or serious betting. Usually, the fans have much less influence on the game than the coach, but they have enough to make the "home court advantage" a reality in many sports. We will look at a variety of metagame activities, including coaching, prediction, and construction. Even so, the range of possibilities is only suggested.

New Views for Spectators and Coaches

The demand for professional sports coverage, in the United States particularly, is phenomenal. The craving, like the very term "fan," borders on fanatic. At first glance, you might think that the driving motivation of this legion of sports enthusiasts is loyalty, the desire for the home team to win. The real appeal of sports though, is not the simple desire to be vicariously victorious, but the whole process of knowing beforehand the strengths and weaknesses, the balance of power, and watching the predictable and the unpredictable work themselves out in suspenseful struggle. If this were not so, the televisions would be tuned out—a simple box score would suffice. Fans would be just as happy with a 64–0 rout as a 64–63 cliff-hanger.

The booming business of sports is the spectators' metagame. The substance of this metagame is not body contact or physical exertion, but **information transfer.** The spectator wants to know what's happening, what can be expected to happen, and what may happen by chance and why, and would like to know it all as instantaneously and graphically as possible. The technological advances are welcomed eagerly precisely on this basis—better television coverage will hardly make your team a winner. The ever-present commentary, the split-screen camera, the presentation of background information and statistics, however crudely they can be handled at this early technological stage, open up new information channels to the viewer. Home computing power will expand the flow considerably.

Present day sports coverage works about as well as building a ship in a bottle: At the scene of play, a dozen cameras cover the action from all angles; coaches and players are making plans and assessing the opposition; statisticians and other analysts are putting the game in perspective and calculating odds. What does the home audience get? Basically, one picture, or half of two pictures, if that's what the crew decides you should see. The coach may be interviewed at halftime. The statisticians and oddsmakers will be allowed to insert a tidbit here and there, squeezed in between Homer Groselli's monolog of recollections and opinions. The wide scope of action has been compressed through the narrow bottleneck of a standard network broadcast. The viewer's options are limited to deciding when to go get pretzels, or perhaps zapping the television sound to get a better commentary on the radio.

Using multiplexing technology (remember the simultaneous chess tournament from Chapter One?), sports coverage for home computer users could be vastly improved. The computer's display screen would provide a bank of selectable channels, under the viewer's control, to display (and store and process, if desired) information from perhaps twenty or thirty simultaneous "chalk talks." The viewer can actively choose the supplementary presentations on the computer screen, while the usual television "dumb show" progresses.

This multiplexing process is already available for various "teletext" systems, where the channels a viewer selects typically have such things as train schedules or market reports. As an added feature to sports coverage, these extra channels could bring in a great variety of graphic and text material for you to select from, obtaining perhaps:

- A play-by-play transcript of the game, which you might store for later perusal, analysis, and reconstruction, as well as feed in "on the fly" to your computer's analysis/prediction programs, developed by yourself or other experts.
- "Scratchpads" from coaches, diagramming and analyzing key plays or anticipated maneuvers.
- Isolated-camera coverage, in diagram form, of every player, as well as the ball, stick, bat, puck, or whatever is involved. (Technically similar to putting those wireless microphones on the referees.)
- Statistical data and summaries, with predictions of all sorts and odds, for immediate viewing or automatic storage for postgame analysis.

You can imagine the excitement and audience participation such coverage would provide. Unless you have played interactive and fairly realistic computer games, you probably have not experienced anything similar. The network might even open up one of these selectable channels for viewer comments, perhaps limited to a few hundred words, or running polls and predictions. Even the homegrown pundit might make it to the big time, based on keen observation, salty wit, or uncanny prediction. The home viewer can have an active point of view, if not a direct input into the game. While you're tracking down player injuries, missed assignments, and comparisons with prior games, Groselli can ramble on if he chooses.

With a wealth of facts at every viewer's command, and a ready channel for feedback to the network, there may even be some Darwinian selection of fact from fulmination.

Going beyond the mere spectator's role, computers can be fascinating assistants for coaches everywhere. Not only "on the field" coaching, but higher level strategies in team construction, training effort, and emphasis can be brought into play, whether your team is in varsity sports from high school to college, professional or recreational adult games, or little league and youth soccer. Computers are already involved in professional sports management, guiding choices from scouting visits to pass patterns. (Once professional sportswriters begin to acquire computer literacy, they will be able to provide you with some insights in the form of programs for your home computer. You can then play along and second guess the professionals. Should the Red Sox trade for hitting or pitching? What will happen to Bleppo's batting average, with Carduzzo in the lineup?)

The preparation of players before a game is often the coach's most important role. How should a team's practice be organized, and what skills are most important for individual players to develop? In varsity or professional sports, the most important question is "What strategy will improve the team's chances of winning?": For less competitive enterprises such as school programs and recreational leagues, other issues can be addressed: "What skill will help a struggling player to actively participate in the game?" Could the rules be changed (e.g., the tee-ball version of the softball version of baseball) to keep the flavor of the game and add to its enjoyment by the players? The knowledge and experience of expert coaches can be communicated in the directly usable form of **programs**, for local coaches, instructors, or parents. A comprehensive program would be based on a range of activities, with specific methods for detailed measurements of player's skills in these activities. (More and more, computer **sensation/action** devices can handle such measurements directly. The radar gun and the pitching machine are already in the baseball coach's arsenal; computer technology and suitable feedback mechanisms can combine them into a programmable "robot pitcher.") The activity-measurement-analysis-activity cycle can be shaped dynamically for each player, while the measurements themselves are accumulated to build a coaching **database**. Continuing analysis of this database will enable the coaching staff to maintain effective training strategies for individual players, as well as develop the strongest configuration of players at game time.

Your favorite "sports" may be parlor games, puzzles or pantomime, requiring mental rather than physical exertion. It is quite possible that you have already played against a computer in chess or bridge, using one of many available electronic games. With only a little more sophistication, a flexible chess, bridge, crossword, or other game program in your personal computer could be not only an opponent but a coach, simply by playing the kind of game which most improved *your* skills as a result. Do you flounder on queen's pawn openings? How many words can you recall that sound like book? What kinds of words are hardest for you to guess, if some letters are hidden? Where should a team or player devote their efforts for the best payoff? In the best metagames, the metaplayer-coach not only introduces a new and interesting role, but improves the overall quality of play.

Prediction

The enjoyment of many games rests on our ability to predict the outcome, regardless of who wins or loses in the underlying game. Horse racing, jai alai, and other betting games are classic examples. Unless you own a horse, you would be equally happy to bet on any horse in the race...

...as long as it manages to win.

A pocket-sized computer custom-tailored for horse racing was an early entry in the consumer market; on the basis of betting volume, you can expect similar products, devoted to football, to appear soon. The information on modeling and simulation you will find in Chapter Seven will help you develop more programs on your own. The main drawbacks of current "horse race computers" and their kin are that you don't buy the data with the computer, and typically must go through some painful ritual of keying in large batches of numbers, and that the special-purpose computer is useless if you decide to change sports, or even simply modify the method of analysis. Since hundreds or perhaps thousands of people are using the same information, a more streamlined distribution system would be greatly advantageous. Rather than buying a paper version of the *Racing News*, you would simply exchange one of your computer's memory modules at the track for a freshly programmed one. Rather than watching the tote board and keying in information manually, your computer could be directly plugged in, perhaps with outlets at the dining tables in the clubhouse section. The computer itself would be completely programmable and equally at home at horse races, jai alai, or hockey.

If we are directly involved, rather than watching or wagering on the sidelines, an important use of prediction is to guide us in the play of the actual game. An expert predictor is guaranteed to be an expert coach, since by predicting accurately the effects of alternative strategies, she can choose the best one. Based on computer modeling and prediction, a basketball coach can estimate how long a player with four fouls will remain in the game, what the scoring effect of removing the player temporarily will be, and so on. Baseball, football, soccer, and other coaches could similarly gain insight about the likely effects of substitutions, changes in player assignments, or other strategic decisions.

Beyond betting and winning, prediction can help in the simple enjoyment of games. The metagame player has the option, if the predicted outlook for a game is pessimistic, to modify or restart the game, or switch to a more interesting or appropriate one. You might have more fun with solitaire, for example, by only playing out those games where your chances of winning are good or excellent. With a computer dealing hypercards, you could simply ask in advance for only these "good deals." Some bridge players prefer to bid grand slams, others would enjoy doubling such a bid No need to wait for dumb luck to provide your chance If you are temporarily stymied in a chess game or a crossword, the computer's predictive programs could supply you with valuable hints.

Construction

You may wish to construct your own games for a variety of reasons. A simple reason is often the desire for novelty—games such as crossword puzzles or mazes are hardly ever played twice. You may also wish to "customize" games, such as puzzles, children's "connect the dots," or coloring books, to match them to your special abilities or interests. As gamemakers know, a scrambled word game in English can be used to make a scrambled word game in Russian, say, by changing the alphabet. By changing the chances of the letters you draw, rather than the alphabet, a scrambled word game could be conducted where pop song titles or professional athletes' names, rather than ordinary English, provided the legal words.

The new game you construct may be aimed at *equalizing* an old game, so that two players of different ability can play enjoyably together. The classic electronic paddle game usually has a range of speeds, from painfully slow to hopelessly fast. Players can choose some middle ground which suits their abilities, and have a good game if those abilities are similar. A metagame alternative would be to have separate speeds for each player's half of the screen, automatically adjusted on the basis of the won/lost records so that each player has the same chance of winning. Every game would be a challenge to both players, and the challenge to each would be to keep increasing the speed on their side of the screen, regardless of the relative speeds for the two players. Similar equalization techniques can be used to produce a "training version" of any game, which gives the fledgling player hints, pointers, and other assistance in the course of the game and then gradually disappears as the player's skill improves.

Art for Art's Sake

Once you acquire a little metagame experience, you may enjoy constructing and combining games as an activity in itself. More traditional art forms such as painting and music often strive for the observer's participation as a central goal. Imagine the gratification of knowing that thousands of players coast to coast are matching wits in a game, installed on their computers, which you have created.

(If you detect the scent of possible pecuniary reward, that also is not unknown in the artistic world.)

Suppose that you have some liking for the spatial interplay of chess, but all in all, would rather play poker. You might look at the various characteristics of both games, and develop a metagame which combines the best features of each. Such a poker-chess game would have:

- Elements of chance, perhaps creating pieces on the board or restoring them unexpectedly after capture.
- Partial rather than complete knowledge of the other player's past moves and present options, bringing guessing into play.
- Spatial reasoning and tactics of the chessboard.
- Attractive displays employing cards and chess pieces.

In combining and creating games, you have all the features and attractions of existing games as a starting point. With many of these games in the form of programs, the recombination process can be quickly accomplished and trial versions produced in many variations. The resulting insights you achieve may lead into entirely new directions.

6

Computing as A Seventh Sense

Let me present you with a short scene of human and computer interaction, and ask you to think about what kind of a human might be involved and when, if ever, such a scene might take place.

The human is watching a display generated by his/her personal computer, not riveted to the images or even intensely concentrating, but interested and alert. The computer is processing and displaying numbers at the rate of roughly one billion digits per hour, or about a quarter of a million digits per second. After two hours or so, the human ends the session, in order to finally buckle down to some more challenging task she/he has been procrastinating about. Several days later, a friend asks this human about the data which were presented in the computer session, not only about the overall magnitude and trends in the numbers, but about the appearance, in the course of the presentation, of complicated patterns and relationships between these patterns. The answers come quickly and succinctly, giving the inquirer a clear and informative synopsis. Based on this synopsis, the friend may well decide to investigate the data himself, and request a second presentation, on his own computer. Alternatively, he may feel that no further review is necessary.

If you speculate that the above scene must describe computer hardware of the distant future, and some human megamind of even more remote descent from the present, you have been snookered on both counts. The scene represents nothing more futuristic than the possible adventures of a present day grade school child, watching a home movie on videodisc (procrastinating about school homework,

perhaps), and subsequently reviewing the movie (and possibly lend-
ing the disc) to a friend. The videodisc player, which is described
in more detail in Chapters Three and Nine, is a bona fide logical
device, which can be used to store and process numerical or other
logical information. The content of a typical movie, expressed in
logical form, would consist of billions of numbers. Nonetheless, these
numbers have been organized and are displayed in a *form* which
feeds directly into the impressive pattern recognition, analysis, and
synthesis capabilities of the human mind linked to its auditory and
visual system. With such aptly organized and displayed data, astonishing mental feats are performed so naturally and commonly by
humans as to pass unnoticed.

In this chapter, we explore the ways in which computers
can assist human thought, by transforming complex and/or massive
data-objects and bringing them within the range of human perceptiveness. Such objects might be:

- Large bodies of data—the computer can help abstract and
  summarize.
- Complex relationships – they can be extracted quickly by
  your programs from the data and presented in graphical
  form.
- Many-faceted observations and records—the computer can
  transform these data into a collection of human faces (or
  trees or castles, as some prefer), so that a human can more
  readily perceive and arrange them.

All of the techniques for transforming data described in this
chapter can be applied **interactively**, in the same way a television
camera operator follows the most interesting parts of a scene unfold-
ing before him. This interaction enables the human to effectively
"track" complex aspects of a situation over time, even as relationships are changing. When the quarterback fakes out the cameraman,
as well as the opposition, all parties are expected to quickly remedy
the error. In addition, we can use the computer to "fine tune" to
aspects of data which are usually lost. For example, as digital coding devices for sound become widely used, these techniques can be
applied to audio information of all sorts. You will be able to cook
up your own "lie detector" by processing voice signals, or develop
sound shaping facilities for music which make today's volume and
tone controls look as sophisticated as stone hammers.

What's Wrong With Ready-Made?

Despite the inherent interest of the topics presented in the rest of this chapter, you may raise a natural objection: Why should we not stick to the simple role of **consumers?** We humans are accustomed to, and have even grown addicted to, a multitude of transformations of the world around us, in order to make it habitable and comprehensible. The methods and implementation of most of these transformations do not concern us, only the end products. We are perfectly happy (for at least a short time longer, anyway) to use gasoline without knowing anything about the chemistry of cracking petroleum or even the physics of combustion. We watch television assiduously, even though we know from explicit warnings that tampering with the inside of the set could be fatal. A subscription to a daily newspaper is seen as a practical, if not perfect, substitute for personal monitoring of the news media of the world, themselves carrying transformations and interpretations of the world of external events. Why, then, should we not just continue to be consumers, rather than producers, when it comes to more sophisticated data-transformations? Why not leave the design and implementations to experts?

At a very mundane level, we must accept a role as consumers. Certainly, in technically developed societies, few people could, and fewer would care to, participate in even a fraction of the fabric of activities which supports their very existence. Most people feel that their time is better spent because of the fact that they do not have to plow, pull weeds, or (perish the thought) collect garbage. Perhaps the time is better spent, despite the fact our consumption of food and production of waste often become thoughtless and even irrational in the process. Even at this level though, there are problems. By giving up involvement in any **process,** we are forced to accept its **products.** These products, from sponge-bread and synthetic cookie filler to cars with hair-trigger accelerators and noxious emissions, may offer nothing but convenience. The prices are only apparently low, since hidden costs continue to accumulate, whether directly in the form of medical bills and other repair and maintenance expenses, or indirectly in the continued erosion of our range of choices, as the market gradually falls to the best advertisers and packagers. Even when we are prepared to be intelligent consumers, so that we define our own needs and values and look for technical products as tools to *support* these needs and values, rather than as standards to *define* them, our most economical and flexible choice is often not the product which requires the least knowledge to use:

Sale
Kitchenware

You would not only have to be rich, but also fairly mindless, to buy even a fraction of all the kitchen appliances offered to American consumers.

Computers and computer-based consumer devices do not yet—but certainly will eventually—outnumber kitchen appliances, and knee-jerk acquisition will be equally ill advised. For example, the sports fan who sees an advertisement for a computerized pocket horse race analyzer may perceive it as a high technology bargain. (The horse race pocket computer, though certainly not the best possible handicapper, uses three separate variables for each horse in a race and has compiled a good track record of its own when tested in over a thousand races.) A better bargain, though, would be to buy an entire pocket computer, also currently available, for about the same price. A program for this pocket computer could still be provided to untrained users by a racing expert, and better yet the users could update their strategy, incorporating more information, or change experts completely simply by changing the program. The versatile pocket computer would have many other uses as well, from note pad to financial advisor, which might continue to be interesting long after the fan has become tired of paying 20 percent off the top to taxes at the track, and switches his betting activities to football pools.

All grubby (if essential) questions of economics and practicality aside, the principal defect with an acquisition-oriented, buy-it-ready-made outlook is that it completely eviscerates the struggle for creativity and productivity in response to challenge which gives our human existence some charm and interest. Even when we are not actively engaged in the creative process, we have learned to choose our friends, and our books and can evaluate movies, paintings, advertisements, scientific proposals, and humanitarian endeavors critically. A similar informed and critical outlook should be exercised toward technologies and interface methods which bring new experience to our doorstep. Consider successively higher levels in a person's possible intellectual activity with regard to world news:

- Ignore the news.
- Believe everything you read in the (most available) paper.
- Realize that you have a choice of newspapers and other sources of information.
- Critically evaluate alternative presentations of the news.
- Become aware of the *basis* of your evaluations, and hence capable of refining them and/or applying them more consistently.

Corresponding intellectual levels, with regard to the "seventh sense" experience of new kinds of data, made possible by computer-assisted transformation and interaction, would be:

- Ignore the new data and ways of perception.
- Pay attention to some randomly chosen (or worse, perhaps the flashiest) data sets, transformations, and displays offered.
- Realize that alternative interface methods can give different data from the same phenomenon, and that different transformation methods can give entirely different views of the same set of data.
- Develop a sense of the kinds of data presentations and displays you find most comprehensible.
- Investigate ways both of transforming data into forms you comprehend, and of combining and improving these forms to broaden your range of experience.

In this chapter you will see some of the ways that you can use computers to acquire a "seventh sense" for data. The three themes taken up are summarization, finding relationships, and finding and making patterns. Appreciation of these themes will give you a feeling for some major approaches to seventh-sensing, as a starting point to develop your own programs or simply to become a more enlightened consumer.

First Theme—Summarize

A natural human reaction to the exploding availability of information is confusion and disorientation, similar to our reaction when we step from a dark room into bright sunlight. It will take years of experience before our sense of data catches up with our sense of sight. The first theme, summarization, is like the human strategy of squinting in bright light to avoid being blinded. It limits the view, but at least it allows you to proceed intelligently. What would you do with a billion numbers, if you needed or wanted to make some sense out of them? Could you answer only simple questions about such a huge mass of data, or would there be any hope of discovering complicated and intricate patterns as well? Suppose, for example that you are considering one thousand of your own physical characteristics. You might have "personal health monitors" which record your heart rate, blood pressure, respiration rate and volume, muscle activity, gland and organ function levels, concentrations of chemicals and nutrients in the blood, and so on. (It does not require strenuous effort to enlarge the list to a thousand features.) If each of these monitors takes one reading per second, your homemade medical charts will consist of a billion numbers in less than two weeks of recording!

Summarizing a set of numbers is much like trying to prepare a committee report. As chairperson, you must give some kind of a "representative" view of the committee's opinions, encourage interaction among the members, and also to indicate in the final report whether the committee is unanimous, strongly divided, or somewhere between these extremes. In summarizing data, you have individual numbers, rather than committee members, to deal with. Your goal is to extract some **representative central number** as a summary of the numbers you have, and also indicate the amount of **diversity**, or **variability**, of the numbers in the group, with respect to your chosen representative.

You might very well want to restrict the flow of data, for example, from the medical monitoring system suggested above. If you felt that one reading from each sensor per hour, rather than one per second, would be more comprehensible, it would make sense to have the "reading" for each hour actually be a **summary** of all 3,600 readings (one per second) reported by the monitors. If you wished to be more sophisticated, you could even let the number of summaries given per hour be different for different physical characteristics, and even change from hour to hour for the same characteristic, depending on the amount of variability found among the original readings. Your weight, for example, will probably turn out to be virtually the same from one hour to the next, while your heartbeat might vary greatly even over a period of minutes. By lumping observations together when their variability is small, it is entirely possible for a computer system to extract most of the **information** from your physical data, while substantially reducing the flow of numbers. Rather than covering less than two weeks, a billion well chosen **summary** numbers could describe the physical record of an entire lifetime.

Without pretending to do justice to the subject, let's take a quick look at how a group of numbers (like the 3,600 readings, one per second for an hour of your heartbeat, or the 5,000 real estate transactions in your town last year) can be boiled down to a report showing a "typical value" and the amount of variability present. The simplest form of summarization, along these lines, is to reduce the original (possibly large) batch of numbers down to just a **two-number report.** The first number describes what a "typical" number in the batch would be, and the second gives some measure of how close most of the numbers in the batch are to this "typical" value.

Two-number summaries are usually introduced in the first chapters of statistics texts, but they are as fundamental as they are simple. When you read in the newspaper that "the cost of new homes in this country rose by 15 percent last year," for example, you are wise to be aware that such a statement must be based on a **summary** of a large number of real estate transactions. More to the point, that "magic number" given as 15 percent may depend very much on how the author of the article (or the person who produced the figures for him) decided to summarize these transactions. Undoubtedly, there are large groups of houses, in various particular geographical locations and price ranges, which have changed price differently than the "15 percent increase" would lead you to believe. Depending on where you live or how much you intend to spend, the house you would consider buying (or selling) might be not 15 percent but 5 percent or 10 percent more expensive this year than last, or possibly even cheaper. Despite all of this variability, newspapers, congresspersons, and people in general often like to have a simple answer (like 15 percent) when they ask a simple question like "How much have house prices gone up."

A specific example is the "cost of housing" figure you are likely to see in a newspaper or magazine. Until fairly recently, the figure given most often would be the **average** price of a house in the area considered. It is more common now to find the **median,** rather than the average, given as the "typical price."

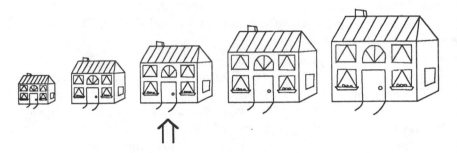

An alternative figure to use instead of the average, the *median* house price is found by listing the houses in the study, from cheapest to most expensive, and then using the price of whatever house is *in the middle* of this list.

For example, if you have seven houses in your study, the fourth one in the arranged-by-price list will be the middle one (three houses cheaper, three more expensive), and its price will be the median. If the study had eight houses, the median price would be halfway between the price of the fourth and fifth most expensive houses; if the study had nine houses, the median would be the price of the fifth; if the study had ten houses, the median would be halfway between the price of the fifth and the sixth, and so on. The **average** house price, in case you're rusty at this sort of thing, is found by totalling up the cost of all the houses in the study, and then dividing by the number of houses.

On the face of it, both the average figure and the median figure would seem to be good ways of summarizing a set of numbers. Computer programs to find either of these summaries are readily available and can handle huge amounts of data, if necessary. A quick example though, will show why the median is now used to summarize things like house prices and incomes, and the "average figure" is only seldom published. Here are two sets of house prices, from the hypothetical towns of Normalia and Statusville. In both sets, the **average** price of a house is the same, $80,000:

Normalia House Prices						
#1	#2	#3	#4	#5	#6	#7
$55,000	$65,000	$70,000	$80,000	$90,000	$95,000	$105,000

Statusville House Prices						
#1	#2	#3	#4	#5	#6	#7
$52,000	$55,000	$55,000	$55,000	$58,000	$142, 500	$142, 500

Although Normalia and Statusville have the same **average** house prices, the situation in the two places is quite different. Using the **median** figure (the price of house #4) as a summary, the "typical" house price in Statusville comes across more realistically as $55,000, compared to $80,000 in Normalia.

In Normalia, house prices are evenly spread around the average, $80,000. In Statusville, over two thirds of the houses are less than $60,000, but there are some "whoppers" that are almost three times as expensive as everything else in town. If you think about the way an "average" is computed, you will discover that it is according to the rule: "one dollar = one vote." By using the average, the two "swell" houses in Statusville get much more than the "fair share" of representation they would if the rule were "one house = one vote." By contrast, the median adopts this democratic "one vote per house" outlook, which is why if you read the *Statusville Times*, you will probably be told that the typical house in Statusville now costs $55,000 (the median figure, not the average, which is $80,000.) In terms of our committee chairperson analogy, the "average taking" person colors his or her summary report according to how strongly each of the members feel on the issue, from right wingers to left wingers, say. If the left wingers are apathetic and the right wingers are apoplectic, then the report comes out right of center. If the two expensive houses in Statusville rose in price to $200,000 each, the average price would jump from $80,000 to over $96,000 for the whole town, even if all of the other houses did not change price. (The median figure for Statusville would stay well behaved, at $55,000.)

It should be clear now why the median figure is more commonly reported for things like incomes and prices, if you are publishing a newspaper, magazine or government document. People do not buy extra newspaper or magazine copies or votes simply because they have more money. It is therefore much more useful to give the median figure to your subscribers or constituents, rather than the average, since the median will always be too low for roughly half of the people and too high for the rest, and not be overly influenced, as the average can be, by just a few extreme values. When wide-ranging distributions like incomes and prices are involved, this compromise solution is about the best that can be done to please a democratically distributed audience *with a single number summary.*

It is worth pointing out, to introduce a theme which will recur in this chapter, that the median is not somehow **the best summary.** If you have invested in a diversified real estate portfolio, the "one dollar = one vote" rule may suit you fine. The average, rather than the median, could tell you what you want to know about overall house prices: The value of your investments is more closely related to the average price in town than it is to the median price. The ideal situation is where everyone obtains exactly the most relevant summary of the data, **for their particular interests,** without wading through a maze of figures they find boring, uninterpretable, or downright misleading. Such tailor-made summarization would require a degree of interaction between the data and the consumer which has simply not been possible with traditional reporting or other static, one-recipe-for-all media. In effect, every user would need to have an individual "consultant," to explain the data and answer questions.

By using a computer, you can obtain not only new data but valuable built-in "consultant service" to help you analyze it.

Your successful use of the consultant will require not primarily mathematical skills, but the **managerial** skills of being able to **conceptualize** your questions clearly, and **communicate** them in some protocol to the "consultant." The consultant will then directly analyze the large mass of data according to your interests. As you might suspect, the "consultant" will actually be a system of programs.

As Abraham Lincoln observed, you can please some of the people all of the time. When a newspaper reports a median figure for something like new houses, the reasoning could be that half of the readers who subsequently buy or sell houses will find the paper's summary figure to have been too low, and the rest of the readers who buy or sell will find it to have been too high. Without any further information than the median, it is impossible for the newspaper to tell its readers just *how much* the median figure will differ from their actual experience. An extreme example can be given for a hypothetical town Splittsburgh, to show how badly things might go, even for the sophisticated newspaper which reports the median. Splittsburgh, like Normalia and Statusville, has an average house price of $80,000. In fact, its **median** house price is $80,000 as well. But it is indeed a small "some of the people" who are going to be pleased with the $80,000 "typical" figure:

Splittsburgh House Prices						
#1	#2	#3	#4	#5	#6	#7
$40,000	$40,000	$40,000	$80,000	$120,000	$120,000	$120,000

In Splittsburgh, the median figure differs from just about everyone's actual experience, by a substantial (33 percent–50 percent) amount. To be honest, the hard fact here is that *no single-number summary* can give an adequate picture of house prices in Splittsburgh. Any publication of conscience should feel compelled, when it gives a median or other figure for public consumption, to also give an indication of the **variability** in the original numbers, as a warning about possible indigestion from that consumption.

The immediate question becomes, "How can the variability of a group of numbers, like house prices in Splittsburgh, be expressed?" One approach, following Lincoln's advice, would be to pick a sizable "some of the people," say, 70 percent for the sake of argument, and try to please them all of the time. When a figure such as the median M is reported, an author can also give a number D, which might be called a "70 percent popular deviation," along with it, and say to his readers: "The actual value (house price, income or whatever) which you experience should not differ from my summary figure M by more than D, either above or below." The typical reader would then know roughly how useful (or useless) the summary figure will be in terms of her own experience. Here are such two-number (M and D) summaries, based on medians M and "70 percent popular deviations" D for the people of Normalia, Statusville, and Splittsburgh.

(Normalia: median = $80,000, D = $15,000): **"The actual house price which you experience should not differ from $80,000 by more than $15,000, above or below."** (This price range, $65,000–$80,000, does cover more than 70 percent of all houses in Normalia.)

(Statusville: median = $55,000, D = $3,000): **"The actual house price which you experience should not differ from $55,000 by more than $3,000, above or below."** (This price range, $52,000–$58,000, does cover more than 70 percent of all houses in Statusville)

(Splittsburgh: median = $80,000, D = $40,000): **"The**

actual house price which you experience should not differ
from $80,000 by more than $40,000, above or below." (This
price range, $40,000–$120,000 does cover more than 70 percent of
all houses in Statusville—and is hopelessly wide.)

       Some popular publications are even sophisticated enough
to temper their one-number summaries with some variability information such as the "70 percent popular deviation." Many are not.
When variability information is not given, or is given in such a form
that it cannot be interpreted easily, the reader must only guess as to
the value of the summary figure in drawing any personal conclusions.
In particular, such statements as

  —figures are given for comparison only; your experience may vary—

serve little purpose beyond boilerplate: The median house price in
Statusville is lower than Splittsburgh's, but useless for "comparative
purposes," if you want to buy a house for less than $50,000; they're
all in Splittsburgh! We may be able to live with the fact that "experience may vary," but we ought to be told roughly how much.

       Many readers, especially in financial and other quantitative
publications, are presumed to be capable of handling many numbers
simultaneously, without dropping any. These readers may get five-
number summaries, or bar charts, pie charts, histograms, and time-
series. If your talent and interests lie in that direction, you should
certainly develop them. The methods of theoretical and applied
statistics provide powerful tools for making the information in a
collection of numbers humanly interpretable. Our excursions in this
chapter give only the briefest of hints. A personal computer, with
its ability to effortlessly do arithmetic, make rankings, sort, select,
combine and re-express observations, will be an invaluable assistant.
The impact of computing on our ability to deal with data though,
reaches many more people than the number lovers or those who
become technically trained as statisticians:

> Most people can deal with a collection of
> data in terms of *questions* which the data
> should resolve, or at least shed light on.

After all, whether the data are prices, wages, population, or scientific
and technological results, the person who collects them or references
them must have some motivation in his own terms from the start.
If every data set were supplied to us with an associated "expert,"

who could answer our questions about the data without telling us more than we wanted to know (but hopefully whatever we needed to know to understand his response), statistical training would be altogether pointless. The ever increasing availability of personal computers promises to provide just such "experts" on a large scale. The catch (and the reason statisticians are not an endangered species) is that the "experts" will in fact be **computer programs** designed by theoretical and applied statisticians. (The label "statistician" is not crucial. Many of the best researchers would call their field "information processing," "database management," or "artificial intelligence.")

As a non-statistician, you will be able to use such analysis programs as intermediaries between unmanageably large amounts of data and the questions you have, formulated in terms which you understand. Even the brief excursion into the topic of summaries and variability here should have been enough to convince you that producing the "right answer" from a collection of data is a difficult, and often downright misguided task. Your personal expert would be forced to summarize, no doubt. The point is, the summary would *respond* to your questions, rather than *restrict* the possible kinds of answers you can obtain.

There may be as many "stories" to a news event as there are delegates to a convention, people in a neighborhood, or products of a technology. Given the data, you may find and be interested in some stories which every other reader discards. No longer will the writer have to make his story the answer to a hypothetical question which the reader, in fact, may never ask.

Second Theme—Find Relationships

Not all of the questions which we might want answered by a collection of data can be handled by a simple summarization. Very often, the interesting features of a situation lie in the **relationships** between various aspects of the data, rather than in any one characteristic alone. If the data we are looking at involve our personal medical monitoring system, we might have questions such as, "How much will my exercising this week affect my blood pressure next week?" or "What foods in my diet contribute the most to my serum cholesterol?" If the data are records of political contributions, we might wish to know how much candidates' voting records agree with the interests of their (largest) contributors. If we are working for political candidates (or are political candidates ourselves), we might like to know where our expenditures of money, time, and effort should go (what localities, which media, what issues), to produce the largest gain in votes. A well planned campaign itinerary, developed with extensive computer assistance, deserves at least part of the credit (or blame, depending on your views) for the election of the current White House resident.

In addition to health and politics, you might also have some interest in financial matters. Financial databases, of course, are prime candidates for relationship-hunting. If you are investing or innovating, the balance sheets of existing companies, market and survey data, and so on, should all yield information as to which companies or products are good prospects either for the short or long term. If you are working from the inside of a company, rather than watching it from outside, "keeping the books" should be a dynamic part of the maintenance, management, and growth of the company. Rather than simply serving to keep Uncle Sam and the shareholders happy, the recording and **analysis** of a company's financial transactions can actively monitor favorable and unfavorable trends as well as potential areas of correction, re-emphasis, or other improvement. You may own your company or simply want to become a more valuable (and valued) member of a larger firm; the relationships you can uncover and capitalize on, using financial and other data you now probably overlook, will be (perhaps literally) a goldmine of information. "What items in a store's stock or a restaurant menu should be removed or replaced?" " How can personnel and equipment be effectively and equitably scheduled?" "Where and what kind of advertising will be the most cost-effective?" The data you need are already available in many cases. With a friendly and manageable computer available (let the company buy it, if you like), you can get more data, and even more importantly, capitalize on the **relationships** a skillful analysis will uncover in the data you have.

Some fundamental types of relationships you might look for in whatever type of data interests you are **association or co-occurrence, predictability,** and **causality.** We can illustrate these relationships here by simple examples, as well as show how the computer provides a "seventh-sense" to find them.

Association—The First Clues

The phrase "guilt by association" is familiar and often apt. If an acquaintance mentions that he is a Nazi, you needn't bother asking his opinion of minority groups. If you have enjoyed reading a book, it is often worth while to check on the author's previous works. If you and your favorite critic both loved Mr. Allen's first four movies, and the critic hated the fifth, you may not bother to see it. You might think of association more graphically as **persistence of association**: If you isolate all the Nazis, and then readmit to civilization all those who are not bigots, you will not even make a dent in their association. In more standard terms, the above relationships are all associations: Nazi party membership is associated with bigotry; liking one book of an author is associated with liking his previous books; your favorite critic's movie opinions are associated with your own.

> To find an *association* requires us to look at our data from two different viewpoints. If the data hang together the same way from either viewpoint, then the two viewpoints are *associated*.

To see how computers can help uncover relationships, let's stay with the movies for a while. If you are not a particularly avid or particularly old moviegoer, you might have seen a thousand movies or so, including television approximations, and remember enough detail from each to rate them roughly, perhaps from zero- to four-star quality. With a computer to present you with the titles of movies and store your remarks, you could polish off your whole backlog of ratings, getting them electronically stored in a matter of hours, and afterwards easily keep up to date with new films as they appear. As things like newspapers and television guides become more computerized, it would be easy to have your computer scan the week's television listings, and tell you how many four-stars are coming up, or which network has the biggest batch of zero-stars (again) this week.

Many other kinds of movie *summaries* could be developed with computer assistance. What about finding *relationships*? There are other viewpoints for movies besides your personal ratings. With good databases and communication networks, you could gather ratings from perhaps a hundred movie critics, on the same thousand movies you have seen. A great deal of insight into movies and even into your own preferences is now possible, provided you can find associations in the viewpoints (yours and the critics') embodied in the assembled movie data. Suppose you find that Myra Snippet, the celebrated columnist, has rated almost all of the movies in agreement with you. The association between your viewpoint and Myra's opens up many possibilities: If Myra is urbane and witty, and you are somewhat awkward, it would be worth going through a collection of her movie reviews, perhaps acquiring a little of her panache to grace the armor of your opinions. You might also find some "uncut gems," movies which you had rated poorly, but Snippet liked. Whether or not you can eventually agree, a second look would be interesting. Alternatively, it may be that you find Snippet personally and philosophically revolting. In that case, the unexpected association between your opinions about movies and hers will probably cause a change of views somewhere. You might simply like to criticize the critics. Do most of them agree with Snippet? What do the dissenters have in common?

Whatever sense you want to make out of associations, you first have to uncover them. In the movie critic example, the combination of one thousand movies and one hundred critics gives one hundred thousand ratings. You are not likely to get far into this data, much less follow up written reviews, produce abstracts, and so on, with old fashioned technology like pencil and paper. (Nor will it do you much good, without a computer and good communication facilities, that there are ten thousand other people also interested in the same movie reviews, with the potential to capture all of the data by typing in ten reviews each.) A computer can easily scan all of the ratings, perhaps in a fraction of a second. The key question for you is, "Can you **define** association between movie critics (or find someone else's definition you can agree with,) in some way that a computer can calculate it from the ratings you have collected?" If you can, the computer is capable of **applying** *your* definition, to uncover interesting associations among the critics. Some possible definitions of association could be:

- *Common winners*: The amount of agreement between any two critics can be judged by the number of movies they both rate as excellent. The more movies they both rate as excellent, the more they agree, by this definition.

- *Common losers*: Agreement between two critics is judged by the number of movies they both rate as awful.
- *Overall agreement:* Agreement is judged by the number of movies both critics give the same rating (0, 1, 2, 3, or 4 stars).

Whichever of the above definitions you settle on, the computer can answer such questions as:

? Which two critics are most in agreement?

? Which critics are least in agreement?

? Of all the critics, which five most agree with your personal ratings?

Starting from your chosen definition, all that is required of the computer is counting, sorting, arithmetic, and other tasks it can blitz through, sparing you the repetitious details of its calculations.

The point to be made, whether your interest is movies or medicine or anything in between, is that the choice is yours. Not just the choice of data, but of fundamental starting points such as the best definition of "association" for your interests. If different definitions give different answers, it is up to you to determine the most appropriate interpretation.

Prediction and Causation

The great interest of finding relationships in many kinds of data is that the relationships extend beyond the data you have, and hold true for new data as well. When a new movie is produced, you will probably have several critics' ratings before seeing the movie yourself. If one of the critics you consistently agree with raves about a new film, you can expect to enjoy it as well. If several critics whose opinions are highly associated with yours all rave about a new movie, you may want to cancel your ski trip to see it.

> When aspects of data which are easy to obtain are associated with aspects which are difficult or impossible to see directly, the association becomes *predictive*. The accessible aspects of the data give clues as to the hidden aspects.

The predictive value of a relationship may be used primarily as an organizing tool. Whether you're tracking down literary references or prospective customers for your used car, you can carry out your search more effectively based on well constructed relationships: The books in a section of the library are related—you can effectively go to a section and browse; newspapers and magazines attract a characteristic audience—you may choose a publication, then effectively advertise.

Very often, the "accessible" means the present, and the "hidden" means the future; "prediction" in ordinary usage means predicting the future. The forecasting angle accounts to a large extent for the economic and technological importance of relationships. As any horse race fancier or investor knows, there are many relationships between characteristics of stocks (equine or otherwise) and historical prices, performances, and payoffs. If these relationships could be reliably found and followed in present and future data, the market analysts would all be working for themselves. The volatility and ease with which markets and races are manipulated should warn off all but the hardiest from wholesale speculation, but other predictive relationships are less variable and perhaps equally profitable. The sales of a business on Wednesday might be associated with its sales on Tuesday, or perhaps more strongly associated with the sales from last Wednesday. A modern businessperson can plan inventory and staff assignments, conduct sales and promotions, and design advertising, guided by such relationships found from recent sales data.

Whatever your gamble is, from bays to business to bridges, a fundamental problem is that data doesn't usually call you up on the phone and volunteer to talk. Nonetheless, we are more and more immersed in a flow of electronic information, but unwittingly throwing most of it away.

> With a little knowledge of computing, you can guarantee that the "computerized cash register" you buy is flexible enough not just to store all of its data, but to transfer it wherever else you need it.

A bona fide computer cash register could be simply an input device, such as a keyboard or a bar-code reader, and an output device for controlling the cash drawer, attached to any garden variety computer. Why pay a fancy price for the label "computerized" on the register, and then have it lack the flexibility to do more than keep books in some restricted manner? The real "computerized" cash register would be the hub of a wide scope of activities, from forecasting to inventory control to communication. Unfortunately, what the uninitiated businessperson may buy is likely to be an overpackaged and overpriced, non-communicative "total machine." Not only will you pay too much for such a device and use it too little, but the instructions and rigmarole you will have to learn to operate it will make very little sense, and have no connection perhaps with several perfectly good computer languages you know already.

As such "computerized" products go, cash registers are not the worst offenders. Devices from auto computers to stereo systems are bound to proliferate, each doing a specific task with unrelated procedures and costing individually what an entire computing system should, as long as customers can be convinced that computers are basically incomprehensible. Rather than seeing a modern business as a den of unrelated electronic appliances, from door openers to scales to cash registers and check printers, your view could be much simpler. What a business needs is an appropriate orchestra of sensation and action devices, able to capture the appropriate information and take appropriate actions. The lifeblood of the organization is information, and the devices should be arranged so that information can flow freely and be commonly utilized among them. Without free flow of information, the assembly of data necessary to find valuable relationships will simply not occur.

Beyond simple prediction, the associations found in data, whether used to schedule doughnut production or automobile construction, often point to **causal** relationships as well.

> If you can manipulate one aspect of a situation, while another aspect maintains a constant relationship, you can put this *causal link* to work, in the same way you would a mechanical link between an accessible object and an inaccessible one.

Causal relationships are the strongest type you can hope to find, and are the backbone of engineering and science. A word of caution is in order here, as you begin to flex your newfound computer capabilities: You will have unprecedented power to find relationships and associations. Once found, an association's *predictive* value can only be established by statistical or empirical induction. The *causal* nature of an association can only be investigated by experiment. All the computer calculation in the world cannot vault you over a single one of these inductive or experimental hurdles.

Third Theme—Find and Make Patterns

What is your response to a new situation? Are you confused? Are you curious? Are you explorative? Do you take the initiative?

However you answer the above questions, the stages they represent are familiar to all of us. In truly novel situations, we must be initially confused, even if only for a moment until we get our bearings. Once we do, curiosity, exploration, and initiative may follow. In this entire process (which Jean Piaget described insightfully as concurrent "accommodation" and "assimilation") the key concept is the idea of **pattern** or **structure**.

> We move through our experience by a process of finding and making patterns. We *assimilate* when we find and make patterns to match our **existing** structure. We *accommodate* because experience leads us to rearrange our expectations and internal structures into **new** patterns.

The abstractness of talk about assimilation/accommodation is not meant to put you off or to fancify a basically simple notion. It is obvious to us all that:

- We change the food we eat. / It changes us.
- We choose our friends according to our tastes. / Our friends influence our tastes.
- We design objects from bookshelves to buildings according to our perception of space. / Objects create our perception of space.

Piaget's accommodation/assimilation paradigm gives the insight that such obvious facts as these are related, and gives perspective to accommodation and assimilation strategies in a wide variety of settings, highlighting the role that patterns play. In our newfound seventh-sensing of data with computers, existing patterns can help us to **assimilate**, giving us a point of view from which to summarize data or look for relationships between sets of data. Beyond that, the strongest influence in our **accommodation** to new data is the attractiveness of new relationships and other emerging patterns. We will highlight just a few possible patterns in data here, and the interplay of patterns, summaries, and the definitions of relationships.

Confirmation: Perhaps the most fundamental action we can take with a new element of data is to confirm it. In this most assimilative context, we have a preconceived notion of what we are looking for, and the only response to a new datum is, "Yes, it is," or "No, it isn't." We all find this mentality occasionally useful, whether looking for a lost contact lens or drilling for oil. Often, with large batches of data, there is just a single yes-or-no question we would like to ask about each item in the batch. In a batch of Yankee box scores, we might simply like to know which games the team won, or we might ask which games were won by the starting pitcher, and so on. Not surprisingly, this all-or-nothing approach does not allow much structure to emerge—if all you notice about a game is whether or not your team wins, your impression of the season will be limited to the won-lost record. For a **summary**, something such as a count of the number of wins and losses, or perhaps the percentage of wins, will be perfectly adequate.

Even for simple confirmation and summary counting, a computer can be very handy, with large amounts of data like sports records or geological readings, or in situations such as traffic monitoring, where we would rather not take up a human's time asking the questions (Was that a vehicle that just passed?) and tallying up the counts (Yes, that's the second one this morning between two and six A.M.). Once we consider more than one yes-no question simultaneously, the possibility of finding **relationships** arises even in this restricted context. If you ask the question, "Did the home team win?" and also, "Did the first four batters in the lineup hit better than their averages?" you may find the same answer for both questions in most of the games. If you do, even this yes-no exploration has led you to find a relationship, perhaps an unexpected one. (You may have asked these two questions originally only as separate angles of interest.) The relationship may lead you to change your mind about why games are won and lost, as well as more assimilative behavior, like tending to switch off future baseball games in the late innings when your team's leading batters are mostly hitting below par. Based on the predictive value of what you've found, the team is probably going to lose. If the two questions are, "Did this person get lung cancer?" and, "Is this person a smoker?", even simple questions can lead to important relationships.

   Classification: A context which gives many more possibilities than simple confirmation/rejection is classification or naming. Each new datum is not just "yes, a crow" or "no, not a crow," but "a crow or a blackbird or a raven or...." If everything fits neatly into a named category, it's all assimilation. When something turns up, like waves that behave like particles and particles that behave like waves, not fitting into any category, people like physicists have to make some accommodations. In the classification context, a summary can be a list of relative amounts of the data in each of the various categories. You might go through your personal expenditures in a month, and classify them as food, clothing, shelter, transportation, recreation, and summarize what you find in a **pie chart**. The size of the labeled pieces of the pie indicate (relatively) how many dollars you spend on that area. To be more graphic, you might summarize with a picture of something more relevant than a pie, such as an...

Summer   Winter

...**ensemble of pie (food), coat (clothing), house (shelter), car (transportation), and tickets (recreation) adjusted to appropriate sizes which reflect each item's share of your budget.**
With several classification schemes operating simultaneously, possible relationships and patterns multiply rapidly. Statistical proce-

dures such as cross-tabulation make it possible to sift large amounts
of data, considering many aspects concurrently to find an interesting angle. Is the nature of a car crash related to the type of tires
used, more than to the color of the car? Insurance companies may
want to know, and if you think the relationship is causal, it will
probably influence your actions. In the past, only large companies
or agencies could expect to acquire substantial data of this type. In
the future, you can expect community and consumer databases of all
sorts, available for your particular questions and analysis, as well as
a potentially large audience for any new insights you might achieve.

Structured Images: Confirmation/rejection and classification are undeniably important, but often too confining. After all,
if you decide to analyze a book simply by categorizing and making
a list of the words used, then give this list to someone, he or she
will hardly have the same experience as reading the original. (The
person might be able to tell you what words should be put in the
book's index though, or even pinpoint the author of a disputed work
by his lexical fingerprints as was done in an analysis of Hamilton and
Madison's Federalist Papers.)

> The essential product of sensing is an *image*. The
> more structure which is available in the *image space*
> where this image is developed, the more structure
> can be captured by the sense.

If you find it unusual to talk about images outside the realm
of art, it is simply because the artist's media have historically been
more closely linked to human senses than the media of data analysts.
The use of computers will change that. Not only will it be possible
to "hear" data if you like (the human auditory system is capable
of frequency analyses and pattern detection that far surpass the
capabilities of any present computer programs), or "walk around"
the inside of a cell, or feel the texture of a microscopic crystal with
your hands, but also to manipulate these objects **interactively** in
the familiar spaces where their images are presented to you.

The statistical and scientific insiders have a variety of images and spaces of their own, whose inherent interest you may begin
to appreciate as the computer interface more and more breaks down
the formidable mathematical barriers of the past.

In these more structured spaces, you might find, for example **ordered categories**, where the naming system is not just categorical (like hammer, scissors, screwdriver ...) but directional. Although ordering is one of the simplest structures for an image space, it enables a new quality of perceptions: Illnesses occur more frequently after more *severe* stress, job satisfaction *increases* with *decreasing* time constraints, and so on. If you can put your categorizations in order of any sort, whether it's severity, strength, persistence or any other aspect which is capable of degrees, you will find computer assistance available to gather data and glean impressions. Other classical spaces have geometric and distance structures similar to the two-dimensional space of photographs, the three-dimensional space of the "real" world, or higher dimensional **hyperspaces** such as the four-dimensional universe of time and distance where physics is done since Einstein. Spaces of "connectedness" like crochet or computer networks exist as well, with the promise that familiarity with crochet or networks will help you get around in these spaces in the future with some of the ease now reserved for mathematical types like graph theorists and topologists. Henceforth, when you are confronted by such analytical buzz words as "correlation," "regression," "multidimensional scaling," "factor analysis," or "clustering," bear in mind that the motivation for all these techniques is the existence of underlying image spaces, whose structure you can investigate, evaluate, utilize, and modify through many computer assisted avenues, beyond classical mathematical skill and training.

Beyond these classical spaces, there are an infinite variety of structures which can be created, in which to subsequently develop our own images of data. The structure-creation/imaging process itself often goes by the name "modeling" or "simulation." There are libraries of material on the subject, but since you're reading this book, you can easily start with the next chapter.

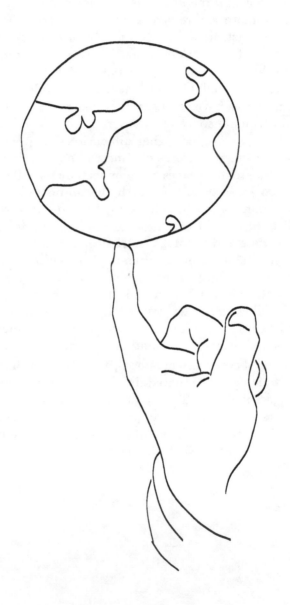

7

Simulation—Modeling Microcosms

A key to the widespread fascination with computers among those who attain a working familiarity with them is the unprecedented capability they provide for creating dynamic systems. One is literally able to create new worlds, specify the laws which will govern their development, and then observe their fascinating and unexpected evolutions. Often, the modeler's purpose may be to mimic real world systems.

Physiological models have been constructed to study systems such as hearts, bones, and muscles.

You could put such models to work for you in designing exercises or preventing injuries. Social/psychological models are also in wide use. The same techniques which produced a winning campaign schedule for the President could be used to help your town councilman, or help you direct an effective phone campaign for your favorite proposition or initiative. If physiology and politics leave you cold, you might be interested in modeling the development of a football game (potentially a lot of physiology and politics, nonetheless). If you read on, you will get a wealth of ideas. Gambling is a great incentive to model building, and the same techniques and principles can guide you, whether your game is football, horse racing, or the Big Board and Wall Street.

This chapter provides examples of possible simulations, set in contexts ranging from the Astrodome to Wall Street. More importantly, we will discuss principles and methods of model construction, verification, and modification, which can not only save you time, but give you a better grasp of and insight into the system you are creating. After that, you can launch into applications ranging from economics, ecology, and sociology to physics and mathematics, according to your taste.

A Few Samples from the Modeler's Workshop

The subject of modeling, specifically the kind of computer-assisted modeling that was not possible thirty years ago, and not practically or widely used even ten years ago, now touches every major area of scientific research. In weather, economic, and business forecasting, computer assisted modeling may be the major investigative tool. Technological applications are equally abundant, in projects ranging from giant bridges to microscopic electronic circuits. Against such a background, the examples given here can only be seen as a few threads picked from a tapestry—a little of the color and a bit of the material of the subject is all they can convey. In each of the subject areas below, examples are given of modeling possibilities, along with relevant questions raised and addressed by the model.

Sociology and Psychology

Manageable Politeness: The processes by which we choose careers and friends are often more haphazard than we would like to admit. Certainly, our occupation is more relevant to most of us than our clothes, but often not as well tailored to fit. Our friends and associates are merely selections (at best, conscious and apt selections) from the limited pool of contacts offered by our job or our geographical neighborhood. Even conscious social "choices" such as clubs, church groups, and political organizations, cast a very haphazard net in the ocean of humans we would find interesting, amusing, and edifying. Imagine for a moment being able to converse with hundreds of thousands of people, not over the course of a lifetime, but in a matter of weeks. Your range of choice for a partner, mate, employer or employee, customer, conversationalist, or co-author would be enormous. Personal computer **networks** will provide such communication ability in the near future.

You do not have to think long though, to realize that the potential for communicating routinely with hundreds of thousands of people, via telephone, cable television, and other network arrangements, can be more of a nuisance than a blessing without careful management. Concepts such as privacy, manners, and courtesy will all have to be carefully examined in this milieu. The "very large neighborhood" implied by computer communication means that new rules of politeness and exchange of information will have to evolve, tailored of course to individual tastes, but nonetheless offering practical protocols for social interaction. Suppose you have talent and wish to flaunt it, to find a prospective employer, customer, companion. What questions should you ask to people you "meet?" What information should you give them about yourself? The electronic boor who imposes upon others without regard to their interests and concerns can potentially be much more of a nuisance than the current cocktail party variety. People will take countermeasures to protect their privacy, appropriate to the new situation. As a salesperson, you may now stoically accept a door closed in your face, or an unexpectedly quick end to a phone conversation, especially if you have called uninvited. You would not expect or appreciate such behavior from a friend or even a casual social acquaintance. When your friends number in the thousands (if you wish), and your social acquaintances, colleagues, and partners form an even larger group, you cannot expect the same standards of politeness to function effectively.

In developing your own rules of communication with others, for example in composing customized "job interviews" or "social questionnaires," you will undoubtedly benefit from examining **social processes** such as communication exchanges, and **psychological factors** of the kind that influence your satisfaction with your occupation or personal situation. Experience with your own models in these areas will give you insight into the widely used social and psychological models of others.

When you receive the electronic version of the first friendly hand wave or nod of the head from your new "neighbor" (some guy from Emporia, Kansas, say, E.V. White, or E.B. White, or something like that) what can you expect to know about him already? What more would you want to know to determine your common interests or possibly cultivate a friendship? Would you prefer to have him respond to a questionnaire (which one?) or provide you with a free-form essay, or both? What are you prepared to tell him about yourself?

Science and Technology

The Scientist as Docent: Many of us are interested in science and the fascinating insights it offers into the world around us, even though we do not have the training or the laboratory facilities to study many areas firsthand. You may find such "hot" subjects as genetic engineering or fusion reactors fascinating, but there are some substantial drawbacks to dabbling in these areas yourself. With a home computer though, you are able to set up a **simulation observatory** to examine and experiment with these phenomena, often obtaining striking glimpses in your model of what the professionals are accomplishing in their laboratories. (Since these professionals often use models themselves to test a process or a calculation before actually trusting it to be implemented, it would not be unreasonable to ask them to supply to the public some of their more fundamental programs describing their work, as an educational and public information service.) Perhaps you have read about current theories of earthquakes or star formation, in articles where these subjects were "translated" for non-specialists. With home computer models, you could observe the earthquake or the star evolve, and the theory expressed in the articles would suddenly come to life.

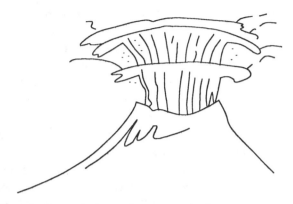

If you're studying the eruption of a volcano, a computer model is *better* than being there.

Appropriate Technology and Resource Management: The resources of the earth are finite. That obvious statement has certainly taken us a long time to appreciate. Mentally, we are slowly but surely being weaned from the "hunting and gathering" outlook appropriate when resources are unlimited, to a mature "husbanding" approach which recognizes the planet's limited capabilities. To achieve self-sufficiency and stability will require individuals as well as nations to set limits and "balance budgets" of all sorts, or suffer disastrous consequences in the near future. Once we recognize that our resources, such as energy, are finite, we begin to be concerned with our possible **choices within limits.** What kinds of food should we eat and/or grow? Within a fixed amount of money for food, what diets are available and preferable? How do we use energy, and how much do we pay for various kinds? Could we develop a personal "energy program," matching every increase in the cost of energy with a corresponding decrease in our need to consume and/or our ability to produce? In particular, what is our "minimum energy requirement," and how much of what we now use is wasted? All of these questions and more can be addressed by modeling our preferences. We can then "spend" our limited resources intelligently to achieve the best quality of life, as we ourselves define it.

Beyond these static **preference-management** models, we can construct simulation models to examine the effects of strategies which are too numerous or too drastic to leap into directly. Will a solar collector pay for itself? What type of a heating or solar or wind energy system could be used (perhaps with modifications) to take advantage of your situation? How much of your "garbage" is in fact *doubly* (you do not use it, and you pay to have it removed) wasted, and what processes could be used to salvage it? If the salvaging requires a "superslave" who possesses a peasant's capacity for dirty work and a professional's technological skill, your personal computer and its associated action devices need to be recruited and trained. What would happen if you dispensed entirely with a personal automobile? How would public transportation serve your needs? Could you share the ownership of **n** cars with **m** other people and have many of the benefits of personal ownership at a fraction of the cost? If so, what should **m** and **n** be? Can you produce alcohol efficiently? Could you if you replanted your lawn in potatoes?

In order to achieve efficiency in processes from cooking and gardening to financial management, *general methods* need to be "custom tailored" to *specific circumstances*. Certainly you will often start with the general recommendations and recipes of experts for solving your particular challenges, but adaptations and fine tuning will be crucial. The computer model provides a general mechanism: your circumstances go into a program as data, making it specifically tailored to you; you then can modify inputs (strategies) and observe outputs interactively to achieve an optimized solution. Chemists and corporations have been doing it for years. You can expect similar results from careful modeling.

Business and Finance

Forecasting: The accuracy of hindsight is universally acknowledged: If we knew then what we know now, we would have done it differently. With a little computer-assisted simulation, business owners large and small can extend their vision and predictive ability in the more profitable forward direction. Theater owners and concert managers can construct and run simulation programs to predict attendance, expenses, and income for their scheduled performances, based on past events and knowledge of performers. When using established performers and a familiar audience, such simulations can predict with high accuracy. When the scheduling has such options as locations for events, types of performances and specific performers, amount of variety, and so on, the prediction program can be used interactively to develop the "best" schedule of events in terms of number of people reached, revenue, or other goals.

In businesses which deal with perishables, from restaurants to greenhouses to truck gardens, computer modeling can help determine schedules of harvesting, preparation, and so on, which closely match customer demand, and so avoid waste and increase both productivity and profitability. For example, an urban restaurant owner might take account of the type of nearby entertainment events, number of conventioneers, and so on, putting them explicitly into his or her program to predict the number of diners expected, and use the results of this program to guide both food preparation and staffing. Other business simulations can be carried out to model traffic patterns in retail stores and warehouses, and to plan the placement of goods and the kinds of equipment and service personnel necessary. Job scheduling and personnel assignment rules can be optimized by "trial and error," gaining experience from the computer model rather than by actually putting the employees through the whole spectrum of unsettling temporary arrangements.

Entertainment and Sports

Player Selection, Game Strategies and Gambling: The use of computers in professional sports is well known by now. Scouting reports and draft-choice information are analyzed by computer for many of the major football teams. A mistaken impression that this publicity may give, (understandably fostered by the people that provide the computing service), is that such analysis is necessarily *difficult and expensive.* It just isn't so. There is no reason why any high school football coach in the country (and simultaneous owner of a personal computer or two) cannot use modeling (along with the statistical analysis techniques outlined in the previous chapter) to adapt his team's play, offensively and defensively, to the analyzed strengths, weaknesses, and patterns of the current opponent. In fact, the portability of personal computers and their decreasing expense make it conceivable that schools can "record" (and analyze) data from football games on the spot, even if they cannot afford luxuries such as extensive film footage, which the "pros" enjoy. The cost of a small computer nowadays is about the same as two hours of color film coverage. The wise football coach, who may also be the physics or math instructor on the side, will find ample opportunity here to teach his entire academic repertoire, as well as to "bootleg" the usage of academic computing facilities. Students who are not able or willing to physically participate in strenuous competitive sports can be recruited to work on the "analysis team." Their contribution, involvement, and personal benefit are potentially far greater than that of traditional ancillaries such as equipment managers and cheerleaders.

In addition to the play of a game, which involves relatively few people, there is the **prediction of a game's outcome,** which typically involves (financially or otherwise) a much larger group. If your personal football modeling program is more accurate than the official line, or the guesses of the people you find willing to wager, your accuracy translates to cash in the long run. If you are not already a gambling aficionado, some sobering things to think about before becoming one are :

- Even "fair" or favorable games can go against you for long periods of time, and even if you have a slight advantage "in the long run," you can well go broke in the short run.
- You should immediately suspect any situation in which the "big fish" are also playing, such as the stock market. You may come up with an insight on your personal computer which beats everything the giants have been trying to do with lots of bucks and very big machines for years. You probably won't.

The inherent joy of gambling is the illusion of getting something for nothing, of finding the pot of gold at the end of the rainbow. If you wish to indulge in this illusion fairly harmlessly, the "best bets" are games with friends and fellow amateurs. By sharpening your skills, you will be able to enjoy an entertaining pastime without incurring large expenses, and may even turn a modest profit.

How To Make a Model

Models are constructed not only in a vast variety of contexts, but for widely diverse reasons. A modeler who is problem-oriented usually begins with a situation and a set of questions or problems posed by that situation. A modeler whose interest is theoretical (and we can include game, hypergame, and metagame players) may not be looking for an answer, a solution, or a decision, but is primarily concerned with constructing a model which is interesting. A model is judged to be "interesting" in terms of criteria such as verisimilitude, simplicity of description, and attractiveness of its functioning and evolution.

The suggestions I will give here for "getting off the ground" with model-making are meant to be useful in a wide variety of contexts, whether your interest is theoretical or practical. Obviously, if you want to be a professional model-maker, you will have to make the designing process more closely matched to your particular interests, and consequently more efficient. If you would like to know about modeling primarily for your own education and amusement though, the suggestions here will serve you as a good starting point.

Getting Started—The Vocabulary List Technique

To get started making a model, you can simply make a **list** of objects and ideas relevant to the situation you are interested in. Possible sources from which you can compile the list include:

- your own ideas and observations.
- questions and goals which motivate you to study the topic.
- background reading and discussions with other people.

The strategy is to search these and other sources and isolate the **major objects and concepts**, by examining the key words and phrases people use. Restricting attention to the level of words and phrases, making only a simple "vocabulary list," is an essential part of the technique. To construct a model, it will be necessary to bring in all of the simplest ideas and concepts first. After that, the more complex features, such as relationships which involve multiple objects and ideas, can be constructed and/or derived.

As an example, suppose that you are interested in modeling the game of football. If you wish to predict the score of an upcoming game, based on the scores of previous games and other information, your list might be something like the following:

- game • score • rating • point-spread • team • player
- weather • momentum • injuries • ability • coaching

Any concept which you can think of (or which has been proposed by sportswriters, statisticians, or sociologists) as being relevant to the outcome should be included, at least at the initial stages. Different people will have different lists, depending on their interests and their range of possible actions. The coach who needs to know what to do with a roster full of players obviously is interested in a more detailed model than the fan who only needs to know where to put a few discretionary dollars.

Quantification

The purpose of the vocabulary list exercise is simply to bring the area which is to be modeled into clear focus. Often (especially if you are modeling a situation which is already well defined, or given to you by someone else such as your boss or the IRS), the simple ideas and concepts involved can be listed immediately. Once the focus is established (and of course the focus and the corresponding list may be revised as your model progresses), the substantive steps of modeling begin. The first of these is **quantification.**

> The complex structure which we wish to describe, by our limited models, must be re-expressed in terms that we can comprehend, store, examine and manipulate in the model.

Often, quantification means that the concepts in the vocabulary list have to be translated into numbers. (Sophisticated modelers may use vectors, matrices, graphs, cartoons, or other representations, rather than simple numbers.) Some quantifications are automatic, such as the score in a game—others are more subtle. For example, if "momentum" is a valid concept for sports teams, we need to know how momentum can be **quantified.** Based on our observations and records of other quantified phenomena such as scores, point differences, and so on, we must be able to give a specific expression (usually a number) to a team's "momentum." (Simple methods of quantifying momentum would be to judge a team's momentum by the length of its current winning streak, or perhaps by the percentage of wins in its most recent games.)

In many applications, the quantifications used are taken for granted as a starting point, and their implications often regrettably ignored. An example would be a study of the cost of a manufacturing process. Any measure of "cost" for this process which ignored the effects ("costs") of environmental damage would get its comeuppance, sooner or later.

All quantification inherently implies **equivalences:**

Cats

If two events in the real world are assigned the same representation in your model, they will be treated in exactly the same way in all your considerations and calculations with the model from that point on.

Despite the fact that this lumping of things together, or equivalencing, is as delicate a part of modeling as any component of the subsequent analysis, it is rarely dealt with systematically.

Bad quantifications doom many models from the outset. For example, if you decide to construct a theory of mechanics based on the physical **shapes** and **sizes** of objects (ignoring their **weights,** in particular), no amount of computing power could give your model any relevance to the "real world" of physical machines. (You should also notice that this "size and shape" model would work very well in a **restricted context,** where all objects are made out of homogeneous materials of equal density. The moral is that success with a model does not guarantee it for any **wider** application.)

It is sad but true that, as a fledgling modeler, you will be subject to a veritable avalanche of bad examples from experts and professional modelers. It would take a bulldozer to handle even a fraction of the advisory and exhortatory literature which has appeared on topics ranging from nuclear reactors to law to education to economics, stemming from models in which the initial **quantification** is both largely unexamined and woefully deficient. Rather than being unduly influenced, you should learn from the mistakes of others. (When economic policy in a country undergoes radical shifts with changing administrations, the phenomenon is predictable, if not comfortable. As you undoubtedly have observed, changes in policy are apt to come quite a bit more frequently than elections.) We must infer for ourselves the severe limitations of economic modeling; there will certainly be no public pronouncements to that effect. Another habitual offender in the bad-quantification category is our legal system. Legal settlements are predicated on the monetary value of things, which is a procrustean enough bed, but in well publicized legal cases, this restriction has meant that aspects of a situation which are not immediately interpretable in dollar terms are ignored. (Equating the damage done by polluting a watershed to the cash value of the fish destroyed is as inadequate as it is expedient.)

As a practical solution, I suggest here that once you make or find a quantification (such as you might if you are in business and have decided to look at dollar costs to your firm of alternative manufacturing processes), you should then think up examples which show the range of phenomena which might be **lumped together** by your model. The prospective widget manufacturer, who has decided on looking at production costs in dollars, should not take the immediate route embodied in the reasoning:

- Widgets can be marketed profitably if the production cost is less than 50 cents per widget.
- Widgets can be made by injection molding for 37 cents each, and by milling for 32 cents each.
- Get into the milled-widgets business.

A little brainstorming along the following lines would not only be enlightening, but often as not produce a better decision, before jumping into the widget business wholesale:

- Make a list of examples of different processes and materials which could be used to make widgets. Do not restrict attention to only processes which are immediately available, but consider other methods which are at least plausible. The only restriction in this brainstorming is that any process which is put on the list must produce widgets for roughly 50 cents, which is the break-even point. All these possibilities, according to cost alone, are **equivalent**.
- After enough thinking to convince yourself that most pos-

sibilities have been covered, examine the list and describe the ways in which the processes on the list **differ** from each other. (By focusing on the differences among these possibilities, which are supposed to be **equivalent,** according to our model, we are challenging the quantification in direct and practical terms.)

- Either consciously decide that the differences discovered are irrelevant, or refine the quantification used. The refined quantification will take note of more features than simple cost, for each process.

Careful scrutiny of your quantification may cause you to change the model substantially. The widget manufacturer may find out that processes which have the same "cost" are vastly different both in the sources they use for raw materials, the byproducts produced/wasted, employee hazards, and so on. The football fancier may find out that his quantification of a team's ability in terms of a "rating," may give equal ratings to one team which has a few superstars and another which has balanced talent and good coaching. Possibly, you will not change your model immediately. Nonetheless, examining the quantifications involved will provide you with a set of worthwhile observations which can be saved and referred to when (inevitably) changing circumstances require the model to be adapted in the future.

Interactions and Relationships

Once you have collected your concepts in the vocabulary list, and given some thought to how these concepts can be observed, quantified, and recorded, the next step is to identify the **interactions between the elementary concepts** of your model. The simplest way to think about such relationships may be in terms of **arrows.** That is, we can write down all of the concepts spread out on a page, (better yet, have them displayed by the computer), so that we can begin to pictorially connect them. Once all of the concepts are put out where we can see them, we can use arrows to connect them as follows: If concept A **influences** concept B, then draw an arrow from A to B in the picture. Nothing could be simpler—an arrow represents some kind of relationship.

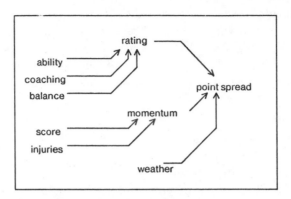

With arrows showing relationships, the football modeler's preliminary picture (technically called a *digraph*) could look like this.

There is a lot of information even in this preliminary picture, and with the judicious rearrangement of the concepts so that the arrows are not tangled, it all comes out pretty clearly. This modeler is primarily interested in "point-spread," which appears to the far right of the picture, clearly the target directly or indirectly of all arrows. (Point-spread is usually defined in terms of a "fair bet." For example, if the point spread is ten points, then it is supposed to be equally likely that the favored team will or will not win by ten points or more. In other words, if the point-spread is ten points, you are supposed to be equally willing to take either side of a bet that the favored team will win by ten points or more.) Two concepts from the initial list, "game" and "player," have been essentially eliminated in the diagram, by being incorporated in other elements. ("Score" and "injuries" are all that will be recorded from previous "games," and "player" effects are incorporated in some measure of team "ability.") From the picture, we can also see the hierarchical nature of the model: Point-spread for a game between two teams is taken to be **directly** affected by differences in the teams' "momentum" and strength as measured by some "rating," and by "weather" (e.g., bad weather may reduce the difference between two teams, if neither can function effectively, or affect the style of one team more than the other.) The other variables in the model only influence point-spread indirectly, previous "scores" and "injuries" affecting "momentum," and individual "ability," "coaching," and "team" balance affecting "rating."

Static versus Dynamic Models

The interactions and relationships in a model can be examined from either a static or dynamic viewpoint. From the **static** viewpoint, the emphasis is usually on obtaining a concise explanation and/or efficient prediction of some of the variables in the model, in terms of others. Statistical analyses, like those introduced in the previous chapter for finding relationships, can give more precise meaning to the rough arrows in the initial digraph. (If you wish to follow up on the football example given above, and see what kind of static modeling can be done, you can refer to the article "Predictions for National Football League Games Via Linear-model methodology," by David Harville, or "Doing It by the Numbers," by J. Marsha. The first article is in a statistical journal, the second was published by *Sports Illustrated*. Both are fully referenced in the bibliography.)

In examining your own static models, you can use many of the ideas outlined in the previous chapter on "Computing As a Seventh Sense." If you understand the underlying strategies, you can capitalize on the fact that most of the more standard approaches, such as correlation analysis, single or multiple regression, and classification routines, are available in packaged form for small computers. Many of these procedures are simple enough that you can build them yourself, equipped with practically any computer and perhaps an introductory statistics text. (Many texts nowadays include programs which you can simply copy into your own computer. Don't forget the versatility **substitution** gives you.)

The other view of models, examining them **dynamically** rather than statically, is equally important, and often more fascinating to beginners. The modeled object is not viewed as a Greek temple or a suspension bridge, artfully constructed and balanced, but more like a planned city or a spaceship, to be initialized with careful rules and procedures so that its evolution in time and space is interesting and well regulated. We will look very quickly here at two kinds of dynamic models. Though they represent only a dab from the dynamic modeler's palette, they can be the basis of many interesting and informative experiments. The first type of model is the **recurrence relation** model, and the second is the **Markov chain** model.

Models Using Recurrence Relations

The recurrence relation model has two components, a **state** and a **transformation**.

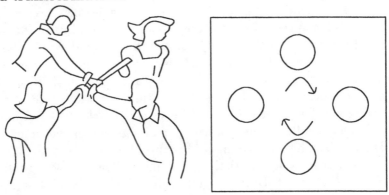

If you like square dancing, you can think of the dancers' pattern as the *state* **and the caller as applying a** *transformation.*

The transformation acts on the state to produce a new state, then transforms this new state to produce a new state, and so on. The **output** of the model is the succession of states as they are produced. In a good square dance or a good model, the starting state and the transformation will be set up at the beginning (places, everyone, your caller tonight is Lew Ramblejaw!), and the whole show will roll on its own from there, weaving a pattern in time and space. (If you infer from this discussion that interesting square dance patterns could be worked out on your home computer, you're absolutely right.)

A popular model based on a recurrence relation is J.H. Conway's game of "Life." This model can be viewed as simply a game which produces patterns automatically, a **hyperkaleidoscope** in the language of Chapter Four. You might also see, though, that the model has the basic ingredients of many ecological systems, where populations grow best somewhere between the extremes of isolation and overcrowding. However you view it, the game is a popular one for computer modeling because of its simple rules and fascinating patterns. The game is played on a board divided into squares, (or, better yet, on a globe divided into squares, so that no squares are on an "edge," and all squares have the same number of neighbors.) The **neighbors** of a square are just the eight squares that surround it.

The initial **state** is formed by placing "cells" (you can call them players, people, square dancers, or whatever strikes your fancy) into some of the squares of the board, and leaving the other squares empty. We might sprinkle these cells over the globe, or start with a pattern, or with just a small bunch like four grouped together.

The **transformation** rule is basically that cells which have not enough close neighbors or too many neighbors die out, and other cells multiply. (You'll have to invent your own version of the squaredance caller's do-si-do.) To be specific, the transformation is accomplished by:

- Looking at all of the cells on the globe, and marking as "survivors" cells which have two or three neighbors among the eight neighboring squares.
- Looking at all of the empty squares, and marking as a "birth square" any empty square which has exactly three of the eight neighboring squares occupied by cells.
- Removing all of the cells not marked as survivors, placing new cells in all of the birth squares, and erasing all markings from cells and squares. This is the new state.

Here is a picture of the transition between one state and the next:

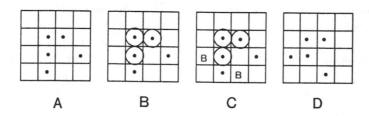

| A | B | C | D |

A) Old State. B) Survivors Marked. C) Birth squares marked. D)New state

As with all recurrence relation models, the transformation is applied over and over again to each new state. The whole secret of the "Life" simulation is to choose an appropriate initial state, so that the succession of generations forms an interesting pattern.

If you follow the rules above, you will see, for example, that in the pattern of four cells bunched together, every cell has three neighbors, and all of the surrounding empty squares have zero, one, or two neighboring cells. Thus all of the initial cells survive, and no new ones are created. The initial pattern simply sits on the globe, in the stablest, and dullest imaginable fashion. Other patterns can shrink or expand, as well as drift across the globe, separate, and merge. At this point, you can do some experimenting yourself with different initial patterns, if you like; Conway's "Life" is a favorite computer game, so you will find programs to implement it readily available in many languages.

Models Based on Markov Chains

Many interesting models, including many serious attempts to model the real world, are based on Markov chains. Markov chains and recurrence relations are quite similar mechanisms, the main difference being that the Markov chain model allows **randomness in** the system's evolution. Whether the modeler is looking at weather or theories of learning, it is often true that knowing all the variables at any point in time still leaves some uncertainty about the system's future development. Rather than overstate our knowledge or throw the baby out with the bathwater and plead complete ignorance, we often wish to use a model to predict what *might* happen, and give estimates of the **probabilities or relative chances** of possible occurrences. Thus, the weatherman, who may very well be using some Markov modeling in his predictions, does not tell you, "It will not rain today, I promise." Nor does he, except on some local stations, cop out on the weather altogether and talk about hog prices or the anchorperson's dress. We all expect something like "precipitation probability tomorrow is 30 percent," and at least know that this pronouncement warrants carrying an umbrella more than a 10 percent prediction. Once you get some Markov modeling experience under your belt, you should have much greater intuition about such numbers.

Specifically, in a Markov chain model, the system is always found to be in one of a (hopefully small) number of **states**.

A simple daily weather model for Sioux Falls might assume that the weather is in one of the four states *sun, rain, hail,* or *snow.*

Just as in the recurrence model, a transformation (usually called a **transition** in a Markov model) repeatedly produces a new state from the present one. In concrete terms, you can think of a player (introducing Mr. George System...) who goes from room to room in a game ("state" rooms, of course.) In each "state" room, System finds a spinner, which has the names of all the rooms, including the present one, written on it. He spins the spinner, and then goes to whatever "state" room the spinner has pointed to. Several things to notice are:

- The spinners do not have to be "fair." that is, the spinner in room #3 may have most of its circumference marked for "room #2," leaving very little chance of System going anywhere from room #3 except to room #2. In particular, the *entire* circumference of the spinner can be marked off for one room. In this case, there is no randomness involved, and no need to spin the spinner—System can just save his finger and go directly to the indicated room.

- The spinners can be different in different rooms. It may be very likely to go to room #2 if you are in room #1, but unlikely if you are in room #4. This feature enables Markov models to mimic real-world systems such as the weather, where snow on one day followed by sunshine on the next for example, would be much more likely than snow followed by rain, and perhaps not as likely as snow followed by snow. In terms of the spinners, this means that the spinner in the "snow" room has very little of its circumference marked out for "rain," more for "sun," and perhaps most for "snow."

- If the spinner in any room has all of its circumference marked out for this same room, the game effectively ends. No need for System to keep going back in and out of the same door. Such a (state) room is called a **trapping state**.

- If you want to set up a Markov model and watch what happens, you have to do two basic things : set up the rooms (at least give them good names) with a spinner constructed for each one, and get somebody (or a computer, of course) to be Mr. System. Start him/it out in some particular room. After that he's off, spinning and slamming on his merry way.

Implementing your Model on a Computer

Recurrence relations and Markov models furnish an excellent context in which to discuss some fundamentals of **computer programming.** Their structure is conceptually simple: Repeatedly update a display of some sort by applying a single transformation (function), possibly calling for some randomness. And, in addition to being easy to implement, even the simplest forms of these models can have unanticipated and interesting evolutions.

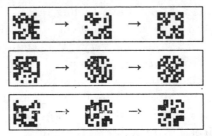

The random mosaics on the left grow by symmetry into the "snowflakes" on the right, by repeated transformations. The recurrence relation model used is simple enough to be implemented on any personal computer.

To set up your own models, the roles of the square dance caller, or the Markov chain's Mr. System, must be implemented by your computer programs. A point worth emphasizing again in this context is how easy it is to change the rules, once you have *any* version of the model running on your computer. Often, a simple substitution will do the trick. For instance, if you obtain a baseball simulation program from someone, which you copy in and get running on your computer, you can easily see how the game would change with new rules. For example, you might allow the batters four strikes instead of three, hopefully to produce more excitement. All you would have to do to the program is change some 3s to 4s. (Probably not all of them!) A well documented program would show you exactly which ones to change. Another, more versatile technique is **function application**, which is closely related to substitution. You could change the baseball game, using function application, so that the batter is allowed a number of strikes which *varies* with his batting average. For example, you might allow four strikes for batters whose average is higher than .300, five strikes for batters over .350, and so on, for much more variety than simply changing to "Four strikes—you're out."

If you like to think in terms of recipes, a **substitution** instruction you might give your cook would be, "Replace *flour* with *cornstarch*," while a **function application** instruction would be, "*Boil* any liquids called for, before using." As you can see, the function application is more versatile—the substitution only applies to flour, but the function (boiling) applies to any liquid which comes up in the recipe. In general, function application is no more than a **rule** which tells the right thing to substitute, not just for one ingredient, but for a whole range of similar things which might occur. You can also substitute one *function* for another one in the program, much as you would tell a cook to *poach* any ingredients which the recipe originally specified to be *boiled*. Especially for beginning modelers, it may be preferable not to start your projects out from scratch, but to find a program that does something analogous to what you want. You can then make gradual modifications with these techniques of substitution, function application, and function substitution.

By the way, there is no need for you to get out of the kitchen mentally if you feel comfortable there. In fact, we will discuss all of the planning of model implementation as if human **actors** were available to take a variety of roles, and our job is simply to be scriptwriters and choreographers. At this early stage of personal computing, it is unfortunately true that "actor languages" for small computers are not common. Nonetheless trial versions of an actor language called LOGO, developed at M.I.T., are already available for many popular computers. If you are biding your time for a more powerful machine such as the 16-bit and 32-bit offerings which are beginning to appear, it would be well worth your while to check up on both LOGO, and a language called Smalltalk developed at Xerox, before you take the plunge. The "actor" mentality can be helpful simply as an aid to ease you into the more stilted communication protocols of non-actor languages. For example, you might well want to learn Pascal as a well designed and widely used conventional programming language. If you do, you will find Pattis' book **Karel the Robot**, which is referenced in the bibliography, a nearly painless introduction. Pattis gets you started in programming by teaching you commands for an imaginary robot, in a very concrete physical world. But whatever languages your first computer understands, you may still find it more pleasant to *imagine* that you have actors available, right down to the point where you have broken the tasks down to extremely simple subtasks. Perhaps then you can look up a friend who feels at home with the standard computer languages. She might teach you a few key phrases, or perhaps just *give* you expressions for all of your low level tasks, to simply copy into your machine and link together. If the tasks are low level enough, she can either write them instantly or fetch them from her library.

As you might anticipate, a step-by-step, **top-down** approach is the recommended method to get a model going, whether you start from scratch or from an existing program. Give the actors ambitious roles at the beginning, and only later figure out how they can delegate subtasks to less inventive subordinates. In addition, I suggest a gradualist mentality. Not only should component roles be isolated and worked on individually, but as small components are finished, try to keep connecting them together frequently for little "dress rehearsals" as the work progresses. There are many reasons to adopt such gradualism:

- You get to see interesting things happen, step by step, even before the whole project is finished.
- You can "pay for" (that is, spend time fixing) problems that arise, on a gradual "installment plan."
- You will acquire information about how your components are working together all during the course of the project. The building of new components will then always be based on well-tested foundations. The constant feedback will often

enable you to make modifications and revisions in your overall plan, or even start over from a different tack, with a minimum of wasted effort.

Now that you are all prepared to be a casting director, let me give you a few of the stock players who figure prominently in most programs, along with a description of what they do:

—The Executive—

Takes a message, interprets it as a set of instructions, and makes sure they are carried out.

—The Advertiser—

If you give her a message, she will display it in printed, video, or other public format.

—The Desk Clerk—

Takes a pigeonhole *name* and a message, puts the *name* on an empty pigeonhole, and pigeonholes the message there. If you subsequently give him that same name with a new message, he will throw away the old message, and put the new message in the pigeonhole. If you just give him the name of a pigeonhole, he will copy whatever message is currently in that pigeonhole, and give you the copy.

There is an underlying reason for the typecasting of actors as executive, advertiser, and desk clerk— these roles correspond to the three main components of most computer systems. (Executive=**monitor** or **central processor**, advertiser=**display**, and desk clerk=**memory**). If you start by thinking of this cast of characters, the ultimate breakdown of things to the fundamental computer instructions will be much easier to manage. You can certainly ask the executive to remember things, or to advertise them if you wish, if you bear in mind that memory operations will ultimately have to go through the desk clerk, and advertising will have to be handled by the advertiser, which is the sole contact of this production with the outside world.

You can start off the whole model implementation process, especially if you're not very familiar with the computer and language combination you are using, by having auditions for the main characters. The logical place to start is with the advertising role—no matter what you eventually get the computer to do, it will be worthless unless it is communicated to the real world. (After all, what's the use of modeling football games, if you get the computer to figure out who's likely to win next week but can't get it to *tell* you?)

The Advertiser's Audition

The idea is to call in a would-be advertiser and put her through her paces. Give her a message, and make sure she can get it advertised properly in whatever medium you request. The easiest advertising task is to display some one-liner such as, "Don't forget the bagels." If the prospective advertising hopeful can't handle that, then it's curtains. In terms of computers, this means you can't really get off the ground until you know how to accomplish a simple display task. Ask yourself: What do I have to say to my computer, if I want it to print out on its screen the one-liner, "Don't forget the bagels?" If you have a computer, and don't know how to do anything like this, stop reading at the end of this sentence (use a bookmark) and go find out, preferably by asking someone informed and lucid. Once you've got advertising bagels mastered, you can of course advertise anything else by simple substitution. If your computer has fancier **output devices** than a simple video tube, your messages might be typed in a professional looking format, laced with graphics, or even etched by lasers. It's best to start simple. Saying

print "DON'T FORGET THE BAGELS"

will work using the BASIC language with almost any home computer, even vintage five-year-olds. If you have a modern machine and dialect of BASIC, amenities like upper and lower case are allowed, and you can say:

print "Don't forget the bagels"

The Desk Clerk's Audition

Give the desk clerk the day of the month and ask him

to put it in a pigeonhole called "day-of-the-month." Now ask him for day-of-the-month, and make sure he gives it back correctly. Try giving a new day-of-the-month and retrieving it. Give him several numbers ("day-of-the-month," "my-height," " my-age," ...) one after another, and make sure you can get back whichever one you want. "Getting back" a number might mean having the advertiser display it, for example. Let's assume that you're (still) using BASIC. Storing and checking the day-of-the-month (abbreviated to "d"ay-of-the-month since BASIC has some basic dyslexia with long names) could go like this:

```
1  d=31
2  print  d
3  print  "d, the  day  of  the  month,  is:";  d
```

The first instruction line above stores the number 31 in a pigeonhole named "**d.**" The second line tells the advertiser to display the contents of the pigeonhole named "**d.**" (Which should be 31, since nothing has happened to change it.) The third line is a better version of the second line, which tells the advertiser to first print the message "d, the day of the month is:" and then print the contents of the pigeonhole **d.** Usually, you would prefer such an explanation, rather than just seeing the number 31 appear mysteriously (long after you've forgotten where it's coming from).

The Executive's Audition

The only general purpose executive around for typical computers and languages is a program (**interpreter, evaluator, monitor,** or whatever it might be called) which is set up automatically when you turn on the machine, or switch to a new language. In some powerful languages like LISP, you can build your own general purpose executive with equally wide-ranging capabilities. Usually, though, there is just one **top** executive, and all the commands (such as the "print" command for display, or the "d=31" command for the desk clerk) are actually given to this top executive, who passes them on properly. The executives you are allowed to set up yourself are **special-purpose executives,** more commonly called **programs or subroutines** or **functions** as discussed in Chapter Two. Here is an

example of a special-purpose executive audition, handled through
the top executive. Directing yourself to the top executive, you say:

******

"I need a *get-from-the-market* executive. Please arrange for
one, as follows:
- Have the desk clerk store the instructions "Go to Schultz's
  market around the corner and buy —☐—." In a pigeonhole
  named **'get-from-the-market-instructions.'**
- Now call in one of the executive candidates and and give him
  the following instructions:
  In the future, when your name is called by the top ex-
  ecutive, accept a single **argument** *from him and then,*
  1.) Retrieve the functional form of your instructions
  from the desk clerk's pigeonhole named "get-from-the-
  market-instructions." 2.) Make a substitution of the
  argument *you received from the top executive into*
  your retrieved instructions, replacing the —☐—in the
  instructions with the **argument.** *3.) Carry out the*
  modified form of your retrieved instructions.

******

You can now conduct the audition by having the top executive relay your command, "**get-from-the-market(sauerkraut),**"
or whatever would be interesting to have fetched, and verifying that
the special purpose, **get-from-the-market** executive knows how to
play his part.

The point of all of this is the streamlined way you can
henceforth just say "get-from-the-market(blah)," without repeating any of the underlying instructions. The ritual is considerably
varied from one computer language to the next for setting up these
streamlined special purpose executives. BASIC is fairly primitive
and Pascal, C, and LISP are more flexible, allowing such things as
recursion, where a special purpose executive is even allowed to call
out his own name, much as one plumber or doctor might call in
another to help out in the course of an operation. Whatever language
you decide to investigate in detail, your main concern will usually be
the definition of useful and correct functions, your special-purpose
executives. Audition them often.

Making Your Model Real, or at Least Plausible

If you have made a model for the purpose of better understanding or predicting the behavior of a real-world system, there comes a time when your creative imagination must face up to the facts. The question, "Is the model believable?" can be asked in many ways:

- How stable is the output if the assumptions and/or the initial conditions are slightly changed? (Be wary if your world population model predicts disaster when the number of children per family is assumed to be 2.52, but not if it is 2.51.)

- Does the model, with all its internal structure, fit the data better than simple statistics would predict? (The football modeler might compare the accuracy of a highly detailed, play-action model with a model based on pre-game predictors, such as the regression models mentioned earlier.)

- Is the model's internal structure plausible? (Just because you have taught your robot camera to recognize policemen's hats and throw snowballs at them, you needn't assume that little children do it the same way.)

The process of modifying a model may be one of tuning, to make the model's output resemble the available data more closely, or it may be simply to make your own microcosm more complex, beautiful, and informative than its predecessors. If your modeling efforts are to predict unforeseen real-world effects, the model must be validated and calibrated by its theoretical base or by agreement with empirical data. Top-down strategies and good programming languages can help you proceed effectively. Your judgment and values must guide you in proceeding wisely.

8

Feedback Loops

The lesson taught by research into biofeedback is that we can gain unexpected control of many of our bodily functions by first becoming aware of them. There is every reason to believe that voluntary control of such things as heart rate and blood pressure will soon be a part not only of clinical treatment, but a useful part of ordinary health maintenance. Current biofeedback research and techniques have already been used to develop therapy for hypertension and migraines. The future promises vastly more sensitive instruments, able to sense the activity of small groups of brain cells or other neurons through implantable devices and computerized techniques such as tomography. Control patterns which can be established at such levels of sensitivity would reshape health and medical practice.

Feedback loops have their large scale impact on maintaining and improving our physical and mental well being. On a smaller scale, they may in the near future help us acquire the physical skills to do things better. An easy experiment to convince yourself of the effect of feedback is to have someone maladjust your television with the "vertical" knob so that the picture flips over and over. It is a simple matter for you to adjust the knob again so that the flipping stops, *if you look at the picture*. If you do not look at the picture, but only rely on someone to tell you when it is flipping up, flipping down, or steady, the readjustment will take a longer time.

The television feedback experiment uses a ridiculously simple and not very delicate task. In interesting situations, the role of feedback is paramount. Suppose it were possible for a pianist, novice or skilled, to feel with his or her hands every subtle movement of the hands of a great artist playing a piece, to vary the pace, to repeat the sections of interest or difficulty at will. Such a thing is foreseeable in the near future. The "modern" tennis coach of today has his pupil hit ball after ball, giving instructions after each hit on the proper release of the ball, the height of the throw, the timing of the swing. His words are poor approximations to the process he wishes to communicate. He may have "sophisticated" videotape equipment, which of course it is impossible for the player to watch while he is swinging.

You may imagine the result of changing this scenario so that sensors connected to the tennis player's arms and hands inform him of his position and guide him into efficient and reliable patterns, based on the coach's knowledge and analysis. At every instant, the player's actions would be compared to an appropriate model and corrective guidance signals instantly returned. With sophisticated display devices, the lesson could even be practiced in "slow motion" for concentration and effect, or "stop action" to isolate weaknesses. It is quite possible that the major advances due to such techniques will accrue not to the stars and professional players, who already operate near their peak, but to amateurs who will greatly speed up the painstaking and painful process of acquiring a skill well enough to enjoy the game.

Biofeedback

Our very concept of what it is to be human involves our self-awareness and ability to control our own actions. Biofeedback techniques, still in their theoretical and practical infancy, show an enormous potential for increasing our "humanness" in both aware-ness and control. We perceive directly such things as hunger, thirst, and physical balance, and relying on this perception, we have evolved strategies for controlling and maintaining these aspects of our physi-cal state. Other aspects of our physical selves are more hidden, and we typically are aware of them only indirectly. Control and care are often too little and too late, in response to problems, with symptoms addressed and treated as if they were illnesses. The "treatment of choice," by overwhelming popular vote, for disorders large and small, is chemistry—drugs which are often systemic sledgehammers rather than medical scalpels. Biofeedback offers a new direction.

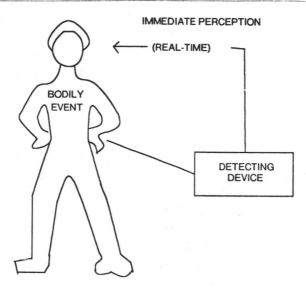

A schematic view of biofeedback

As the diagram shows, biofeedback starts from bodily events (such as heart rate, or the amount of activity of a particular muscle cell or collection of brain cells), which are ordinarily imperceptible to the human involved. These events are detected by an external device, and displayed in such a way that the person becomes aware of them. The often startling consequence is that the person not only develops a sense of himself and of the bodily event, which had been totally absent before, but actually becomes capable of consciously **controlling** this newfound aspect. The key feature of the paradigm is the immediate, or **real-time** display, so that the subject develops a "tracking" of the phenomenon of interest and is able to separate it out from the background events and other sensations of his consciousness. Electronics, and more recently **microelectronics**, have had the central role in developing this real-time detection and display mechanism. (You can't effectively develop a strategy for controlling your heart rate if you need to count heartbeats for fifteen seconds to get a new reading. Precise timing enables a new reading with every heartbeat.) Going beyond mere electronics, **logical** devices will be the underpinning of vastly more sophisticated and reliable systems. From uncertain and faddish beginnings, biofeedback bids well to compete with the millennia-old methods of medicinal drugs.

Major types of biofeedback currently in use include electromyographic (EMG), electroencephalogram (EEG), and temperature displays. EMG feedback provides a person with a constantly up-dated picture of the activity of muscle cells. The sensitivity of the devices used can vary from monitoring whole groups of muscles, down to probes which measure only a millionth of an inch at the tip and record at the level of single muscle cells. EEG feedback directly monitors the electrical activity of the brain. Temperature display, of course, is familiar to anyone who has ever used a glass thermometer, but electronic devices enable a person to become aware instantly of temperature changes as small as a hundredth of a degree Farenheit, rather than the tenth of a degree or so you can read on a glass ther-mometer, or the five degree change you would notice yourself (in your hands, say) without a thermometer.

The theory of biofeedback, especially in indirect applica-tions, is only in its infancy. On the face of it, it would seem strange that one could remove a **cause**, such as migraine headache, by train-ing oneself to remove a **symptom,** such as unusual cranial blood flow or temperature patterns. The effect nonetheless is real, whether it is the observed fact that a soldier in battle may feel no pain from serious wounds while his ability to devote conscious attention to them is blocked, or the clinically established fact that systematic relaxation relieves headache significantly better than the predicted "placebo" effect (that giving the sufferer any medication which he or she *believes* will work typically produces some improvement). In other cases, for example where EMG techniques are used specifically to shape muscular response in stroke rehabilitation, the effects are not only dramatic, but more easily understood theoretically. Even in these cases, theoretical questions may remain as to the neurological or other pathways used by the patient to control the response. The autonomic system which controls such bodily functions as heart rate and blood pressure has been traditionally thought of (and called) "involuntary" in Western medicine. Biofeedback radically proposes to place such systems under conscious control. Any such technique is rightfully viewed with initial skepticism, and subsequently with a good deal of caution when our ability to intervene in (and pos-sibly damage) the body's self-regulating mechanisms is firmly es-tablished. Nonetheless, the evidence for both the reality and the value of properly understood biofeedback techniques is inescapably accumulating.

Despite the substantial successes of present biofeedback techniques in clinical areas such as rehabilitation of stroke patients, and other areas which we shall discuss briefly, much development is needed to make the display tools sufficiently finely tuned to be widely useful. The entire subject of biofeedback, in fact, still suffers from the faddish aura of the "alpha wave" biofeedback of the sixties. At the grossest level, we find a frequency pattern to brain electrical activity, give it a name like "alpha waves," and discover that it can be brought under conscious control. The credulous or unscrupulous are tempted to make vast claims, but real progress will only be made when global phenomena such as alpha wave patterns can be more finely and locally understood, and globally integrated by study of other, simultaneously occurring physical processes. Continued development of biofeedback will require both the kind of microelectronic technology which is becoming technically feasible (due in large part to the development of large scale and very large scale integrated systems—electronic processors on a chip), and also the widely available processing power (personal computers) of the coming decade.

Miniaturization is not a severe challenge for the technology which reduced a room-size computer down to a chip of silicon. More importantly, microelectronics can produce devices which are more sensitive, directed, and adaptable to everyday use, rather than only suitable in protected and expensive laboratory environments. One needs, for example, to make the instruments insensitive to various types of background "noise," as well as to calibrate and adjust them for different individuals.

As an illustration, consider what an impact a "dumb" technology such as x-ray photography has had on medicine. Admittedly, your physician could find your broken rib by thumping your chest, but both you and he would prefer an x-ray. If you have had a lot of x-rays lately, and/or are worried about possible side effects, you might want to be probed with something a little less disruptive than x-rays, such as sound waves. Such acoustic (ultrasound) probes exist, and can give accurate pictures, but only with the help of "smart" computer processing to transform the tangled net of signals they send back into a picture which resembles a photograph. A large hospital in the early eighties is likely to have an ultrasound imaging machine and its associated computer. Your personal physician is not likely to have one, and you almost certainly do not have one at home. Continued development of microelectronic devices and their associated computer "interpreters" in the eighties will not only radically change the tools of the physician, but greatly enlarge the range of devices which can be informatively and intelligently used at home for medical self-help, oriented toward maintenance rather than remedies. Biofeedback is one aspect of this new technology for health maintenance, along with better understanding and control of long term external factors such as nutrition, exercise, and environmental hazards.

A brief look at the successes already achieved by biofeedback will serve both to establish the proven value of these techniques, and also to illustrate how little is presently known, and how wide-ranging the potential uses may be. Rehabilitation of stroke victims has been already mentioned, and deserves further comment. The analogy it suggests, that we all are currently "crippled" by lack of awareness and self-control, should not be missed. A typical scenario of a recovering stroke patient is that he first has no sensation or control of the affected part of his body, perhaps muscles required for arm movement or walking. Sensation gradually develops, and the muscles may be activated consciously, but typically produce spasms, with antagonistic muscle systems working against each other, rather than in coordination. For the fortunate patient, a final phase is reached in which the muscles can once again be both consciously and effectively utilized. Biofeedback (EMG) monitoring enables the patient initially to sense even minute amounts of muscle activity, of which he would otherwise be unaware, and gradually to enhance this level of activity. Once large scale muscle activity has been established, the separate activity levels of opposing muscle groups can be displayed simultaneously, so that the subject "tunes himself" to de-activate an opposing muscle group while he is bringing a desired group into action. These techniques have aided not only stroke victims, but cerebral palsy patients and patients who have undergone reconstructive surgery, enabling muscles, tendons, and nerves, transplanted from a healthy part of a body, to assume new and coordinated roles in rebuilding a damaged part.

By several recent surveys, the two most popular prescription drugs are a single sedative, marketed under various brand names, and an ulcer remedy. Patients are undoubtedly taking the sedative for a variety of ailments ranging from headache to tension to insomnia. A list of substantially different kinds of headache, however, categorized by their physical locations and origin, would include twenty or so varieties. A satisfactory approach to treatment (never mind prevention!) would require recognition and accommodation of these differences. Inasmuch as any headache may be in fact a symptom, while tension or anxiety is the underlying cause, a general approach to reducing tension is nonetheless worthwhile.

Whether one is dealing with migraine or tension headaches, insomnia, or "psychological" difficulties such as anxiety and depression, the fact is that these conditions are invariably associated with high levels of physical tension. Substantial evidence shows that producing "relaxation" in strictly physiological terms, such as that evidenced by low levels of (EMG-measured) muscle activity, has psychological effects which counteract those caused by "psychological" stress.

It is worth arguing that there are sources of anxiety and depression which individuals should work actively to remove, rather than treating their consequences. In this respect though, biofeedback and other relaxation techniques are comparable to sleep: It would certainly not be responsible or advisable to deal with all of our stresses by sleeping them away, if that were possible. Nonetheless, humans find a certain amount of sleep both necessary and beneficial. If it were possible to treat headaches or feelings of anxiety effectively by allocating ten minutes to sleep whenever these symptoms arose, the therapy would hardly be objectionable. In contrast to current methods of stress reduction, which account for ingestion of vast quantities of alcohol and other drugs, systematic and conscious relaxation seems innocuous. Biofeedback **relaxation techniques,** at the very least offer an "organic Valium," which is in almost every way preferable to the drugstore variety, in effectively treating a wide variety of stress-related diseases.

Although relaxation has been correlated with the EEG pattern of brain electrical activity called "theta waves," the most common form of biofeedback relaxation training in use does not deal with the EEG information directly. Rather, relaxation is achieved through relaxation of muscular activity, which can be precisely monitored and tracked using EMG, or through increase in peripheral blood flow, as measured and displayed by temperature sensors. The advantage of biofeedback techniques over older methods, developed under names such as "progressive relaxation," "autogenic training," etc., is that while the older methods indeed work for many people, provision for feedback greatly increases the speed and reliability with which the technique can be learned, and objectively identifies (rather than relying on subjective reports or impressions) the amount of relaxation produced, signaling difficulties and allowing the training to be tailored for different individuals.

The display capabilities of EMG and temperature devices in pinpointing the physical appearance of stress are useful even beyond the context of a "relaxation break," in which an individual consciously reduces these physical symptoms. These devices can provide us with valuable information about our responses to external events, in order to help us deal more effectively with them. An actual example is the case where an instructor is explaining biofeedback to a parent and child. He explains that peripheral blood circulation is a good indicator of anxiety or stress, and that a sensitive temperature gauge attached to a person's finger will show the temperature to increase as the person becomes more relaxed, and to decrease under stress. The child asks for a demonstration of something stressful, and the instructor responds with a mental arithmetic problem for the child, pressuring him for a quick answer. Sure enough, the child's peripheral temperature drops by 1.5 degrees. In addition, the *parent's* peripheral temperature drops by 5 degrees! This information provides a practically useful insight; the parent now thinks about various "educational" interactions with the child, and sees many of them in the light of the parent's response to stress, rather than in response to the child's needs and capabilities.

With a sensitive and portable biofeedback thermometer, you would discover that your body temperature is definitely not 98.6° or some other magical constant, but fluctuates according to a daily rhythm much as the ocean tides or daylight and dark. (The entire subject of such **circadian**, or daily, rhythms suffers currently from lack of extensive data.) Your personal temperature cycle affects, among other things, the quantity and quality of sleep you get. In recent studies, people who chose to begin sleeping at the high point of their own personal temperature cycle slept about fourteen hours on the average, or nearly twice as long as those who began sleeping at a low temperature point. Not only is sleeping at the right time (a low temperature point) beneficial in producing the right amount of sleep, but also in producing the most relaxing kind of sleep. When personal temperature monitoring and recording devices are as common as wristwatches, you will be able to be aware of exactly where you are in your own circadian pattern.

The circadian pattern must be discerned from many days of temperature data taken in succession. Other practical applications include drug-free birth control. By looking at the records of many people, it will also be possible for medical researchers to better delineate the effects of this internal biological clock we all have, and methods of attuning ourselves with it. In animal experiments, shifting the body clock artificially (as rotating-shift work might do for humans) decreased the animals' life span by twenty-five percent!

In attempting to estimate the importance of biofeedback, one must also remember that the presently used devices will look extremely crude from the standpoint of the technology available ten years from now. A device the size of an aspirin has already been produced which will travel through the entire digestive tract and transmit temperature and motility information by radio signals during its entire trip. Microneurography, a technology which attempts to study the nervous system in a similarly non-disruptive fashion, is also only in its infancy. Another present limitation is that the logical processing power to synthesize and coordinate the information from *many* biofeedback devices operating simultaneously is unavailable or prohibitively expensive in the early eighties. That, too, will change.

Wristwatches are everywhere, despite the fact that most of us have little practical need for the exact time. Heart rate monitors, in wristwatch form, already are being marketed. In the near future, we can expect to see extremely useful wristwatch biofeedback monitors. With such a monitor, one will be able to take an effective and refreshing psychological catnap, at a desk or waiting in a ticket or supermarket line (much like "transcendental meditation" without the mysterious trappings). Rather than just leaving your wristwatch on the nightstand, you can leave it on. During the night, it will transmit its stored data on your physiological states during the day to your home computer, as well as monitoring your sleeping patterns. This information may be for strictly your own use, or can be made available to others for medical or research use. Imagine being rushed to the hospital after a heart attack or an accident of some sort. By checking your "watch," the doctor sees that you have kept these extensive physiological records, and that you will allow them to be used for treatment. A quick phone call to your home and the information is automatically transferred to the hospital computer, along with other medical history such as allergies, current medication, etc. Extensive epidemiological studies can also be done, by distributing such "watches" to samples of people, and analyzing patterns which appear. Based on such analysis, your watch should in the future be able to summon help and guide you through effective countermeasures in a situation, for example, where conditions signaling an imminent heart attack occur, *before* these conditions actually produce a disaster.

Acquiring and Improving Skills

Two examples will be given here to indicate the methods by which logical devices can provide feedback loops for learning and improving a skill. The skills I will discuss are...

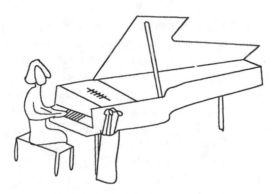

...piano playing and golf.

Beyond choosing these topics as a simple matter of taste, the choice of keyboard and golf club has some merit in suggesting the *variety* of activities which will be affected by feedback techniques. In addition, the electronic gear necessary for making effective feedback loops has been produced and is in fact being put to limited use already in golf and in keyboard music. It is only a matter of time until suitable devices are packaged in a form suitable and affordable to some extent for home use, and certainly for shared public use. (Most people do not expect or require the ownership of a private golf course, and many people, such as college students, become proficient pianists on borrowed pianos.)

Crystal Fingers

Here is your complete piano lesson:

> Put your fingers in the right places at the right time, and press down with the proper force. Once you've got that down, you can start off on the concert tour.

The reason, of course, that airplanes are not filled with pianists on tour is that the piano-playing recipe requires **real time** processing. Anyone can play the minute waltz, given a few hours to work at it. It is obvious that effective piano *instruction* should take place in real time as well. Unfortunately, by the time the instructor can say "presto," the notes have often marched away several measures, and by the time the student understands the correction and decides what to do about it, it's too late. Better luck next time.

If you have ever wished that you could play the piano, and regretted not having the "talent," you will be pleased to know that all humans have the underlying "talent" for piano playing in large supply. This talent, universal, common,and wonderful as pattern recognition but more primeval, is **balance**. Without balance, we could not stand or walk. When experience is linked in direct **feedback** to our sense of balance, we can intuitively find and follow astonishingly complex "paths" through that experience. If you know how to ride a bicycle, you have learned by exploiting your sense of balance. (If you are impressed by computerized guidance systems which put a man on the moon, you will get a big ego boost from knowing that these guidance systems could not control a freehand bicycle for more than a few yards before crashing.)

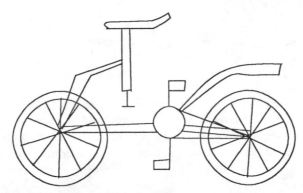

The role of feedback loops is to put us in immediate contact with a new dimension of experience, where we can sense our "position" and learn to balance.

Imagine resting your hands on top of those of your piano teacher while he plays a slow and simple exercise, such as a scale. Your task is to use the feedback from your sense of touch to move your fingers on top of his so that they stay in contact. Provided the piece is played slowly enough, you will be able to follow his hands continuously by balancing your fingers on top of his, much as you would balance a wobbling book on top of your own fingers. As you repeatedly practice the scale, your balancing act, like early bicycle riding, changes character from *reaction* to *anticipation*. Rather than reacting to the sensation of the fingers underneath slipping off, you would gradually have the motions learned "in your fingers" well enough that contact would never begin to slip. The piece could soon be played with the apparent ease of bicycling or horseback riding over familiar territory, and the fingers underneath would gradually become unnecessary. At your own pace, you could develop your individual interpretive and expressive approach, based on a solid foundation of technical skill.

Since few piano teachers, if any, have the physiology and temperament required for thousands of choruses of "hands on hands" play, this performance-as-balancing scenario has not previously been realistic. But, with a feedback loop linking the **sensation** of finger position through a personal **computer** to tactile **stimulation** back to the pianist, this "ideal" configuration becomes practical. All of the information involved in playing a piano piece, even subtleties and nuances of individual artists, can be captured in a fairly compact form. (You would not be unusual as a reader of this book if you have not seen a personal computer. It *would* be unusual if you had never seen a piano roll.) From the computer's high speed processing perspective, human piano playing at any speed appears as extreme slow motion. If the computer is provided with a **sensation** device to detect the position of each finger continuously, it can take this position data, compare it with its stored information about where that finger *should* be, and feed back a corrective signal when necessary through a corresponding **action** device. The whole process can be carried out so quickly that even though the computer is processing one finger after another in succession and performing a computation and signal generation for each in turn, the human performer perceives the feedback as instant and continuous for ten fingers simultaneously.

As you know from Chapter Four, there are many useful sensation and action devices possible. **Piezoelectric** crystals are a likely choice here, to communicate by vibrations back to the student's fingers. In fact, a portable reading device for the blind was developed using piezoelectric crystals several years ago. Vibrations from the crystals in an array, initiated by optical scanning of ordinary printed materials, enabled printed letters to be felt through the reader's fingers. For piano playing, each finger might have three crystals, to denote left, right, and downward movement. The crystal could communicate to the fingers by vibrations or pulses, and individuals could have control over the strength and pattern. As the student progresses in learning particular pieces or general skills such as improvisation and understanding of written musical notations, the external feedback loop could be reduced and eliminated. Even skilled players would find uses for the loop, perhaps in rapidly expanding their repertoire, or experiencing in an unprecedented way the style of great artists by playing along "in the fingers" and simultaneously receiving the feedback of touch and sound.

Feedback For Fore Time

The abbreviated piano lesson above has a counterpart for the golfer:

> Move the club into the ball with the proper force,
> holding it at the right position and angle to send the
> ball to the pin.

No amount of computing is likely to eliminate all of the mystery between the telling and the doing of this feat, or to make holes-in-one commonplace. (The sense of balance enables humans commonly to stand; it would be little reassurance for most of us on a tightrope. Small matters of strength are enough to remove well balanced cowfolk from reluctant rodeo partners.) Whether or not you ever make it to the (W)PGA, you would still have a quicker and more pleasant time learning the game, using feedback loops. As good instructors know, practice does not make perfect routinely. The practice must reinforce effective patterns and prevent bad habits from becoming ingrained.

Unlike the pianist, a golfer in the past has had to carry out her performance at a reasonably high speed, or else it would be pointless. Although she might improve her swing somewhat with slow motion practice, there would be no reason to use a ball at all until the swing was fast enough to launch it. This essential involvement of speed is characteristic of many sports. If you play back a film of a golfer in slow motion, the club moves slowly, hits the ball, and the ball moves slowly away. It only happens that way in films. Similarly, a slow motion baseball player might wait five seconds for the ball to reach the plate, but no physical baseball can possibly stay in the air that long on an approximate straight line from the pitcher's mound.

Bringing a computer into play, with sensors for various parts of the golfer's body and the club, and action devices to feed back the important information immediately, the player would not only get "real time" feedback, perhaps limited to concentrate on problem areas, but could also slow the process down, with the physical ball replaced by a computerized version. For example, a special club with a mirrored surface could be very accurately measured as it approached the tee, by its reflection of a pencil of laser light. No matter how slowly or quickly the club passed the tee, the information could be used to display the trajectory of an imaginary, speeded up ball. Similarly, an imaginary baseball could be continuously and gradually brought up to realistic speed, all the while maintaining the trajectory of a curve or a slider, as the skill of a batter improves.

The incentives for adopting any effective training technique are undeniably greatest for professional athletes and teams. Given the high stakes of professional sports, there will undoubtedly be scandals involving telemetry of feedback signals to players during the course of a game. It's easy to imagine biofeedback producing a spectacular improvement in novice bowlers; the effect on polished professionals may be less noticeable but more controversial. Baseball's raging controversy over "spitballs" could one day seem like the simplest of pleasantries. Whatever the risks and rewards for high rolling athletes, feedback techniques have tremendous promise for bringing the enjoyment of diverse forms of physical recreation to amateurs.

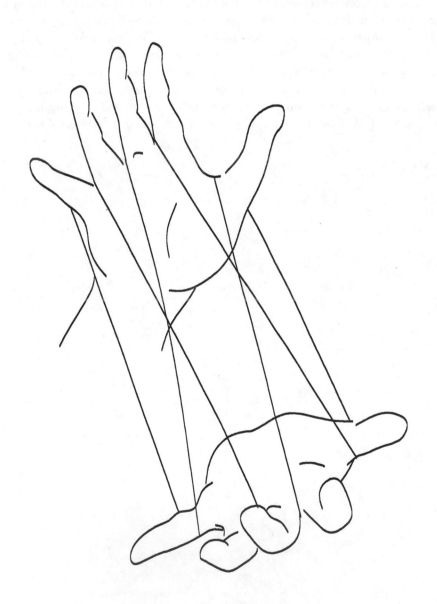

9
Teaching and Learning

The promise of personal computing for teaching and learning is that instruction can be uniquely adapted to each individual student. From simple features, such as the ability to select a sequence of topics which makes sense from the *learner's* viewpoint, to more advanced capabilities, such as facilities to generate examples of concepts and provide practice material on demand, the computer promises to provide a tutor of unique value. The key advantage is individual control, and the great attraction will be the opportunity to learn subjects of one's own choice in a self-paced, supportive environment. An analogy can be made to traveling: As a student you now tour the countries of someone else's choice, firmly handcuffed to the tour-guide/teacher.

> How much better to be free to roam about at will and speak the language, with teachers as "natives" eager to assist you!

Learners may see personal strengths and weaknesses in a variety of areas charted frequently as they progress, and vary the format and conditions of presentation for enjoyment or efficiency (3,000 words per minute is not an unheard of rate with computer presented speed reading.) The potential use of computers for learning exploring is vast, not only in traditional intellectual areas, but in physical skills, arts, crafts, and sports.

As confining classroom walls are broken down, and teachers begin to be cast in new roles, entirely new opportunities and challenges emerge. Can computers be used to *increase* the kind and quality of interaction between students and teachers, students and other students? If traditional classrooms and textbooks are no longer dictated by the necessity of getting a large group within earshot and developing a single instructional package economically for all, who will choose the topics and the methods of presentation? All of the parameters of "public education" need to be re-examined. The reassuring boundaries of named times and places, such as "elementary, middle, secondary, college, lunch room, playground, study hall," may vanish in the process. Policy issues and personal issues raised by the computer revolution in education will not go away if you ignore them. Someone else will simply make your decisions for you.

Self-Images in Learning

In seeking to improve our mental, psychological, or physical skills, it is invaluable to know both the strong and the weak points of the way in which we approach any task. Shotputters and tennis players may seek to improve themselves by simply doing what they have always done, only harder. Frequently though, the effort would be better spent in changing and tuning their approach for maximum effectiveness. A personal computer can be an invaluable help to us in analyzing the way we carry out a whole host of mental and physical tasks. Keeping a **diary** can do more than provide enjoyable reading in retrospect. If the diary is maintained on a computer, it can enable us to keep tabs on "how we are doing" in a variety of mental and physical ways. "Home movies" of activities from piano playing to tennis to children's play with blocks and puzzles can be analyzed to shed entirely new and productive light on the subjects. Feedback is a vital part of learning, whether the immediate loops we use for "balance" or the more analytical descriptions which give vital detail to our many self-images as they develop.

Let's take some specific examples. There is a company in Amherst, Massachussetts, called Computer Biomechanical Analysis. The stock in trade of these folks is improving the performance of athletes. Their techniques consist of such things as high speed motion pictures, converted to stick-figures for computer analysis. Detailed calculations can then be automatically made of the forces exerted and experienced by various body parts in the course of physical activities. The computer programs involve elementary physics, and are nothing that wouldn't fit on a good-sized personal computer. Other activities involve "bugging" sports equipment such as golf clubs, tennis rackets, ski bindings or weightlifting gear with electronic sensors, such as those for pianists and golfers described in the previous chapter. These sensors transmit information about speeds and forces directly to the computer. Analysis of the information provided can help an athlete eliminate a weakness, capitalize on good technique, and/or avoid an injury. Feedback and analysis techniques like these have been used to improve Jimmy Connor's serve by 10mph, change the angle of Al Oerter's arm and enable him to throw the shotput 15–20 feet farther, and lend a hand in the achievement of world records in the discus as well. If you become computer literate, and get your hands on the microelectronic devices which are going to be available in the next few years, you can do this type of thing for yourself and your friends.

Your own psyche might also benefit from a little more conscious attention. Self-awareness and self-improvement are perennial topics for bestsellers, despite the fact that most of what can be written as a general prescription for the public (take two aspirins and call me in the morning) is either a placebo, scientifically suspect (don't ask biorhythms to predict your period), or vacuous, untestable generalization (astrology). It would be much better to have a home "psychologist," doctor, lawyer, or mechanic, in the form of a computer program, able to respond with information (whom to call, where to look, etc.), as well as advice for *your* particular situation. You simply provide your personal information, your particular questions, perhaps in response to some intelligent and appropriate questioning. Rather than putting psychologists and psychiatrists out of business, personal computers should enable good practitioners to gain from a widespread use of their work. (Rather than interviewing five patients a day, a psychologist may wish to develop and distribute an interview/analysis program to tens or hundreds of thousands of users.)

You can expect to see "how to" books on subjects ranging from depression to party games gradually replaced by a new computerized format. The new format will have text material integrated with interactive exercises and data collection programs, all packaged in a format such as tape or disc which "plugs in" directly to a variety of home computers.

The self-help books of the near future will be embedded in computer programs that make the "how to" book a "what with" book as well.

With widespread use, and with results recorded precisely and automatically, the worth of various medical/psychological regimens might soon become as much a matter of public knowledge as the service records of various types of automobiles. Do holistic health methods work better than psychotherapy? It might depend on who the patient is, or whose version of the methods you decide to follow.

"Know thyself" was a worthwhile piece of advice when Socrates gave it. Putting it into practice effectively means having some specific facts about what things are happening to us, how we feel about things (even in relation to how we felt about them yesterday), what our priorities are, how well we are communicating with those around us, and a whole host of physical and environmental events, such as how much of what kinds of drugs (medicines) we are taking, and how much sleep we get. As an example, clinicians often use a scale to measure stress, where a client is given so many "stress points" for different types of traumatic events occurring to him or her in the recent past. Such events as loss of a spouse, birth of a child, change or loss of job, major purchases, and so on are weighed in together. Persons who have accumulated too much stress according to this measure are likely to experience physical or emotional problems, and are cautioned to take countermeasures, such as slowing down, engaging in more enjoyable and relaxing activities, and working through the residual effects of any of the crises which still make life difficult. There is, of course, no reason why an individual cannot keep track of his/her own "stress level," or any of a host of other perhaps more useful physical and psychological indicators. Experienced modelers will have their own opinions about this **quantification** of stress, as well as the ability to develop their own alternatives.

Often, even when there are no easy answers for problems, a "support group" of like-minded people who are now experiencing or have recently been through similar difficulties can be a lifesaver. This principle underlies the success of groups from Alcoholics Anonymous to pre-school play groups and professional associations. A personal computer will help you to obtain, evaluate, and utilize questionnaires and other new kinds of diagnostic tools to get enlightening insights as to "where you are" psychologically. You may use these insights to seek out and interact with those who are your mental "neighbors," or simply to relate your experiences to those of others. The best medicine may be a tailor-made "Dear Abby," or a chat over the psychological back fence (whether by old fashioned telephone or the latest computer networks) with a few of your spiritual kinfolk. In addition, it would be beneficial for all of us to make frequent excursions from our own thought-neighborhood to interact with those who see the world differently. The good ideas underlying "pen-pals," "computer dating," and guidance counseling for education, careers, etc., all deserve the technological boost they will receive from widespread personal computing.

New Tutors: Choice and Construction

Our concepts of teaching and learning are shaped by the kinds of experiences most of us have had with books and schools. In a classroom full of other children, or in following a conventional book, the learner must pay attention, avoid interruptions and distractions, and refrain from unpredicted behavior. The format of a book is essentially straight-ahead. A daring writer may invite you to choose the order in which you read his chapters, but certainly not the order in which you read his sentences. In school, we have grown used to following a pattern and presentation predetermined by the teacher and the textbooks used. In this conventional environment, we are taught to think of the learning process as based on lessons, lectures, and other passive experience. Even when the school allows for laboratory work, the student is usually told what experiments to do, and even often knows beforehand what is supposed to be "discovered."

Providing a tutor for every student, able to organize and guide the presentation of material in the best direction for the student's interests and abilities, would indisputably produce superior learning. (Even beyond conventional performance criteria, the main benefit would be the active involvement of the student in choosing and directing what he or she learns and how to learn it.) Ordinary classrooms and curricula now exist simply as an uncomfortable compromise between the ideal of individualized instruction and realities such as the historical expensiveness of facilities, equipment, and teaching personnel. By the end of this decade, cheap and powerful personal computers will be in widespread use as "tutors," providing one-to-one interaction with students for a large fraction of their day.

> The style and the techniques of these new "tutors" will be entirely dependent on the ability of the human **metateachers** who design them.

Goals for instruction must be consciously set, in the context of the new freedom that personal computers as tutors can offer. We must not think that the programs which are easiest to write (and hence appear first in the "educational software" market) are the best efforts which can be made. As an uninitiate, you would either have to "approve or disapprove" as you read the typical headline **COMPUTER TEACHES ARITHMETIC FACTS.** If you are a bit more sophisticated (and by now, I hope you are), you will realize that the "computer" which is teaching arithmetic is in fact some person's *program* for teaching arithmetic, being carried out by a computer. You should no more care about the "computer," except for technical reasons, than you do about the movie projector which is used by your local theater. You should be asking yourself, for example, whether or not this teaching program enables a child to interact easily, without imposing unnecessary or confusing restrictions for input. Has the author arranged an interesting **display**, not to you (you already know arithmetic), but to the child? More to the point, how could the program be changed—even by simple substitutions perhaps, made by a human parent or other teacher who personally knows the child involved? Beyond that, you might ask yourself whether, given all of the potential kinds of programs which can be written for computers, and the capabilities of these programs for such things as modeling and simulation, storage of vast amounts of pictures and data, and the control and production of physical actions, the very idea of a computer program presenting "2+3 = ?" isn't embarrassingly primitive.

Despite the fact that computer tutors are often developed (and undoubtedly will continue to be developed) simply by looking at all of the tasks that conventionally restricted teachers do in conventionally restricted classes, and then writing programs to mimic these efforts, such tutors are fundamentally misguided. The constraints historically dictated by efficiency and economics no longer hold. There is no educational advantage, for adults or children, to receive material passively without the need to react to it, or to be instructed in any synchrony with the time or space of others. If the schools are intended to have a social (as opposed to a strictly custodial) function, that function will be best realized by small groups of students learning to cooperate actively in common tasks. It's time to break out entirely from the "classroom mode" of thought about learning, and begin to think of learning as an invitation to travel and explore. What tools and guides can be provided for the student/traveler? How can we determine what she or he wants to see? What should be offered and suggested? Your role as learner of any age will no longer be passive, but directing and active!

The Computer as Tutor

In describing the learning process as a tour, the emphasis is on the choices the learner has—to select material, rates of presentation and other features. An equally important part of learning (and what traditionally educators have concentrated on) is the teacher's active role as counselor, coach, and disciplinarian, in addition to the more passive function of being a reliable source of information about the subject matter. If the literature of education has any content at all, then good teaching must be able not only to present the student with (a choice of) material, but also to guide him or her in **effective strategies** for dealing with the material.

At the simplest level, a computer accomplishes a good deal by simply being able to provide continuous feedback to the student, and present alternate types of material for each response. For example, with a simple program, such as the kind available on many of the first home computers offered, you might obtain the following

kind of dialog between the "subtraction teaching program" and your
child:

Program:	3–2 = ?
Child:	1
Program:	Very good. 7–2 = ?
Child:	5
Program:	That's great. How about 23–16?
Child:	6
Program:	Oops! Want to try again?
Child:	7
Program:	Now you've got it. How about 44–38?

This simple dialog exhibits many of the features which even
the simplest computer aided instruction programs have:

- Learners receive **immediate feedback** for their responses.
  In this case, every answer to a subtraction problem is either
  praised as correct or flagged as wrong. If the answer is wrong,
  the student has the opportunity to try again.
- The program is able to automatically **branch,** or proceed
  with a variety of different displays, based on the responses
  given by the student so far.

At the simplest level, this always means giving positive
feedback of some sort for correct answers, and negative feedback for
incorrect ones. The phrases "Very good," "That's great," "Oops!"
and so on used in the subtraction example are just schematic suggestions. More pictorial feedback, such as smiling or frowning faces, and
even animated cartoons with sound effects such as a bright trumpet
fanfare for right answers, screech of tires and collision sounds for
bloopers, etc.), are more effective and entertaining. (If you're cooking for children, experts warn not to make the wrong-answer displays
too thrilling, or the student may opt for entertainment over learning.) Adults may appreciate the added variety and change of pace
from textual material that sight and sound provide. Our beginning
subtraction student, perhaps even more tentative about reading than
about arithmetic, *needs* sound, visual, and spoken cues to progress
effectively.

The type of presentation selected by the program may be
extremely varied. In the simple example above, the program was
intended to present successively more difficult problems, as soon

as it was established that the student could do simpler problems easily. Thus, the sample program moved quickly on from the one-digit subtraction problems such as 3–2, 7–2, which were easily done. This decision might be based on more than the obvious fact that the student got two of the problems right in a row. The computer's built-in clock might also have recorded the time taken to answer the two questions, and found this to be quite short. In addition, data from a previous session might have been saved, indicating that (unless the student has forgotten since then) this level of problem had already been mastered. In any case, the more difficult two-digit problem "23–16" was presented next, and then "44–38," etc. Besides presenting different levels of problems, the program might offer the student the opportunity to change topics (perhaps switching from subtraction to a program of poetry reading, rock music composition, or a football simulation) or to end the session, especially if the time between responses or the quality of responses indicates the student is becoming tired or bored.

Primitive as the above example is, its approach is far superior to the use of a standard subtraction "workbook" which might be used. The student presented with a workbook can only proceed to do the problems in the specific order they are given on the page, whether or not they are appropriate (if they are either much too easy or much too hard, he learns little). In addition, the student typically receives no information about the correctness of her work until she turns in the entire page, and perhaps not immediately then. If she gets the problems back the next day, dutifully marked right and wrong, she may not even remember them. Both the amount of interest and the level of learning are kept much higher when the student is given the correct answer immediately after each problem.

You might also pause to consider that "workbook" methods are, sadly, not restricted to grade school classrooms and subtraction lessons. You can walk into a lecture hall in any university in the country and find the speaker rambling on, deflected little if at all from his chosen course by the occasional student question. The students mechanically copy word after word of notes, perhaps including a homework assignment to be completed within a few days and then probably not seen again for a few weeks. In some science and mathematics classes, instructors may thoughtfully provide the answers to homework exercises immediately when the students submit their papers. Providing immediate answers is certainly a step in the right direction, but the student who made an error may not have a clue when he receives the solutions, if ever, as to *why* his or her answer got off the track. There is no fundamental reason why the same simple techniques of immediate feedback and branching, which demonstrably improve the teaching of arithmetic to children, could not be used to more effectively present courses in any subject, from integral calculus to real estate licensing to the language of Shakespeare. In some cases, the attempts are being made; in most cases not. It will be interesting to see what response high schools, colleges, and universities make, when personal computers are as common among students as stereo sets are today. It is then likely that students will come to expect interactive techniques to be utilized, providing appropriate feedback and examples individually in the course of instruction. In addition, schools will not miss the profitability, in the days of declining enrollments, of exporting (**transportable** and **negotiable**) "courses" able to be transmitted, either in mass-storage form or through a communication network. High caliber and aggressive schools will soon have active students scattered over countries, if not around the world.

A good question to ask here (and elsewhere in the book) is, "What specific advantage does the use of a computer provide, in the subtraction lesson example above?" The answer for that example is honestly, "some practical advantages of *administration*, but not really a great advantage to the *student*." After all, a teacher with a set of flash cards could do as well or better than the computer program, if one teacher were available for every student. The practical advantages in administration of the lesson should not be dismissed lightly, but to go much beyond these, one must make very different use of the computer as a tutor, capitalizing on much more than its capabilities for bookkeeping and raw output. By using the computer's **processing** power and capability of **interactive display** more fully, sophisticated programs can provide the student with a much more powerful learning tool than does a simple presentation-response-branch program like the one in the above subtraction example.

Before discussing the more powerful methods of using the computer as tutor, it would be wise to give the practical advantages of even the simplest computer techniques their due. The type of instruction in our simple subtraction example above goes under various names, such as "programmed instruction," or more technically for this case, "frame-oriented computer-assisted instruction (CAI)." In frame-oriented instruction, the material for the lesson is broken down into "frames," like the individual frames of a movie. The student is presented with a frame, and required to make some response at the end of each frame, before going on to the next frame. There are typically hundreds if not thousands of frames in a programmed instruction sequence, but the frames *could* be (have been) printed up one after the other in an ordinary book. The only technology required is a sheet of paper which the student can slide down the page to uncover each frame in succession. Typically, a question which is posed in one frame is answered at the beginning of the next frame.

As you can surmise, printed versions of programmed instruction involve a lot of paper and ink. In a full blown programmed instruction sequence, branching takes place, so that a student does not see frames one after the other, but skips after each frame to the "best" next frame for him or her. (If you had a programmed instruction frame right here in this book, it might ask you to explain "frame-oriented" CAI, giving several alternative answers for you to choose from. If you picked the right response, you would be directed forward, and if the wrong one, you would be directed back to the previous point in the text, where "frame-oriented" CAI was defined.)

Even lessons which use such multiple-branching programmed instruction can still be presented in book form. The author simply numbers each individual frame, and gives instructions at the end of each frame, along with the question which is asked, such as "If you pick:

- answer 'a,' go to frame 10.15.
- answer 'b,' go to 3.14.
- answer 'c,' 11.07 . "

At this point though, the printed-book format begins to (literally) fall apart. The reader must constantly be turning back and forth from one page to the next (the frames must be sprinkled through the book in pretty much of a random order. Otherwise, the student would quickly realize that the right answer to any question is the one which directs her farthest toward the end of the book.) With all the possible options available, the total number of frames in such a book can be ridiculously large, both in absolute terms, and especially relative to the number that any given student actually reads (even if he perseveres through the entire course). In the extreme case where each student who responds *differently* to the instructions gets a *unique* set of frames to read, the book format is entirely out of the question, since to present twenty frames, for example, where only two responses are allowed after each frame, would require the book to have over a million frames.

Advanced Techniques

The most exciting developments in the use of computer-assisted instruction involve much more extensive use of the computer than the traditional "frame-oriented" methods. In some sense, these traditional methods have used the computer as little more than an automatic page-turner. Let's look briefly at some more ambitious prospects.

Interactive Display: In the chapter of this book on games, we have discussed the ability to create new materials and dynamically interact with them through the use of the computer. Rather than simply marshaling children through rote subtraction exercises, the computer offers the possibility of presenting them with experience which is exciting and fun, and teaches them not only subtraction, but the more important lesson that "numbers are your friends." Imagine for a moment a display of three apartment buildings, with floors numbered 0 through 9:

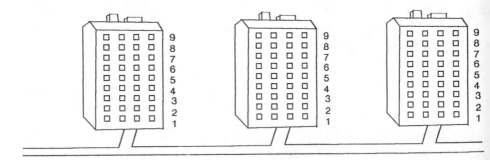

**These apartments can represent the "hundreds",
"tens," and "ones" digits of a number, in teaching arithmetic.**

People come into the apartments and fill up the floors from the bottom to the top. Whenever a floor is filled, the windows on that floor and the appropriate digit (1, 2, 3, 4, 5, 6, 7, 8, 9), both light up. It takes only one person to fill each floor of the "ones" building, ten people to fill up each floor of the "tens" building, and a hundred people to fill up each floor of the "hundreds" building. Teaching programs can be written to play arithmetic games, allowing the student to bring people in and out of the apartment buildings by interacting with the computer display, automatically changing the numbers and lighting the windows to demonstrate addition and subtraction processes. We might have buses, for example, as well as buildings, also labeled "hundreds," "tens," and "ones." A child can learn addition and subtraction by transferring people from the buildings to the buses and back again, using the digits of the numbers to control the display, gradually learning to "guess" the answers, from her developing knowledge of arithmetic facts.

Some of the best work done to date in computer aided instruction has utilized the computer's ability to be a laboratory/game room, where the student can make things happen and see their effects, in subjects ranging from arithmetic to geography to physics and electronic circuits. In this context, the computer is used as a **tool**, as well as a tutor, and these lab/games show an ability to hold children's (and adults') attention which is remarkable. To a large extent though, all of the **action** has so far been confined to pictures on a television screen. Pioneering exceptions, such as the LOGO programs and devices of Seymour Papert and his colleagues at M.I.T., give some indication of the eventual potential for learning which will be realized when the action moves off the screen and into the classroom. (In his book **Mindstorms**, Papert describes much of his work and philosophy.)

In an environment like that of the LOGO project, children take the initiative to **use** the computer, and learn from their interaction with it. With the "turtle" as a physical object moving in the real world of the classroom, the children can develop powerful and precise concepts through physical movement and visualization, as well as through language.

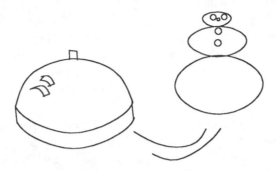

In Papert's LOGO environment, young school children have learned to program computers by giving commands to a "turtle" which can actually move around in the classroom, drawing pictures on the floor with a pen it holds.

The Computer As Laboratory: Many students react to theoretical subjects such as physics, chemistry, or mathematics as no more than an elaborate collection of rituals and numerology designed to give esoteric delight to insiders and thoroughly intimidate any others. Why should a student appreciate the crystallization of experience which a theory represents, if he has never had any of that experience himself, or if she has never attempted to simplify things with a theory of her own?

With widespread use of computers, a student will be able to quickly and easily experiment with many situations, using a stored model developed by experts and teachers. In addition, the students' own programs will serve as a familiar and flexible language in which they can develop their own "theory" of a situation. The simple pendulum of classical clocks and physics can be set up by the student using a computer model, examining long and short rods, heavy weights and light, wide swings and narrow, and so on. Rather than starting with mathematical formulas, a teacher could introduce a Gravity Actor, a Rod Actor, perhaps an Air Actor, and so on, suggesting some possible ways they might interact, and asking the student to determine which protocol seemed to bring about the observed actual behavior of the pendulum. Once the students have this familiar "model" as an explanation, they can readily grasp the shorthand notation of classical mathematical formulas.

In elementary mathematics, there are always both *abstract* and **concrete** forms that can be given to basic concepts. The area of a figure, for example, is just the number of standard sized tiles it would take to cover it. We can thus say either:

"The area of a rectangle equals its length times its height," or...

Area: 5x8 = 40

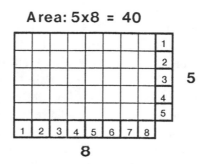

...**the number of square tiles needed to cover a rectangle equals the number which can be lined up on the bottom edge, repeated for each tile which can be lined up on the side edge.**

And *"The area of a parallelogram equals its length times its height,"* or...

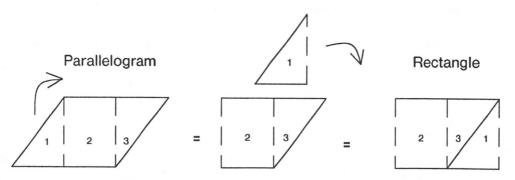

...**any parallelogram can be cut in two and the pieces rearranged to make a rectangle with the same width and height. The rectangle can be tiled as above.**

With their history of *experience* in the computer laboratory as a resource, students can assimilate theoretical knowledge not as mere rote, but as a simple and effective **program** for understanding that experience.

Modeling Teachers: If we use the analogy of the computer as tutor, based on the fact that there will eventually be one computer per student in many learning environments, the task we are faced with is to capture, in the programs we write for teaching and learning, the best aspects and strategies of interaction for human students and tutors. In his work, Ira Goldstein distinguishes three tutor's roles which can be individually modeled by a computer program. Specifically, he discusses the roles which would be needed for a "computer coach" which assists a student in learning to play a game well: The **teacher as expert** role for the program requires it to determine, at any stage of the game, what the best course of action for the student to take would be. The **teacher as psychologist** role requires the program to infer, based on some model of the student's conceptual structure, the reasons behind moves which the student suggests, especially when these moves could be substantially improved. The **teacher as tutor** role requires that the program be able to incorporate the advice of the expert and the inferences of the psychologist, and *intervene* in the game at appropriate times to offer advice, exercises, questions, etc., to the student, which will lead to consistently better play in the future. If you are a student or a teacher, you can implement models such as this for programs you develop, or use this reasoning to evaluate programs you might find already available. The more skilled you are in conceptualizing and developing programs, the more you can adapt strategies to your particular perspective.

Learning from the Learner: As more flexible and powerful **interface** methods between humans and computers become available, students will have a wider and wider range of actions available to them, at any point in the course of a session. Pictures and text can be selected and manipulated; the student's own strategies (programs) for approaching the subject matter can be tested; physical objects can be constructed and arranged; and actual and modeled experiments performed. From one point of view, the advantage of such flexible interfacing is that the tutor (programs) can communicate information much more effectively **to the student.** Equally important in the long run though, is that a versatile interface, offering the student a multiplicity of options at any point in a session, also provides a greatly increased flow of information *from* the student.

Without sophisticated input and output capability, a typical teaching program simply waits "in the dark," while the student works through a variety of mental tasks, perhaps even using a pencil and scratchpad or other devices inaccessible to the program, and finally comes up with his next "move." With integrated graphics capabilities, "scratchpad" facility, and other planning tools, the student would not only complete any necessary intermediate mental steps more quickly, but would be effectively "thinking out loud" to the computer, in a variety of ways which could produce better responses from the program. A complete log of the interaction between student and teaching program can be automatically and reliably recorded in the course of a session. The combined data of many such logs, obtained from perhaps thousands of students and programs, will be a goldmine of information, immediately usable without further intervention in the form of observers, coding, or recording. Using this database as a firm empirical base, the development of better programs and other educational and psychological research will be greatly enhanced.

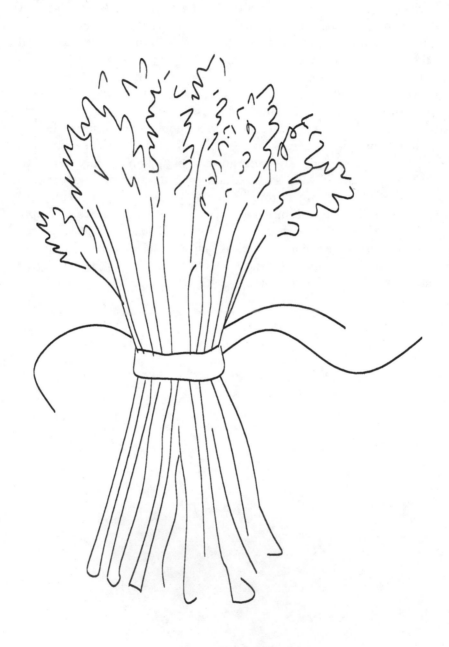

10

Harnessing the Information Explosion

Transportable and Negotiable Information

The most intensively used resource of the coming decade will be not oil or coal but information. The personal computer of the near future will be an **access port** through which an individual can **receive, transmit,** and **interactively interpret** data. A characteristic feature of logically coded information is its transportability, and even beyond that, its negotiability. Not only can you get information, in logical form, where you want it, as easily as television or radio broadcasts or telephone hookups, but once transmitted, the information can be stored, reutilized, recombined, and used directly to drive programs for whatever application, from music composition to shipbuilding, that humans find interesting. The ability to find, abstract and utilize existing information, to locate applicable and available technology and resources can not only benefit the individual but perhaps alleviate some of the strain on an overworked planet as well.

As you will see, the transfer of information is no longer going to be confined to books or paper, or even to the two-dimensional format of the printed page or picture. This chapter outlines a few of the ways in which you will be able to tap this vast information flow with a personal computer. The availability of information in transportable and negotiable form, will bring a new perspective to:

- Newspapers and magazines—both the materials and format are open to radical changes.
- Information distribution—materials from airline schedules to seed catalogs can be distributed rapidly and selectively.

- Network communication—two-way information flow will occur with an unprecedented immediacy and versatility.
- Libraries—as books literally dematerialize, libraries will take on new roles.
- Information economics—consumer blocs, word of mouth advertising, and other buyer inputs will reach unparalleled significance.
- Political debate and decisions—new ways to examine representatives on their records and determine their views will emerge, as well as effective ways to mobilize constituencies for "grass roots" lobbying.
- The human interface—logical devices will make many forms of interaction between humans and data possible, from books that read themselves aloud to children, tax instructions which answer your questions, to hi-fi remote transmission of batik or backrubs.

It is very important, at this early stage of development, not to think of information primarily as something that large corporations will develop, manage, and monopolize for subsequent distribution to the masses. If individuals can begin to think of themselves as cooperative producers, rather than consumers, the communication capabilities of burgeoning computer networks can be a great asset in organizing their efforts. The uninitiates will remain simply "dumb terminals," to their corporate or political suppliers, selecting from a limited menu, and more easily misdirected and manipulated by news coverage, advertising, and other "PR" strategies than ever before. With a little computer literacy, you will be able to command your own processing facilities, transforming, processing, and originating information as well as receiving it.

The entire character of life in developed countries is shaped by the fact that *electrical power,* as well as the devices, from electric motors to air conditioners to television sets, for using this power are universally available. The development of large scale distribution systems for *information* and matching logical devices to tap into this system will have an equally profound effect.

> Over the next decade, information "power
> lines" in the form of computer *networks* will
> develop to link together workers within an
> office, neighbors within a community, and
> citizens within a country.

In many cases, the groundwork for networks is already in place, in
the form of telephone, cable television, satellite, and other technology. It is commonplace to call a co-worker on the telephone; it
will soon be expected as easily to call for a selected review of things
from stock trading to consumer information to airline charter status.
Your information may come from the nation's capital, a community
electronic bulletin board, the office down the hall, or the public
library. Whatever the source, network communication will enable
you to obtain information rapidly, as well as sift and search through
large databases to retrieve just the material that interests you.

Retooling Conventional Media

Early writing and information transfer were carried out by
means of clay tablets. Symbols could be pressed into the clay when
it was wet, where they remained more or less permanently when
the clay was dry. Try to conjure up for a moment the image of
your *New York Times* being delivered to the doorstep, impressed
on clay! You'd be lucky to find the door under it, much less the
doorstep. When you stop and think about it, information is not
much better suited to being pressed on paper than it is on clay,
once you have large amounts of it to contend with. In a gradual
but ever-accelerating tide, the paper wave is ebbing just as the clay
did before it. Information, the inherently massless concept, is once
again finding a more mobile medium.

It is possible already to subscribe to several major newspapers electronically. No smudgy package of newsprint arrives daily at
your door. Instead, you are given a phone number and a password.
When you wish to see the day's news, you simply sit down in front
of the television screen on your home computer, call up the number
given, and are automatically linked up with the newspaper. You
may read the news page by page, if you wish, simply pressing a

button to see new text appear on the screen.

Despite what salespeople and far-gone hobbyists would tell you, it is obvious that a newspaper does not undergo any substantial improvement simply by virtue of becoming "electronic." You may be able to subscribe to *Teen Crush* magazine with your educational computer, or *Hollywood Scandals Review* on the computer news network, but you will get little education or news in the process. Once the magic aura of "computerized" is dispelled, you will not only be less susceptible to hype of products from toasters to toys, but you can also get through to some basic questions about how computing power is used. The computer revolution is proceeding as a number of disjoint pieces, such as hardware development, program development, distribution mechanisms, maintenance, and public education. These pieces are moving at wildly different speeds.

> In most areas, the technological capability to produce computer power is far ahead of the human understanding of how to use that power effectively and cooperatively.

Another key stumbling block is the lack of information and programs in a widely and easily accessible form. Computer experts and enthusiasts often feel like do-it-yourselfers with a garage full of power tools, an attic full of plans—and no lights or electricity. Imagine for the moment a country where a color television standard has been adopted and transmission facilities and receivers are just becoming widely available. You might well hesitate in such a situation to rush out and buy a color television set, due to the simple fact that very little programming in color may be available. It would certainly not impress you if stations varied their old black and white programs by sending them in red and white, then green and white, then blue and white, etc., and advertised "extensive color programming." If most of the transmission is still black and white, you may be better off with your old black and white television, which has a sharper picture (in black and white) than the new sets.

This imperfect analogy is close enough to bear in mind whenever you hear anything touted as "computerized." In particular, a computerized newspaper which is nothing more than the logically coded duplicate of the printed edition is making severely limited use of the technology. The attractions of speedy delivery and ability to impress your friends are undeniable, but hardly require computers. Many computerized data services are accessed, in this early stage of development, through very small "windows" based on available home computers and data terminals. If you have only twenty or so short lines on a small screen, and if the transmission of new data to your screen takes longer than you would like to wait, you may very reasonably prefer to walk to the corner and buy the "old fashioned" printed newspaper, which gets its information to *you* much more rapidly and interpretably.

It is only a matter of a few years until large screen terminals and high speed transmission of data, perhaps ten times faster than in the early eighties, are widely available. Such "wide window" facilities will make it possible to truly *add* features by making a newspaper electronic, rather than *trading off* advantages of computer power against the drawbacks of greatly restricted display. The advantages of a true electronic newspaper, designed from the ground up to use computer processing and display to the fullest, would be substantial:

- Rather than paging through the newspaper from front to back, you would be able to use an exhaustive index to scan through the topics of the day, then bring the most interesting stories into view immediately.

- The entire newspaper text could be searched to find key words and phrases (stored on your personal computer and automatically looked up when you access the newspaper). Occurrences of these phrases would be reported to you, along with the location and perhaps additional information about the stories involved. An automatic "clipping service" could store away all stories which pertain to your various "topics of interest."

- Wide access to the past issues of papers and magazines could be available, allowing you to trace back events leading up to a topic which suddenly becomes interesting. If it strikes you that several politicians have changed their tune substantially between campaigning and holding office, the public record will be there for you to peruse. A quick rundown of the past few months' stories containing the key words "President" and "navy," or "President" and "social security," or other combinations, would give interesting perspectives. Depending on your tastes, your searching and summarizing could cover world affairs, financial acquisitions, or box scores.

- A much broader spectrum of information and opinion could be accessed, once it is assumed that the *reader* will be able to define a point of view, as well as an editor or group of editors. You will not ordinarily find the same news story covered by more than one writer simultaneously, or more than one editor's point of view on the editorial page, in a conventional newspaper. Routine multiple and parallel coverage would burden newspaper carriers and readers beyond patience. In completely electronic form though, you could well subscribe to scores of newspapers (perhaps through your public library), picking and choosing the most knowledgeable, well written, or thought provoking coverage, on a story by story basis. Individual reporters would develop followings, as well as editors and news staffs. Editorial judgment and organization would remain extremely valuable, seen now as *suggestions* rather than hidebound *restrictions* on how the reader may approach the day's news. The reporter or group whose story is spurned would still have a public forum—you can simply look them up in the day's "reject" file.

- Even individual stories could be rearranged to allow different levels of reading. The casual reader may wish to see a story only in the conventional straight-line narrative. Below the "surface" of every sentence, a display could be retrieved, showing the reporter's notes, references to previous news and commentary, and other valuable information which typically goes into the preparation of the story, but is too detailed to supply to every reader. Who knows, one level beneath the "surface" story might be a simple listing of indisputable facts, as counterpoint to the typical weave of fact, opinion, and subtle injection of attitude which characterizes early eighties journalism.

It is interesting to compare broadcast and "printed" media as they currently exist, since technology may eventually make the two indistinguishable. Why, for example, would you prefer to read a news story about a particular event, rather than view a television documentary? The television presents much more visual and audio information. The advantages of the newspaper are that you can start and stop reading any time you like, you can skim over unwanted material, and go back over sections as you like. All of these "newspaper" advantages can be achieved by electronic transmission, coupled with temporary storage for processing by a personal computer. Broadcast material can be stored for review at leisure, much in the same way that television programs are currently able to be stored by conventional (non-intelligent) home videotape recorders. But with intelligent processors, much more can potentially happen. Newspaper reporters can routinely insert both sound and pictorial material into their stories. With a logical device for storage, material can be skipped over, scanned, and searched for automatically. The home viewer can process and evaluate this "firsthand material" personally, whether it is background interviews for public opinion (too lengthy to be presented in today's newspapers or television) or political candidates' speeches, or sports replays. The viewer can then use his own programs and judgment to operate on the material and decide such questions as, "Is the official convicted of bribery actually innocent?" or "Did Merzy Putzwell really drop the ball before he was tackled?"

Moving to a "paperless society" will save forests full of trees, and enable you to weed out a lot of noise quickly to get the information you want. As valuable as these benefits are, they are only the beginning of the technology's impact. Because the information coming to you is going to be in logical form, it is inherently portable and adaptable, essentially negotiable in an unprecedented way. Rather than sitting passively in front of a screen as the information passes by, you are able to actively select and extract relevant information, to be assimilated by your personal computing system. Information can be combined with previously stored information, patterns can be sought out and displayed. Whether you are following stock prices, keeping an annotated list of your senator's public statements, or collecting recipes and do-it-yourself projects, the language is no longer stuck to the page, but flows freely to and from whatever programs you care to use it in. The stock prices you note may send you an automatic signal to buy or sell; the recipe you "clip" may actually cook dinner tonight.

However comprehensive electronic newspapers, magazines and other written media eventually become, the attractiveness of "live" radio and television presentations will continue to be a distinctive feature. With advances in computer support though, the "live" quality of broadcasts will make a quantum leap in realism, through direct feedback between broadcasters and the viewers. Television and radio will then emerge as just one level of a pervasive system of interactive communication. This developing system of **computer networks** deserves a discussion in its own right, and will get one shortly in this chapter.

Interim Technologies

Electronic readers for **bar codes** are already available for microcomputers, and should become even more popular as an intermediate technology. You have undoubtedly seen bar codes, since they are printed on most products in stores everywhere. If you assumed, perhaps naturally, that the only thing bar codes are good for is to help the checker get your money faster, you should reconsider. If the grocery ads in the newspaper had bar codes with them, in the same way that the packages on the shelves do, you would be able to go through the ads from several stores in a matter of minutes, automatically transferring data to your personal computer. If you already had a "shopping list" in mind, the computer could print out a list for you of what to buy in each store, or which store to go to, if you wanted to buy everything from one store, and tell you how much the trip would cost. Alternatively, since the computer would have your favorite recipes stored, along with their ingredients, you might ask it to suggest some menus, based on current supermarket prices, and even have the shopping list itself developed automatically for your approval and modification. What bar codes represent, simply put, is a way to patch the outmoded printing-press technology into the development and transmission of highly mobile data.

The lack of such mobile data in the early eighties is a much greater stumbling block to the usefulness of computers than the availability of personal computer hardware. It is beside the point, for the next few years anyway, that communication will *eventually* be accomplished by direct electronic/optical connection of your personal computer to an information network. Bar codes and other innovations with printing (including improved programs and optical devices which can automatically translate printed data into logical form) will be valuable for quite a few years to come, making good use of our existing technology as new channels and devices are gradually put into place.

Other technologies, perhaps less ephemeral than bar codes, are already being utilized, and are far from achieving their full potential. Chief among these is the use of **storage discs** as a sturdy and somewhat transportable memory medium. Discs for computer storage come in several forms, including the magnetic **floppy disc** which resembles a small phonograph record. Discs are less transportable, of course, than telephone or television signals, and require more sophisticated equipment to (re)produce than bar codes, but their high density capability makes them extremely valuable, even if you do have to go to a store, check one out from the library, or wait a few days for the postperson to bring you one. The oldest type of disc technology for computers is based on magnetic effects, in the same way that cassette tape recorders are. It is fairly easy to keep track of millions of words of information in a library of magnetic computer discs, and most home computers have the capability to be connected to and use magnetic disc storage of some kind. For example, if you have a personal computer and are interested in the stock market,you can arrange to have a disc sent from Standard and Poor's each month (for $20 or so), with far more information about stocks for that month than you would ever type in by hand. Mount the disc on your machine, and the information is ready to be sifted, sorted, and displayed as you like.

Another disc technology, which is only in its infancy in the early eighties, is the **videodisc**. Videodiscs can be produced to hold truly vast quantities of information, but have not been as widely developed as magnetic disc, to match up with the storing and retrieving technology of computers. Videodisc *players* though (with no recording capability at all) have already begun to appear in the mass market. These devices use a laser beam to read microscopic tracks in a plastic-coated metal film. The tracks, which are also made by a laser, consist of holes burned through the film. In this dialect of the binary language, the translation might be "hole = yes; no hole = no." Because the laser can be focused to such a narrow beam, the holes burned are extremely small, and it is possible to write enormous quantities of information on a single disc. For the entertainment purposes, this means you can buy an entire movie on one small plastic disc, which is entirely digitally encoded, never touched mechanically to be read, and hence has no noticeable wear, regardless of the number of times it is used. This, like many immediate uses of a technology, misses the larger point. The fact is, that "home-entertainment" disc is the densest mass-storage device likely to come down the pike for quite a while. To put things in perspective, you can compare the videodisc to several other technologies for storing information. The videodisc of a small size can hold about ten billion bits of information. If you figure an English word as about fifty bits, that means that a single videodisc can be used to store 200 million words of text, which amounts to a library of about two thousand volumes. I don't know how large your current home library is, but it is probably less than one videodisc worth.

Networks

The greatest immediate social impact of the computer revolution may well come about due to **computer networks**. These networks, which can be based on telephone, cable television, or simple co-axial cable connections, provide channels for the extremely rapid and selective data transmission which computers make possible. With your personal computer as an access port, you can communicate to your office copying machine, across town, or across the country. The data transferred and processed could be supporting anything from electronic interactive games to investment strategies to building plans.

Whether the social impact of networks will be remembered by history as beneficial depends both on government and corporate policies and the intelligence and vigor of public reaction. Will the main result of computer networking be large scale cooperation in business, educational, social and artistic endeavors and an increasingly informed and active public for economic and political processes, or will "interactive television" give us a new breed of electronic zombies, hooked into hour after hour of spacewar shootouts rather than the passive "boob tube" fare which has characterized video technology before the eighties? In the long run, computer networks will establish sharing and cooperation as a routine element of the social ambience. Whether this activity will be as banal and trivialized as the classic C.B. radio, or as productive as public libraries, frontier barn raising, and food coops, is entirely up to us.

The economics of implementing electronic networks are very favorable; network use is predicted to involve tens of millions of people by the end of the decade. Two of the earliest computer networks, **The Source** and **CompuServe Information Service** will have perhaps 100,000 users by the end of 1981, and more firms seem to be entering the market daily. The CompuServe network of

Columbus, Ohio, offers to its subscribers the opportunity to retrieve a wide variety of information for display at a home terminal, or direct transfer to a home computer. By purchasing this service, you can display news, food information, stock and commodity prices, as well as receive commentary and statistical summaries. Electronic mail can be sent and received, as well as many varieties of games from blackjack to electronic pinball or the latest intergalactic space war. Other network services, such as those provided by Boeing Computer Services and Lockheed's DIALOG, the law specialists of Westlaw, Lexis, and so on, are tailored to information retrieval in scientific, technical, and other areas.

A typical package deal gives the purchaser both the right to connect to a network and the necessary computing equipment to set up a personal *data terminal.*

A word of caution to be said is that many package-deal offers do not give the user much of a computer, but merely a terminal capable of simple request and display commands, and the display itself often very limited. Like instant film photography, the initial equipment may be cheap, but is useless without continued and fairly expensive purchases of supplies. In this case, the "supplies" consist of hourly charges to network users for any time they are connected. The accumulated costs can rapidly exceed the price of a small computer system. Certainly, it would be cheaper over the span of a year or so for many people to maintain a conventional newspaper subscription, and play their games on a computer system which they have purchased outright, rather than use a network service extensively for these same activities. Ideally, a network should provide users with just those services that they cannot economically and practically maintain themselves, in addition to its function of transmitting mail and messages. With a proliferation of companies and competitive arrangements, as well as more educated and discerning network customers, much better package offers will be forthcoming.

You probably realize, at this point, that there is no fundamental distinction between a "network" computer and any other kind. The simple fact is that the telephone system has been built to handle audio data like voices and tones. If a computer network is implemented over phone lines, that means that the **electrical signals** which the computer deals with internally must be converted into **sounds** (to go into the telephone handset) or **waves of electrical voltage** which can go directly over the phone lines without being severely distorted. There are many other devices worth connecting your computer to, beyond or by means of the telephone system:

- large **memory systems** based on discs.
- **output devices** to produce high quality typing and pictures, or speech, or signals to control household electrical components.
- **input devices** such as television cameras and monitors for temperature, sound, motion, and so on.

The key fact to be aware of is that some personal computers have versatile **communication interface** circuits built in, enabling you to directly or easily hook up to telephones, to large memory devices and so on, while others keep their processing "locked up" or virtually impossible to relay to other devices without purchasing expensive add-ons from the specific manufacturer. The best strategy in the long run is to evaluate the computer's **processing** capabilities, and its **communication** capabilities somewhat separately. A well designed personal computer, with a good library of available programs and an elementary, standardized communication interface, will typically cost perhaps 20 to 40 percent more than any single mass-market device such as a "data terminal," "talking computer," "video input computer," or whatever. Once you develop a variety of uses for computers though, a comprehensive system of devices built around the more versatile computer will not only be the only manageable solution, but cheaper as well. It may very well be, at the early stages of personal computing, that a special-purpose device is both cheap and useful for some initial experimenting. For offices and businesses and other such serious or ambitious use, the penny-wise strategy of buying cheap and uncommunicative devices to do individual, specific tasks can easily lead to a pound-foolish cacaphony of non-cooperating subsystems.

Despite some acknowledged limitations of speed and restricted accessibility, the telephone represents a great "natural" resource for developing computer networks. To implement many of the features of a network, including electronic mail, text retrieval and processing, facsimile and image transmission, one can use the existing telephone system. This "value added" concept relies on the fact that the information carrying capacity of the telephones is currently vastly under-utilized. The situation is reminiscent of a group of rural California families who made their own telephone exchange, long before any other farm areas in the country had one. They connected crank telephones to the top wire of their interconnecting barbed wire fences! In fashionable terms, they were merely capitalizing in a "value added" fashion on the underused "barbed wire channel."

Logical techniques are able to improve the use of a channel, whether it is a telephone line or a piece of television antenna cable, in many different ways. **Multiplexing** enables many transmissions to be sent out over the same channel simultaneously. Multiplexing is possible because most transmissions of analog signals such as telephone conversations are highly redundant. (If your mother-in-law always complains for the first five minutes of her phone call, or if your son in law always brags about his job for the first five minutes, you can safely put the phone down and read the newspaper, just checking occasionally to make sure things are going predictably.) Even transmissions of digital signals often have "dead spots" where nothing is being sent.

Channel sharing has been used extensively, to implement nationwide research networks as well as office communication systems linking word processors, graphic devices, and file systems. Such networks would simply not be practical if every pair of communicating sites required its own dedicated channel. Typically, the input channels have a fair frequency of "dead spots" (when nothing is being sent), so that when any individual message needs to be transmitted, the high speed output line is usually not busy and there is no noticeable delay.

Electronic networks can also be expected to replace traditional postal service to a large extent. Not surprisingly, one of the first large scale studies of the feasibility of electronic text networks has been carried out by the post office in England. It does not make much sense, after all, to have a paper-delivery system, which is what the traditional postal service is, doing a job which is mainly information transmission. At present the British post office's Prestel teletext service (for sending messages electronically from the terminals of individual subscribers) is growing by one percent per day, and is expected to have 250,000 terminals in use by 1985. Users of the early computer networks have quickly grown spoiled with the idea that they can write a paper or a memo and "post" it on an electronic network, to be picked up by the recipient whenever he or she next checks for messages. A delay of days or weeks to deliver a short message cheaply by conventional mail systems then seems impossibly slow.

Unlike standard national and regional broadcast networks, computer networks promise to be efficient and practical for relatively small groups as well as large ones, and over short distances which span a typical office, institution, or neighborhood. A trial program of such a **local network** facility linking top level administrators at Stanford University has become quickly established, eliminating the paper memorandum between offices. The university officials simply sit down at their electronic "typewriters" and compose the memo (editing and revising via instant word-processing capability), then send it off to its recipient with the push of a few buttons. When the recipient next checks his messages, he may respond to the new message and/or save it, automatically filed for later retrieval. The phrase "try to get so-and-so on the phone for me" has virtually disappeared from the language.

The goal in establishing local networks is to link people together over the short distances covered by a company or institution, and convert all documents and data communication, whether memos or training manuals or final reports, into transportable and negotiable form. Business data processing, in particular, will be radically changed by this approach in the next few years. It is already possible, for example, to obtain a complete local network facility, including the required computers, storage and graphic devices, and necessary programs, in a single modularly constructed system developed by the Digital Equipment, Intel, and Xerox Corporations to require only coaxial (tv-antenna type) cable connections between locations. Other approaches, such as Wang Laboratories' broadband system, capable of dealing with television transmission as well as logical data simultaneously, are being followed, and both small companies and the traditional data-processing giants may have a role in the eventual development of standards. Undoubtedly, more possibilities and vendors will emerge, but even the initial efforts appear to be easily used and cost efficient in many environments. Xerox, in particular, has put great emphasis on developing programs which enable humans to manage computers, rather than vice versa. Using video displays which can be rearranged much like sheets of paper on a desk top, users of Xerox workstation computers can invoke commands by simply pointing to a descriptive picture or **icon** on the screen.

Highly Informative Television—In Two Directions

We are all familiar with television technology, and its amazing ability to present visual images with realistic color, dynamic action, and on-the-spot closeness. Most of us are also unhappy with the inane uses to which this technology is regularly put. Fortunately, trends are beginning to develop based on cable television, which promise to make better use of the the medium's vast information carrying capability and integrate it as a useful part of an overall communication network.

By using **cable** (optical or electronic) to connect television sets to a central station, rather than sending the station's signal through the air, it is possible to transmit hundreds of channels simultaneously without interference. Optical cables presently exist which are capable of transmitting information at the rate of one billion bits per second. (That's something like 200 complete books of English text per second, if you recall the earlier calculation in this chapter for videodiscs.) In addition, the individual subscriber to such a cable television network has the capability to transmit program material **back to the station.** With the material coded in logical form, it is then possible to automatically sift through the information going in either direction, store selected portions, and direct other portions to further users or computer programs for analysis, synthesis, redisplay, and so on. What this means is that television programs, from stand-up comedy to political speeches, can proceed interactively, with the comedian/speaker responding to and asking for information from the audience. The politician can take an on-the-spot poll of his constituents, and respond to questions they present to him. The comedian (and the audience) can gauge the success of the show by something more plausible than canned laughter. The audience may even be able to embarrass the actors/network involved in a particular program, if the occasion warrants it. In addition, home viewers can supply their own programs, transmitted from their home cameras or video recorders through the station, to other viewers.

A key economic factor in cable television of any sort is its profitability. People have proved to be willing to pay for non-commercial "cable" television in the past. The rates for a "smart," multi-channel cable connection, with two-way capability, should not be much more. Early pilot systems (the Teletext System in Salt Lake City, Utah , the QUBE system in Columbus, Ohio, and a full two-way system in Higashi-Ikoma, Japan) have been enthusiastically received. In many areas, the technology is only beginning to be available, but public policy is being set *now* that will shape the future uses and usefulness of cable television. You would be wise to realize that the technocrats and cable suppliers may define an "optimal" solution differently than you would. Before your community buys a package-deal cable system, the package is worth careful scrutiny. There is sufficient profit involved that suppliers will be competitive, and communities can be choosy. Some locations, by dint of strenuous bargaining, have managed to install a community *owned* cable system, rather than giving both ownership and control to a licensee. All sorts of bogeymen, from technological complications to uncertain revenues and loss of a large initial cash return, will be flushed out to discourage such initiative and involvement. At long last though, the public has an opportunity to change television, rather than simply complain about it.

What Is A Library?

Widely accessible computer networks will erase many long-held prejudices about storing and using information. The impact on the development of libraries will be profound. The word "library" itself conjures up images of a repository for scrolls and books. The library of the future will take a more active role as a **community information center**. Such an information-processing center can serve as a high powered resource, able to be shared by individuals on a limited basis as needed.

As a communication resource, libraries can provide access to a wide variety of different networks, allowing their use by individual library "cardholders" who do not need these networks except occasionally. Such specialized networks might be devoted to high speed transmission of massive amounts of data, access to exotic or expensive computing facilities, or long range international communication. "Exotic" might mean such things as direct astronomical observations transmitted from powerful observatories on earth or in space, or special-interest coverage of conferences and political sessions. One "exotic" connection already handled through libraries in the early eighties is to put the user in touch with a large database of specialized knowledge. This use is only in its infancy, but is already important and valuable. The catalog of machine-readable databases of the American Society for Information Science includes more than 1,400 suppliers, some of whom have billions of words of data accessible by specific topic.

Public library systems are built upon the belief that access to information is a public good, which should not be regulated by simple economics. In that vein, the public library as a community information center can be oriented to providing basic computing facilities to the public at large. Citizens with only the simplest computers (the phone company may eventually find it cheaper to give you one than print phone books) would have the ability to use the library computing facilities for word processing, storage, communication, and other basic information services. (Of course including reading, seeing, and listening to transmissions of the library's books and materials.)

Your library may well have a copying machine. With all of those materials around, it's not surprising that people would like to *do* something with them, as well as peruse them momentarily. Photographic copying is a fairly limited capability, but the use of copiers in libraries illustrates that it makes sense for them to be there. As more and more information is expressed in transportable and negotiable form for computers, the range of special-purpose devices to *do* something with the information will go far beyond their ancient ancestor, the copier.

The community information center might develop, in fact, as primarily a studio/laboratory facility for sophisticated processing of cardholders data. We are all familiar with photo-processing laboratories to support our cameras' output. Experienced photographers may develop and print their own pictures with fairly inexpensive equipment, and then invest in expensive printing of only their best efforts. Recording artists and filmmakers also make use of such "production facilities" to capture their creations and produce them in polished form. As the mentality of *doing things* with information becomes more and more prevalent, a wide variety of action devices and fabrication systems will be in demand, but many of these will be too expensive (as golf courses and concert halls are now) for individual ownership. It makes eminent sense for communities to develop their information and education resources, including libraries and schools at all levels from infant to adult, around the concept of shared facilities accessible by network. A "trip to the library" might then be most commonly used to pick up the finished product, generated by the library facilities from your programs, perhaps at the end of a "hands on" course of instruction from the local school. Depending on your interests, you might be picking up full color animated films, tapes of electronic music generated by sophisticated synthesizers, airbrush paintings, pre-cut fabric for tailored clothing, or furniture pieces.

Enlivening the Human Interface

The Computer Speaks Up

A relatively new computer technology for interfacing people to information, which has only begun to be widely available in 1981, is computer speech. Computer speech has a tremendous number of potential uses, from the sublime to the ridiculous. The ridiculous uses are more likely to hit the market first. The uninitiated may be tempted, as they see an onslaught of talking word games, automobile dashboards and washing machines, to think of computer speech as another flashy gimmick.

It only takes a moment's reflection though, to realize the significance of devices (already available but costing several hundred dollars) which connect directly to many personal computers, and contain both the physical hardware and the necessary programs to enable the computer to automatically transform any text (typed in or retrieved from memory) into **spoken output**. Especially as the cost of this capability drops (the huge market is as yet untapped), speech development will be far from gimmickry:

> In functional terms, it will very soon be unnecessary for anyone—school children, foreign visitors or the visually handicapped—to be able to read.

With computer speech ability, it suddenly becomes true that all **machine-readable information**, that is, information which can be stored and transmitted by computers, is immediately available in spoken form. Reading instruction in primary schools will be re-examined, once it is no longer an inescapable prerequisite for the great majority of all other instruction. Those who are not visually or otherwise disadvantaged in reading can hardly understand the impact of this liberation. The goals of the disadvantaged are now those of the society at large—to get as much of the information around us as possible into logical, transportable, and negotiable form. With a little thought and creativity, you will find many of your own uses of computer speech, from games and educational programs to simple bookkeeping and secretarial tasks.

An essential quality of the computer speech breakthrough is that the computer becomes capable of **parallel channel output to humans**. To the blind, this means that their usable channel, hearing, can be effective *in place of* sight. For humans who both see and hear, this means that they can receive auditory and visual information *simultaneously*, increasing the speed, comprehension, and enjoyment of activities ranging from armchair travel to foreign language learning to proofreading. (Why not let the computer read the original to you, as you scan the written version?) Parallel channel input and output to humans of many other conceivable kinds would be enormously useful, practical, and efficient. The territory is only beginning to be explored. Based on pilot projects though, it is easy to envision a human communicating with a computer by speaking, pointing, typing with one hand, and using other body movements, all simultaneously. The computer, in turn, might respond by parallel output of displayed symbols and text, high fidelity speech, music, and other sounds, and physical movements of its own.

High Quality Graphics

Photographic reproduction, as it now stands, is a fairly baroque procedure. When you take a snapshot of the proverbial bowl of fruit, let's say, the light reflected from the bowl of fruit bounces back all in a mishmash to your camera. The camera has a lens which transmits rays of light in different directions, depending on the direction they came from. If this lens, which is made by a mechanical (hence never completely accurate) process, does its job...

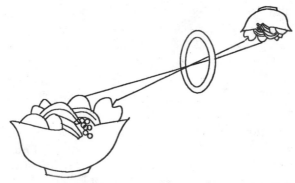

...the light from one point in the bowl of fruit (the stem of the apple, for example) hits the film behind the lens in one place, and the light from a different point (the navel of the orange) hits the film in a different place.

When your camera is "out of focus," any one place on the film is being hit by light from *more* than one place in the bowl of fruit, so that a clear image (point for point) of the bowl of fruit is not made. Good lenses produce better pictures because, when you have focused a good lens as well as possible, it sorts the light out more accurately than a poor lens would. (Other complications arise, for example, because the stem of the apple is a combination of colors, and a lens made out of a single kind of glass would tend to send each one of these colors, all coming from the same point on the stem, to different points on the film.) Complications aside, the way to make a better lens is to make its physical dimensions closer to some ideal shape (typically by grinding) and to make its composition as uniform as possible. If great accuracy is demanded, both of these processes are expensive.

Once you obtain an image on film, you may want to use this image to make other images. If you have taken a "color slide," you may need to do nothing more than look at it or project it on a screen. If the image on your film is a negative, you probably want to make positive images of different sizes. The end result in any case is to arrange things so that the bowl of fruit can be taken away (even taking snapshots in the refrigerator, it won't last forever) and an image of some type substituted such that with proper illumination, it can transmit roughly the same pattern of light to your eye that the original bowl of fruit did.

Cameras without Lenses

For simplicity, I will describe here a lensless black and white camera. The ideas can be used perfectly well for a color camera, except that the process will have to be done separately for three "primary" colors, rather than a single kind of light, and the resulting images will be superimposed. The process I will describe is analogous to "flash" photography, or other situations in which the photographer provides the light source for the subject. "Natural light" processes are entirely possible, but more complicated.

Let's look at the usual flash photography for a minute. When the flash goes off, the entire subject is illuminated, and light from all parts of the subject bounces back, so that the camera needs a lens to sort it all out. What we need is a different kind of flash, which could be very **rapidly and precisely** directed to any single spot on the subject. Such a flash can be made from a laser. We will use this laser to sweep over the entire subject, point by point. The light that bounces back at any time is now coming only from a single point on the subject. With such a "flash", the camera can be replaced with a light meter and a laser "pen." As the flash laser sweeps over the subject (left to right, top to bottom say), the pen laser is exactly synchronized with it, and traces a path, left to right, top to bottom, across the film.

If the flash (and the pen) stay for a microsecond, say, at each point, the amount of light coming from that point on the subject can be measured by the light meter. If the light meter shows maximum illumination (highlights on the subject), the pen laser would be turned on for the entire microsecond it is at that point on the film. If there is less light coming from that point, as measured by the light meter, the pen laser will only be turned on for a smaller fraction of the microsecond it is at that point. At each point, more light coming from the subject will result in more light being sent to the corresponding point on the film, and less light from the subject will result in less light going to the film.

When the flash and the pen have finished their sweep, there will be an image on the film exactly recording the amount of light, point for point, coming from the subject. The "camera" has no lens. To make sharper pictures, it is necessary to reduce the size of the "point" on which the flash focuses in any time period, and the corresponding "point" which the pen writes on the film. Both of these reductions can be demanding, especially if speed is essential. An inherent limitation exists in that if the light meter used for the camera has a fixed sensitivity, then reducing the size of the point where the flash hits the subject and/or requiring the entire sweep of the subject to be faster will require higher energy illumination from the flash laser. Suitably powerful lasers are certainly feasible, but such "flashes" would vaporize all but the most hardy subjects.

The overwhelming advantage of the lensless camera is that it is easily converted to a digital device. One merely uses a digital device for the light meter in the camera. The pattern of light captured from the subject is then exactly embodied in the successive readings of this light meter at each of the successive points where the flash reads. One may dispense with photographic "film" entirely if a better, digital storage device, is available for storing this pattern of successive readings. Lensless digital pocket cameras, which store their pictures electronically for subsequent processing by your personal computer are certainly possible, if not practical in the near future. The overwhelming advantages of digital technology for reproducibility, ease of communication, and flexibility in subsequent processing though, are already making lensless cameras of various types valuable and useful. The original image of the page you are now reading was "composed" by a laser pen writing on a photosensitive drum. The information to drive this pen did not come from a lensless photograph, but perhaps more interestingly, from a harmonious interplay of Donald Knuth's font creation and graphics programs, Max Diaz's collection of book patterns, and the author's text and judicious substitutions, all working harmoniously together. The result of such "conceptual art" is what you see before you as the photographic image of a typeset page which *never existed* in reality. In the near future, this **conceptual graphics** technology will be used by artists and filmmakers to produce totally realistic images of their equally imaginary creations.

The Three-Dimensional Image Emerges

The realism of images presented by ordinary television, and hence by computers which use television output devices, promises to take a quantum leap forward in the next few years. A spinoff of the materials research for magnetic bubble memory, for example, may lead to the development of a "supertube" for television sets, which could replace the standard picture tube. Coatings being tested for this tube can be illluminated under high voltage to the brightness of the noonday sun. These supertubes would be only a fraction of the size of the conventional television picture tube, and rapidly make projection television as cheap and as common as color television of the early eighties. Projection television, however, does not really introduce a quantitative change in realism. That change comes about when the images, life size and in full color, are made to be **three-dimensional**, and appear to move around in the entire space of a room. The three-dimensional effect can be achieved by the **stereographic** method of projecting two images simultaneously, one for each eye (a pair of untinted polarized "sunglasses" worn by the viewer will direct the correct image to each eye.) The changeover in broadcast and recording technology to adapt to stereographic three-dimensional image transmission would be inherently no more complicated than that required to implement stereophonic sound.

There are other three-dimensional image production techniques which produce much greater realism than stereo projection, as well as not requiring the viewer to wear glasses or other special equipment. Images which are truly three-dimensional, so that the viewer can obtain different views from different angles, move around the image and so on, have been produced experimentally by a variety of techniques. Perhaps the most widely known method is by **holograms**, which are attractive in many ways, but present serious technical challenges in transmission and full color reproduction. Other methods are based on the multiplexing concept described above: Three dimensional images can be divided into thin two-dimensional slices from front to back. The individual slices are transmitted one after another.

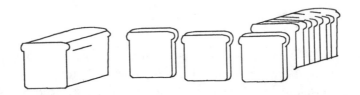

As the images are received for projection, a vibrating mirror or some other arrangement stacks the projected appearance of the slices into the proper front-to-back position.

Even beyond the *illusion* of a three-dimensional object, it is possible for transmitted information to cause the *construction* of an object in real, physical space. Conceptually, there is simply a three-dimensional, sculptural analog of the two dimensional mosaic:

- A two dimensional mosaic is made by choosing tiles, from a limited collection of possibilities, to fill in a grid. The smaller the tiles, and the greater their variety, the more complex the picture can be made.

- A three-dimensional mosaic sculpture can be made by choosing pins to insert at each location of a central, spherical core. The pins would differ in length, and possibly in other characteristics as well. The thinner the pins and the greater their variety, the more complex the sculpture can be made.

You may want to try out this idea by using a styrofoam sphere, and sticking straight pins into it to different depths, but practically speaking, the process is much better carried out by a laser and mirror directional system, burning holes to precise depth at each location of a larger sphere. Although special materials and laser systems need considerable further development, three-dimensional "photographs" of this type have already been commercially produced, and there is no reason to doubt that three-dimensional mosaics will one day be as common and subtle as the two dimensional mosaics which form the pages of this book.

Economic and Political Clout

In speaking of transportable and negotiable information, the ordinary use of the term "negotiable" should not be ignored. Free flowing information can have tangible and eminently practical influence in areas such as economics and politics.

One of the earliest features incorporated into any commercial computer network is always the capability to peruse and order from the catalogs of major retail stores. Electronic shopping by means of cable television and two-way video terminals is already possible through pilot projects in Los Angeles, San Diego, Omaha, St. Louis, New Orleans, and other cities. One cable broadcaster expects to have 300,000 cable subscribers in the United States by the end of 1983, and expects that 60,000 or more of these will subscribe to the electronic shopping service as well. Not only shopping can be handled by these subscribers electronically, but also bill paying and bank transactions as well as network information retrieval.

If the rush to electronic shopping services leads you to hastily conclude that computer networks are the electronic version of junk mail, you may only be perceiving the advertiser's intended use. (In fact, a significant "feature" of the shopping service will be the ability it gives customers to instantly/impulsively order products when they are advertised on television.) The customers' inherent capability though, once they are able to communicate widely and effectively, must not be overlooked. Specifically, if 100,000 customers are looking at the same catalog from the same store at the roughly the same time, there may be a thousand of them who want to purchase a single particular item. If these thousand people have an effective means of communicating with each other, they may wish to inquire as a group to see whether the manufacturer of this item is willing to give them a discount, or perhaps whether or not his competitor would.

Other opportunities for cooperative consumer communication abound: Any item in a catalog may have a corresponding, automatically updated commentary file from network users who have purchased and used the item. Manufacturers would be wise to watch these commentaries as closely as consumers, and modify their offerings or their prices accordingly. I have personally seen the effects of consumer-and-computer power in local community bulletin boards and nationwide computer science networks. Nothing gets around quicker than news of a bargain, or combinations thereof. Kits, combinations, customizations, and modifications may also give the wise customer a better value, from components and a little time, than the all-in-one consumer who buys everything whole hog. The components in question may be for anything from hi-fi to dressmaking to diesel engines. The necessary wisdom to assemble the whole may be developed by a few and shared with many. With versatile displays and action devices, the **instructions** for a kit, in the form of computer programs and text, may make the **construction** both semi-automatic and virtually foolproof.

With computer-assisted communication technology, consumer groups, coop organizers, and other dropouts from the plastic world of the conglomerates can take real initiative, as well as react to current markets. Individually, you probably will not convince your local baker to change his bread. A few hundred like minds and definite orders will produce some action. It is already possible for individual computer owners in major cities to dial "electronic bulletin board" telephone numbers to send and receive messages of general and special interest. As the amount of use of such services increases by orders of magnitude, the need to actively select and process the available information, and the benefits from being able to do so, will multiply correspondingly. The idea of "generic products" has caught on beyond all expectations, as a way to eliminate the cost of worthless advertising. The most severe drawback to such products is the "pig in a poke" uncertainty of the product's quality from one purchase to the next. The antidote for uncertainty is information, and with networks to provide it in good supply, generic products could provide continuously coded and monitored quality products, offered at face value without extravagant packaging, advertising claims, or prices.

Electronic competition in the form of auctions, sealed bids, and other organized efforts, coupled with rapid feedback to the public of the performance of suppliers and their products, could easily lead to a far more efficient marketplace than the current system based on catchy jingles, endorsements by expensive celebrities, and multiple discounts of impossible claims. It's a sure bet that the uninitiates will not find this the path of least resistance.

The Electronic Forum

The members of Congress are currently supplied with computer terminals if they wish them, as well as access to the Dialcom service, which provides newspaper services, computer programming capability, and access to all other members of the network. As their constituents become more informed and computer literate, the importance of network connections for legislators will grow. The old fashioned communication process, where you may write a letter to your representative, which she may respond to in a private and partially or completely "canned" fashion, and where the supply of information to you consists of such things as a newsletter briefly covering a scattering of topics and self-congratulatory notes, could be made substantially more informative, interactive, and public by the use of networks. You would not only know what your representative has said to others, where the votes have been cast, and what future plans are, but you would also become aware of the issues which other voters, lobbyists, and so on, are pressing or concerned about. Such an "open mailbag" environment for public officials would be informative and useful to most of us.

Network communication will enable officeholders and candidates to directly poll their constituents and develop a greater degree of responsiveness. Even "canned" correspondence, if directed by the legislator's computer program to find relevant references and highlight new areas, rather than being carried out by filling in blanks on a form, can more directly answer the points of an inquiry and be registered in greater detail for future reference and analysis. "Town meetings" conducted electronically for the voters back home, perhaps through the public library facilities, will enable the representative and the represented to interact on a personal basis more frequently than the time and expense of travel would allow.

Networking will allow voters to have access to nonpartisan databases to retrieve detailed dossiers and analyses of candidates' histories, including writings, speeches, and voting records and campaign contributors. No longer will having a "book" on public officials be a privileged and expensive undertaking, available only to candidates for high office themselves.

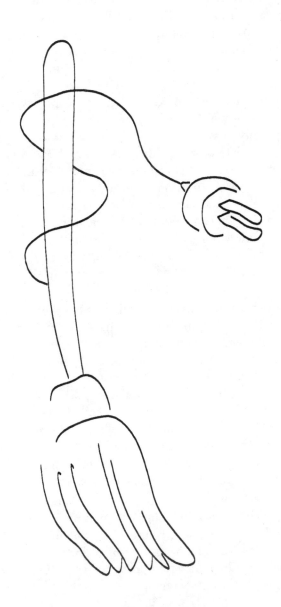

11

Chores and Drudgery:
Computer As Slave

Having Your Cake And Deserting the Kitchen

Many of the prospects for computer usage in the future involve relieving people of the need to do things which they do today only under grave monetary motivation. From such everyday tasks as shopping wisely and balancing checkbooks to major ordeals such as buying a home, making investments, and developing strategies to give IRS exactly as little of our cash as is legal, we engage in many time consuming and painfully boring mental activities under the relentless goad of making or keeping a buck. Given a choice, most of us would gladly prefer to make or keep the buck, while devoting the mental activity to something more appealing.

A personal computer can be a great help in getting the monetary monkey off our backs, as every manufacturer of home computers has been quick to note and advertise. (No personal computer owner should be caught dead sweating through checkbook balancing.) The fortunate few among us who don't give a damn about money and/or don't have to worry about it, as well as the less fortunate who don't have enough financial freedom to plan anything much more than paying their bills, might take all of this advertising to mean that computers belong squarely in the domain of the bourgeoisie. The mistake is serious, but the confusion is understandable. After all, if you do not know about computers, then you must presume that they are best suited to the tasks for which people most commonly use them (possibly known only second-hand from writers and advertisers). If you have read any significant portion of this book, and still believe that the best use of a personal computer would be to balance your checkbook, I think you deserve a refund (and you will probably be interested in one).

More likely, I hope you share to a substantial degree my conviction that the ability to shuck some of our financial chores off onto the computer is a nice fringe benefit of the technology, but able to use up about one percent at most (with good programs and documentation) of a reasonable computer's total time, and motivates the use of computers about as much as the desire to read subway signs motivates ordinary literacy. Nonetheless, you will do well to look at the services and options typically offered by computer purveyors, some of which are described in more detail in this chapter. Reading Shakespeare while the train goes past your stop is usually inadvisable.

The world of chores certainly does not end with personal finances. Other kinds of mental tedium are endured, to solve logistical problems in matching the supply of food, libations, babysitters, transportation, and so on, to their corresponding demand. The problems of getting what you need where you want it when you can still use it, without a great deal of waste and confusion, can pose such mind bending puzzles that most of us are accustomed to accepting the waste and confusion. Trial and error will often provide a solution if enough different arrangements, schedules, and combinations are tested. Generating and testing combinations may be interesting for humans, for the first dozen or so, but when there are thousands of possible arrangements, it's a good time for you to make some rules and let a computer sift the possibilities by applying them systematically.

Many chores which we do are foisted on us by our pursuit of gainful employment. *Repetitious* and *boring* are two key words which ought to mean people out and computers in. As you get more experience with perceiving patterns, many tasks in your line of work which at first sight seem to be not repetitious but merely boring will turn out to be boring precisely because they are basically **repetitions** with identifiable **variable elements** of certain patterns. Computers can repeat the pattern, while the human supplies the variation. Often, your employer or customers will be glad to supply you with the necessary computing facilities. Even if they will not, you may find it is worth the time, money, and mental relief to make an investment and strike out on your own.

If your job has kept you at a desk or behind a counter for a sufficiently long time, you may have lost the immediate association of the word "work" with actual physical labor. It would be well worth thinking about physical chores, and strategies for getting some brains into the brawn that underlies even the most sophisticated home or society. The robot is already in the paper mill, and there is every indication that he will soon be in the moderate-sized manufacturing plant. On the scale of personal computer usage, there are a number of applications which are not theoretically very exciting, but eminently marketable and handy to know about. You may want to have your lawn watered, dinner cooked, or electricity use reduced. There is little that human maids and butlers do that a work oriented computer could not. (The practical issues in making simple and effective robots will be discussed in more detail below.) The do-it-yourselfer can have an untiring, cheerful drone-apprentice-master-planner for the bothersome tasks which come up in everything from sewing to woodworking (how to use material efficiently, make modifications scale changes, and so on).

Wanted: A Live-In
Secretary/Accountant/Consultant

Imagine placing an ad in your local newspaper for a financial and secretarial assistant, able to manage all of your clerical, secretarial, and accounting chores, as well as provide sophisticated advice in such areas as investment and money management. (More to the point, imagine what kind of salary you would need to offer, in order to hire anyone competent.) Against that kind of a background, the prices of many of the currently available personal computers begin to look pretty negligible. Perhaps you are ambitious, or have a small business, or have the hobbyist's fascination with machines. For these or a hundred other reasons (all equally agreeable to manufacturers), you may go out and spend several thousand dollars on a full blown system, the "live-in" assistant, and feel that the money has been well spent. Then again, you may well be a little more hard-headed. You could remind me that the title of the chapter is "Computer As Slave," and suggest that if expenditures in the thousands of dollars are involved, a better title would have been "Computer As Racehorse" or "Computer as Yacht," or as some other proverbial sink to throw money into. All right, let's look at the nitty-gritty a little bit, and ask point blank: If we put aside all the intellectual fascination with computers, and even their undeniable *eventual* practical and physical importance for humans, and narrow it all down to the hard facts of income and outlay, what is the conclusion—will today's personal computers pay for themselves, or not? The answer, I believe, is surprising in the light of the relatively primitive state of personal computing in the early 1980s: If you shop carefully, buy exactly what you need, and share the facilities you do not need, even your first computer, bought right now at the dawn of the era, will be dirt cheap, if not free.

I believe this answer is surprising because so many of the ways in which computers *could* save people money are currently blocked. The ability of personal computers to pay for themselves will improve tremendously as time goes on. You will not go bargain-hunting for groceries with a computer, for example, as long as you have to enter all of the items and prices by hand. In many other areas like this, computer technology gives us sophisticated "power tools," but the necessary "information grid" to plug into is only slowly being installed. It takes some time for the elements of a society such as utilities, businesses, and government to gear up to a newly available resource. Anomalies abound in the transition. An electric company reminds us frequently about its increased cost of fuels and yet refuses to buy back power from customers able to generate it, until forced to do so. The phone company is attempting to thwart dial-in information, but an automated "directory assistance" databank would eliminate the need to print and ship millions of pounds of phone books. As a personal computer user, you could easily keep your own automated file of phone numbers, using the dial-in service only rarely. Perhaps if you offered to forego any future phone book deliveries, the phone company would send you an appreciative note. It would be more appropriate for them to make an adjustment in your bill.

We will suppose that you have decided not to advertise for the "superperson Friday" described above, but instead plan to invest in a personal computer. In doing so, you can be motivated not just by the practical and often money-saving things you will do with it in the immediate present, but by the desire to build up your communication and planning skills, and what these skills will enable you to do in the future.

Secretarial Services

Most of us keep track of appointments, coming events, chores, and messages with a variety of paper-and-ink devices like calendars, appointment books, and bulletin boards. One of the major functions of real-life secretaries is to handle these reminders and scheduling intelligently, with or without paper-and-pencil assistance. Even with the simplest of computers, you can set up an electronic and intelligent "bulletin board secretary" for yourself. As messages, appointments, and chores come in, you can enter the information into your computer, along with a note as to when (and how insistently) you want to be reminded about each item. Your "dumb" paper calendar can then be replaced by the computer's video display. Notices which are simply for interest or amusement can be displayed unobtrusively on the screen—perhaps a few choice clippings from the morning's electronic newspaper. Messages which require you to respond can be highlighted, for instance in a bright flashing marquee. Truly urgent or insistent messages can be displayed in "alarm clock" fashion, with sound and picture nagging you until you take some action. For example, if you have bills to pay which will incur a penalty after a certain date, it would help to have the bulletin board audibly nag you on the day you must pay them, either by simple beeping or by spoken messages, until you indicate (truthfully or otherwise) that you have done it.

It is a simple business fact that accounts receivable are collected as early as possible, and accounts payable are paid as late as possible. Businesses may be making a substantial amount of interest on your money, if you always pay their bills when they first notify you, rather than on the last day before late charges. It is not uncommon to be billed by a company many months before the account is due. Before the days of computers, it made some sense to pay up immediately, rather than risk forgetting the bill and incurring penalties. With your electronic secretary, you can easily insure that you are reminded to pay all bills, and the timing of the reminder and the payment will be under *your* control. Given the present high interest rates, and the amount of money paid by most people in installments of some sort, this single application for bill reminding and management could offset a good part of the price of a beginner's computer.

An added advantage of a computerized message service is that you can *process* the information in the calendar once you have it. That means, for example, that if you have five errands you have been saving up to run, you will not only get an occasional reminder that they have to be done, but if you wish, you can have the computer figure out *in what order* they should be done, to minimize time, travel, or some other criterion you have set up. If you have five errands and chores to do, there are 120 possible orders to do them in. In case you've never counted up for yourself, here is a list for the chores a=auto, c=clean, d=doctor, l=laundry, s=shop:

a-d-c-l-s	a-d-c-s-l	a-d-l-c-s	a-d-l-s-c	a-d-s-c-l	a-d-s-l-c
a-d-l-c-s	a-d-s-l-c	a-l-c-d-s	a-l-c-s-d	a-s-d-l-c	a-s-l-c-d
a-s-d-l-c	a-s-d-c-l	a-s-l-d-c	a-s-l-c-d	a-s-c-d-l	a-s-c-l-d
a-c-d-l-s	a-c-d-s-l	a-c-l-d-s	a-c-l-s-d	a-c-s-d-l	a-c-s-l-d
l-a-c-d-s	l-a-c-s-d	l-a-d-c-s	l-a-d-s-c	l-a-s-c-d	l-a-s-d-c
l-a-d-c-s	l-a-s-d-c	l-d-c-a-s	l-d-c-s-a	l-s-a-d-c	l-s-d-c-a
l-s-a-d-c	l-s-a-c-d	l-s-d-a-c	l-s-d-c-a	l-s-c-a-d	l-s-c-d-a
l-c-a-d-s	l-c-a-s-d	l-c-d-a-s	l-c-d-s-a	l-c-s-a-d	l-c-s-d-a
s-a-c-l-d	s-a-c-d-l	s-a-l-c-d	s-a-l-d-c	s-a-d-c-l	s-a-d-l-c
s-a-l-c-d	s-a-d-l-c	s-l-c-a-d	s-l-c-d-a	s-d-a-l-c	s-d-l-c-a
s-d-a-l-c	s-d-a-c-l	s-d-l-a-c	s-d-l-c-a	s-d-c-a-l	s-d-c-l-a
s-c-a-l-d	s-c-a-d-l	s-c-l-a-d	s-c-l-d-a	s-c-d-a-l	s-c-d-l-a
c-a-d-l-s	c-a-d-s-l	c-a-l-d-s	c-a-l-s-d	c-a-s-d-l	c-a-s-l-d
c-a-l-d-s	c-a-s-l-d	c-l-d-a-s	c-l-d-s-a	c-s-a-l-d	c-s-l-d-a
c-s-a-l-d	c-s-a-d-l	c-s-l-a-d	c-s-l-d-a	c-s-d-a-l	c-s-d-l-a
c-d-a-l-s	c-d-a-s-l	c-d-l-a-s	c-d-l-s-a	c-d-s-a-l	c-d-s-l-a
d-a-c-l-s	d-a-c-s-l	d-a-l-c-s	d-a-l-s-c	d-a-s-c-l	d-a-s-l-c
d-a-l-c-s	d-a-s-l-c	d-l-c-a-s	d-l-c-s-a	d-s-a-l-c	d-s-l-c-a
d-s-a-l-c	d-s-a-c-l	d-s-l-a-c	d-s-l-c-a	d-s-c-a-l	d-s-c-l-a
d-c-a-l-s	d-c-a-s-l	d-c-l-a-s	d-c-l-s-a	d-c-s-a-l	d-c-s-l-a

With only five tasks, you may have intuitively guessed the best order, or nearly the best order to do them in. If you have seven errands to do in a week or so, there are 5,040 possible ways to schedule them, and it's likely that you have missed some interesting, timesaving, or convenient possibilities by not examining them all. Provided you can specify what factors are important to you (perhaps simply the total distance you have to travel), a computer will slog through the 5,000 possibilities without complaint, and display for you the best (according to *your* definition) possibilities. If you are trying to make an appointment, your computer can find the best match, by your definition, between your preferences and existing commitments, and the available time slots of the doctor, dentist, or hairdresser.

A good deal of a traditional secretary's work involves document preparation, which goes nowadays under the more trendy name of **word processing**. Far from eliminating the writing of ordinary prose and poetry, the growth of computer languages bids well to make this writing easier to produce, evaluate, polish, and present. Beyond that, the growing power of language will make it ever more important, in contexts from writing programs to planning cities or transit systems, to mean what we say and say what we mean. Instant communication may be fine for off-the-cuff conversations with family and associates, but it would be a sad mistake to take the availability and high gloss status of electronic communications as any indication that carefully structured, extensively mulled over language is at all on the wane. An old proverb may have to be rudely relearned, as electronic instantaneity and friendly computer interfaces make it ever more possible to get *effects* simply by speaking loosely and spontaneously:

> *A gram of planning*
> *is worth*
> *a kilo of cure.*

Document preparation is such a prevalent and important activity and so well suited to automation, that you can expect to have an editor/word-processing program supplied with virtually any computer system you buy. In fact, editors have progressed well enough at this early stage that you can afford to be discriminating, rather than take whichever happens to be offered first. If you can not obtain the editing features you want for a particular computer system without paying extra, then that extra cost should be figured in when you compare it to competing systems which have the features. Editor programs vary considerably in both the **power** of the available commands and the **ease of use** of these commands, as well as their ability to **display** the document you are working on rapidly and effectively. The most hardened critics of paper-and-ink technology cannot deny the fact that a bound book or a desk top full of sheets of paper gives you both rapid access and a wide field of view for your document that no inexpensive personal computer of the early eighties can match. (The reasons for using computer editors, such as the ability to **modify** the contents and format of a manuscript without redoing the unchanged parts, as well as to automatically find, change, and manipulate words or larger patterns in the text, are now working *against* a display capability which is typically limited. That drawback will be effectively removed for inexpensive personal computers within the next few years.)

The best way to compare editors, like computer systems in general, is by hands-on experience. By making a few visits to stores, friends, and local computer clubs, you should be able to have a variety of editors demonstrated, and try doing some things on them yourself. How much of the document can you see at one time on the screen? How easy is it to move portions of the text from one place to another in the document? How easy is it to make **substitutions** extensively and automatically in the text? (A lot of the documents you deal with, as your computer literacy increases, are going to be in fact **programs**. Substitution capability for these is essential.) Does the editor give you good **feedback** at all times on the screen, so that you can easily see "where you are" in the document, and what commands you have recently done? Is there an **oops!** facility, allowing you to instantly undo any command which you enter by mistake, or regret at leisure?

Some operations on a text, for example, to find all of the paragraphs containing the word "videodisc" and copy them into another file, may involve repeating a sequence of commands over and over again, working all the way through the document from the beginning to the end. Does the editor let you give this whole sequence of commands a single name, like "getvideoreferences," "getv", or even "g," to be dredged up automatically and applied automatically as often as necessary, whenever you simply give a single command with that name? This capability of automatically remembering and executing a *group* of operations under a single command defined by you is important both practically and conceptually. The **metacommand** you define in this fashion is commonly called a **macro** by computer types, who often speak more obscurely than necessary. The term "repertoire" command would be more apt, since what the computer does is use your command "getvideodiscreferences" not directly, but as the name of a whole set of actions in the repertoire of things it already knows how to do. (For anyone who has seen the Laurel and Hardy movie, the image of the word "Niagara," which triggered a whole sequence of comic behavior, is right on target.)

Editors which you should try to see and use for comparison are **Wordstar**, which is widely available for small computers, and **MINCE**, which is not as extensively marketed but well worth finding in order to try it out firsthand. Here, as in general, the computer magazines such as those listed in Chapter Twelve are your best source of up to date information on availability and prices, as well as descriptions and reviews. Widely used programs like editors are available by mail, in the form of discs or magnetic tape to load automatically into your system. For any particular editor program, different tailor-made versions are sold for a wide variety of store-bought computer systems. Just as a wise automobile buyer may buy a "stripped down" car from the dealer, and add accessories from undercoating to high fidelity audio herself, from other companies which are better and/or cheaper, the smart computer buyer may do well to buy the most popular and cheapest computer, similarly stripped down to a minimum of features (and price). The chocolate sprinkles, chopped nuts, and maraschino cherry for this stripped down "vanilla" system may then be obtained from other and better sources. (You may think of the editor as the chocolate sprinkles, if you like. We will discuss the other possible add-ons shortly.)

The Supermarket Alert

The personal computer secretary and electronic messsage system can also serve as an unprecedented means of cooperative advertising. If advertisers' notices of sales, price changes, new products, and so on, are relayed to you electronically (easily done over the phone—all of the necessary equipment is already available in stores or by mail), you can select and have displayed only the items which interest you. A "supermarket alert" can be efficiently organized for several hundred subscribers, with a single automatic dialing device and a central, small scale computer. By sharing the facility in this fashion, the cost to individual shoppers would be comparable to that of a newspaper or magazine subscription. The supermarket alert could operate as follows:

- Participating stores (and it would profit a store to participate, even if the necessary equipment costs were subtracted from conventional advertising) would phone in daily to the central computer, giving only the prices which have *changed*. This relatively small amount of information, by computer standards, could be transmitted by the store's computer in a matter of minutes to the central computer.

- By taking data from many stores, the central computer would have a complete databank, updated daily. It would then go over the list of its subscribers, and prepare a short report for each of them. The report could be based on a **summary** measure of the cost of food in each store, determined on a customer by customer basis. The summaries would be *different* for different customers, due to differences in the "market basket" of foods and brands from one person to the next.

- The central computer would then give a daily **information delivery** (just like the old milk wagon) to each subscriber, either by calling on the phone at a prearranged time, or allowing customers to dial in if they prefer. For subscribers without computers, the central computer would just give a spoken summary of the "customized totals" for each market, so that the customer could decide whether price differences warranted making a trip or changing stores. Other items of interest, tailored to each individual customer, might be price reductions on favorite items or by selected manufacturers, as well as quality ratings for the "no label" generic products currently in stock at various stores.

- Customers with computers of their own would get much better service, since data could be transferred rapidly and automatically between them and the central computer. After accepting the standard customized report, additional information of possible interest could be transferred to be reviewed at the customer's discretion. The customer's computer could then **transmit** to the central computer, giving perhaps a shopping list for the day or asking for recipes of a certain kind. The central computer would match the customer's request with the stores' price data, and return suggested markets, recipes, and so on.

Financial Services

All of the popular computer systems offered for home use have some sort of financial programs included or available. As with computer editors, it is well worth your while to try before you buy. In particular, it would be worth experimenting with the **dynamic worksheet** approach, as exemplified by programs such as **VisiCalc**. Such financial programs are in effect **hypereditors**, which you can use to edit a balance sheet, but which in addition **automatically recalculate** any other entries on the sheet which change, due to a change you make in one particular place. Thus, if you change the projected widget sales forecast with the editor, the entries in the dynamic worksheet for gross and net revenues will automatically change as well. Because of their ease of use and adaptability to different kinds of layouts, dynamic worksheet financial programs have been tremendously successful. If you have a small business or are just a fiscally minded person, your entire computer system could "pay its way" on the basis of the power of these programs.

The range of uses for dynamic worksheet and other financial programs includes not only management of checkbooks and bill handling (accounts payable and receivable, if you are in business for yourself), but new areas of money management. If you have several investment possibilities open to you, you can "try out" alternative scenarios of future economic behavior, such as interest rates, inflation, salary scale, and so on, to see how each of your options would perform in the different "crystal balls." You may decide to put all of your eggs in one basket, or hedge your bets, or leave your money in the mattress. At income tax time (or before), you may wish to try out many different legal ways of allocating costs, depreciation, deductions, and so on, for the minimum tax. Once your data is entered, it can be rearranged in many different ways. (Few of us can bear computing out our taxes more than once with paper and pencil, or even paper, pencil, and pocket calculator.)

The economic value of information will become increasingly apparent as time goes on. The difference between wholesale and retail prices is a prime target for conversion of bits into bucks. With a home computer, buyers' cooperatives can be formed and efficiently managed for everything from food to films. As you may know, good food can be bought directly from producers, at substantial savings over retail prices, if you are willing to forego advertising and individual packaging, and can use large quantities of each item. Since advertising and packaging are not only expensive but increasingly indigestible, buyers' food cooperatives have sprung up in many places, from college campuses to apartment complexes. Members are invariably ecstatic about the prices and quality, but the organizations often founder due to logistical problems. Who will go when to pick up what, and when will it be parceled out and when will I know if my order is in, and so on, are questions best fielded by your personal computer running the "food coop" program.

In fact, good food coop programs, or buyers' coop programs of many sorts, would be no more difficult to develop than other financial programs, and would be highly marketable. What that means to you is that if you are reluctant to initiate a food coop yourself, and/or develop the necessary programs to keep it going smoothly, you can expect in the near future to be contacted by a neighbor who knows of a complete coop program (**VisiMunch?**) which will work on your computers. From then on, you may be joining together to buy cheese, fish, or salami in lumberjack quantities, and hardly noticing it at all, except for meeting the neighbors more often.

In financial matters, as elsewhere, communication is essential. Once your personal computer is linked up directly, through the telephone, cable television, or other means, to the outside world, you will find it less and less necessary to reinvent the wheel for each programming vehicle you require. Services from small business accounting to printing, graphics, and artwork, tax preparation, and investment counseling can all be provided via home computers. In many cases, the personal computer will not be exercising any real "brain power" to develop programs, but serving as an automatic and flexible **access port** to communicate with established programs elsewhere.

Computers at Work—Your Place or Mine?

For many people, the first contact made with computers is through their workplace. Often, management will be introducing computers to do something which from the employees' point of view was going well enough already. Misconceptions and negative reactions abound in this scenario, but it is worth pointing out that:

- The goals of the owners, managers, or whoever else is introducing computers into the workplace may not be the same as those of the employees and customers directly affected.

- Advertising overkill leads to all sorts of claims for what computers can accomplish (immediately) in any given work situation.

- Computers are highly visible and uncomplaining scapegoats upon which to lay blame when things go wrong. It is more than convenient to forget that the computers are carrying out some *person's* plans, in the form of programs.

Imagine for a moment a company where no one knows how to read or write. (Certainly, commerce preceded writing historically, and probably produced it.) It would undoubtedly be a big deal if "reading and writing technology" were suddenly introduced on the scene. People would question the disruption of the *status quo*. The increased accountability of having one's actions on record would be resented, management's motives would be suspect as the paper mounted and longtime staff members departed. Promoters would claim mystical powers for writing, and employees would point to badly scrawled and misinterpreted notes as representative results. Novice writers would blame their faulty penmanship on poor quills and ink, and so on. No one in this furor would be able to get much of a view of the long range impact of literacy, or dream that the new "illuminated written rules of employee conduct" were no better or worse, now written, than they had been when spoken. Only the farsighted would recognize practically that writing could express employee demands as well as employer's requirements, or think creatively about taking the vile technology home to help communicate sonnets.

Whatever your business, you might remember this fictitious scene occasionally as successive waves of "computerization" wash over your workplace. No matter what field of endeavor you imagine, computers can be as helpful as writing and drawing, provided that you can think of the application **systematically** and **find patterns** whose variable elements are identifiable. If you are a commercial artist, and your boss buys a computing system for art that was designed with an accountant's mentality, don't blame computers or insist that they are only good for numbers. If you work in a restaurant and are told that foods (and customers!) have to be remembered by number, don't blame "binary code" or the "computerized electronic remote-activated auditing cash registers." The best way to keep from being snowed by salesmen, systems analysts, and other vested experts, is to have hands-on experience yourself with programs that you have written. When presented with other people's programs and systems, you can then reasonably ask for an explanation in your own terms. You are even permitted to laugh out loud at such explanations as "That's how computers do it," or "Because of the *computer*, employees are not allowed to take their vacations in more than two calendar months."

If we were illiterate and innumerate, we would have to suffer the expense of paying scribes and reckoners to do tasks we could certainly better do ourselves. (In the midst of such large scale inexperience, scribes and reckoners would certainly be held in mystic esteem, far beyond the capability of individuals to manage or hire permanently for their own use.) Letters and numbers, of course, are currently within our ken; our inexperience is in the tools and symbols of programs and functions. The hallowed aura is not accorded to scribes and reckoners, but to "programmers," "systems analysts," and other denizens of Computerland. Your goals in the workplace, to make your job interesting, pleasant, and profitable as possible, can hardly be expected to coincide exactly with those of every superior, subordinate, or customer who wants his order yesterday. In order to get computers on the job *working for you*, you will often have to be capable of obtaining and/or supervising them yourself.

As a manager, for example, you might very well find that your knowledge of the company and of particular employees enables you to produce, on your personal computer, excellent forecasts, schedules, and so on (in a fraction of the time required by paper and pencil methods). Other tasks which you find annoying and repetitive can be tackled. If you can do paperwork in fifteen minutes that takes your fellow managers a day, they may well emulate your example of trading up from an attaché case to a personal computer.

As your skills improve, you may produce some surprises for both yourself and the rest of the company. Wouldn't it be interesting if week after week, your personal computer managed to duplicate the entire payroll and accounting process of your small company, which is presently farmed out to "computer specialists," at expense comparable to your total salary. Whether or not you decide to compete actively with external specialists to do jobs which you know in more detail, or whether your programs simply run as a check for you and a reminder to them that they *can* be replaced, the effect will be both healthy for your business and perhaps profitable for you.

For many of us, the physical environment of our workplace is less convenient or congenial than that of our homes. You may prefer to work at odd hours, play loud music, drink whiskey rather than coffee, or indulge in any of a hundred habits which do not fit comfortably into the typical office environment. Then again, you may be perfectly able and occasionally willing to work in a traditional office building, but simply *prefer* to do your work in the social environment of your family and other lifemates, rather than the company determined by your work. **Telecommuting**, the ability to work "at the office" while physically still at home, is not a science fiction concept, but a reality even for the early eighties. Whatever your reasons, from personal habits to the desire to save transportation costs to the conscious decision to devote more attention to your family environment than to your workplace, the personal computer and telephone interface combination make it quite easy for you to telecommute. You can prepare and review documents of any sort, do financial calculations, planning and a host of other tasks, on your computer at home, while fellow workers cooperate, kibitz, review and revise as appropriate, from miles away at the office or in their own homes.

Robots and Other Assistants

Unpleasant physical tedium confronts most of us on a fairly regular basis in our homes. The rich may be able to buy off on housework, and some personalities either thrive on it (next to godliness, after all), or serenely ignore it (and count the resulting blessings in fertile chaos and/or longsuffering mates). The topic of household cleaning (in the abstract) does not ordinarily hold much interest except among detergent manufacturers and the populace of their commercials. When it comes down to "When are you going to ...?", though, some vigor may enter the debate. Rather than carping about the common cold, I, for one, lament that the nation which put a man on the moon can't even manage to have my bathroom cleaned once a week.

Lets take a quick look at the prospects for **Tidyduds ex machina:** To sum it up, I would say that the chances of a computer maid/butler/cook/dishwasher eventually bailing you out are reasonably good, but "handshaking" devices which are both affordable and reasonably inexpensive will not appear within the next five years, at least. Robotics designers, for a variety of reasons, have been testing their wings (and knuckles, etc.) in the factories, and will have to accumulate a larger body of knowledge and techniques, and a gradually expanding market before VacuRover comes home from their direction. In familiar terms, your ability to fix your lawn chair easily depends on a design which uses components such as screws and bolts, which you find so affordable only because their usefulness is more widespread than in fixing your garden furniture.

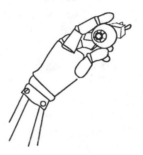

Comparable "nuts and bolts," elementary components which would be widely and repetitively used for sensation, action, and communication in robots of all sorts, are not yet available.

If you look at what the professional robot makers are doing, though, you may get a false impression of how far away the era of useful robots is. For example, a project at the National Bureau of Standards robotics lab has developed robot systems which are already capable of simple sorting tasks, en route to developing a completely automated workshop. This shop would take a set of instructions, generated by anyone's standardized program elsewhere, and be able to automatically produce and handle moderate-sized objects. All operations such as milling and drilling would be precisely specified and under constant computer control, for unprecedented accuracy and reproducibility. Instructions, in standard program form for such an automated factory, are revolutionary **logical blueprints.** Transportable and directly negotiable, they not only show *how* something should be built, but are actually capable of independently supervising its actual construction.

It is admittedly a long way from such sophisticated projects, which pay greater attention to precision than you might, and probably less attention to expense, to common and affordable home helpers. For a variety of reasons though, the home robot may not come about as a spinoff of such high class efforts, and hence possibly appear much sooner. Robots which do physical tasks "in the same way that humans do them" are indeed not likely to be seen for some time. No current technology could be used to make an inexpensive, self-sufficient robot arm capable of loading a dishwasher (without catastrophe), scrubbing floors, raking leaves, pulling weeds, and doing other "manual" labor. In industrial applications, the requirements can be made more restricted and specialized and the economic incentives are greater. In such things as weapons development, economic considerations hardly seem to matter. Unless screwing 1,000 widgets per minute or dropping bombs turns you on, you can't expect much from these developments, except by (lack of) accident.

My own feeling is that the desire to produce a "humanoid" home robot is also something of a red herring, and gives a false impression of how quickly the technology can come along and do some useful physical chores in people's homes. Such "humanness," or at least adaptability to a wide variety of changing and perhaps hostile circumstances, is a goal of much theoretical research aimed at producing truly "intelligent" machines. For the purposes of getting the laundry done or the sink scrubbed, a lot of the theoretical questions and elegance can be scrapped in favor of some tinkering and (Yankee or other) ingenuity.

A good example is the thermostat which is found in buildings everywhere. This is perhaps the first popular "logical device" to make its way into people's homes. The thermostat's single-cell brain is enough to make an earthworm look like a prodigy, and it's decision making capability is ridiculously simple: Too cold?—turn on the heat. Warm enough?—turn it off. Nonetheless, the thermostat performs a valuable and widely appreciated function. The evolutionary descendants of the thermostat are logical feedback loops of all sorts, which are much too amorphous in shape and much too specific in function to satisfy any anthropomorphic image of "robots" or scientific definition of intelligence. Like the simple thermostat though, logical devices incorporated throughout a house in feedback loops can do a great amount of practical and moneysaving work. By means of such loops, many conditions inside and outside a house can be monitored simultaneously and automatically, and action devices such as furnaces, fans, pumps, and shutters all operated to maximum effect.

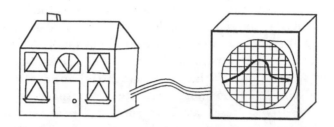

Feedback loops can "tune up" your living space by monitoring time, temperature, and humidity, in the same way that computers in modern automobiles automatically keep the engine in tune as you drive.

For example, you have undoubtedly observed, on a muggy summer day, that a human's *perception* of temperature depends on both the actual temperature and the humidity. If you are heating your home in the winter, or cooling it in the summer, it would be economical to control the humidity as well. The minimum use of energy needed to make a house more comfortable might well be to adjust the humidity, rather than turn on the furnace or air conditioner. Other refinements such as **zone heating** or cooling of only the proper rooms (people) in a house or apartment, as determined by the time of day or by actual people-sensing mechanisms, can produce additional savings. Programmable thermostats which allow the time of day to be taken into account are an off-the-shelf item already from several manufacturers. Simultaneous temperature/humidity monitoring is equally standard, if not yet commonplace for home use. What these feedback loop devices illustrate is that the "robots" which do important jobs in people's living space, in the near or longer term, may have virtually no intelligence, technicolor cuteness, or other redeeming social value beyond their function. Nonetheless, the scope of application of these devices, from comfort monitoring, energy capture, and utilization to active home production of food and fuels, make them far more practical and valuable than their more mobile relatives are likely to be for some time. Even the more personable and mobile robots of the near future are likely to work much better, and certainly be less expensive, if they are developed without any notion that their operation will copy human behavior.

Program Chic

Rather than assuming, as the weapons designers do with evident practical sense and the artificial intelligence researchers do out of theoretical preference, that the world a robot sees will be hostile or at best ambiguous, we can simply remove all of the ambiguity from objects with which our robots will have to deal. This strategy is so eminently practical that it has already been implemented on a vast scale. The bar codes which are now a part of virtually every manufactured product furnish a graphic example. It is theoretically possible, but largely irrelevant, that a supermarket computer system could be built, using the most advanced artificial intelligence techniques, which would see by means of a television camera and recognize all of the products (without any bar codes needed!) in a store, and automatically tally them up as they are checked out, keep track of inventory, suggest advertising, and so on. The complexity and expense of such a system would keep it out of supermarkets for a long time, and beyond that, public resistance to being stared at might keep it out even longer. The bar-code solution avoids all of this complexity and expensive perceptual programming, and is simple enough to have been quickly and almost universally adopted. Rather than making a smart machine, able to figure out that blob A in its lens is a box of Spudchips and a very similar shaped blob B is an upside-down can of Bowlblaster, we simply "brand" all of the items with a code which a relatively dumb machine can instantly and unambiguously comprehend.

"Oh, no," I can hear you muttering, "don't tell me those depressingly automated bar codes are going to start showing up on more things." I am most certainly not going to suggest any visible bar-code proliferation. The first thing to remember (and I suggest you look back to Chapter Four if you can't instantly come up with examples,) is that "labels" we can put on things to make them immediately perceptible and interpretable to computerized sensing devices might be completely (and desirably) unnoticeable to humans. Beyond this, one might even develop a "program chic" style for everything from dishes to clothes to rows in a vegetable garden, where what appears to be the "form" of an object is artfully constructed to be simultaneously a "function" to the perceptive computer.

A few examples of the craft of hidden labels (we'll get to the art of program chic in a minute) : Security systems for many office buildings are based on "plastic" cards which actually contain a code spelled out by magnets or other objects invisibly embedded in the card. An authorized cardholder inserts the card like a key, and the door is automatically opened by a computer, which also may make an entry in the building's log as to who is coming in, and when they leave. There is no reason why each of your dishes might not have such an invisible "slate" incorporated in its construction. Although the dish would not be noticeably different from the ones you now use, it could be "programmed," perhaps by the manufacturer at the time of your order, or perhaps by means of an accessory device from your home computer.

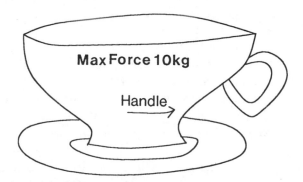

Once such a dish was "written," it would be completely self-explanatory to even a fairly simpleminded home robot.

Not only could your "fetcher program" read how to safely pick up and move the dish, based on the "label instructions," but other programs such as the "washing routine" could give it exactly the optimal processing. (A washing device which can handle pots quickly and efficiently is likely to be a dangerous thing to turn loose on a china cup, without these explicit instructions.) If you go out to buy a set of "smart threads," you may come home with exactly that.

We are used to seeing complicated patterns in clothing fabrics, and historically, looms were the first sophisticated computers. By using two kinds of thread, indistinguishable to humans but obvious to a computer sensor, an invisible "pattern" of instructions could not only be woven into every piece of clothing, but in fact **repeatedly** woven, so that it could be found and read no matter where the garment was picked up.

Examples of program chic are easy enough to generate, but visual programs, like any art form, will take considerable time and talent to be fully developed. One avenue of approach is through the use of symbols and patterns. The bizarre shapes of letters you might have seen presented as "computer writing" or "optical characters" result not from any artistic intent, but a restrictive requirement to make an alphabet which both looked like the old alphabet (somewhat) to humans, and was quickly decipherable by dumb programs. If the goal is to create a visual design, rather than an alphabet with noticeable Roman ancestry, more pleasing forms can be created.

Specifically, suppose that we design fifty "atomic symbols," and use these symbols together to make "designs." One code might be to use fifty-bit binary words, assigning a position (1, 2, 3...50) in the binary word to every atomic symbol. Every design (combination of atomic symbols) can then be read directly by the computer as a fifty-bit binary word—the binary word which has a "1" in the position of every atomic symbol the computer finds in the design, and a "0" for the positions of all atomic symbols it does not find in the design. By using part of the design "word" to specify an instruction to the computer, and the rest of the word to specify when the instruction should be carried out, the designer would have complete freedom to arrange a long program (up to about a quarter of a million instructions for a 32-bit computer or about sixteen billion instructions for a 16-bit computer) by placing the designs anywhere on an object to form a pattern.

12

Off the Shelf: Practice for the Future

This final chapter provides a brief description of some personal computer systems and their organization. The emphasis will be on the equipment and systems for programming which are inexpensive enough for you to buy without taking out a loan (although many a business person might be well advised to do just that). Given the vast *potential* of personal computing, the devices and services which are presently available can only be seen as offering you a way to "get your feet wet" and become literate. By today's standards, the first personal computers of 1975 seem hopelessly primitive. Planning strategies and good conceptual techniques which you learn now though, will be an asset even when your own vintage five-year old computer has long since been replaced.

Any inexpensive computer you can buy today will be a quaint antique by the end of the decade. In ten years' time, computers will not only be able to handle vast quantities of data at speeds which make today's machines look like snails in an air race, but will be routinely supplied with equipment for connection to communication and fabrication facilities which may not even be conceived of now. I strongly encourage you to take this long view when you think of investing your time and money in the first system. In particular, the parts of a computer system which handle **communication** are likely to give it its most lasting value.

> *No human's computer
> is an island.*

If the communication facilities of your first computer are well designed (specifically the telephone interface and the computer's high speed **bus wires**, which we will discuss below), you will be able to extend the machine's useful life considerably, saving plastic, metal, and money. (It is quite common nowadays for the *box* or casing of computer equipment to cost more than the chips and other electronic devices which are doing all of the work.) With good communication, you will be able to:

- Keep in touch with the rest of humanity and learn how to write and use programs, and work on projects which are mutually productive.

- Gradually expand the computer you have by adding auxiliary devices for input, output, sensation, and action as they become cheaper and more readily available.

- Recycle the plastic, metal, glass, and other durables of the computer's package by using them, connected to more modern or remote equipment, even after the machine's vestigial silicon brain has long since lost the spotlight.

In the choice of languages as well as equipment, I also urge you not to be shortsighted. You may be tempted, for example, to choose a computer system which is *entirely* menu-driven, so that all sorts of things, from games to checkbook balancing, appear in full color on your screen with the simplest of "pick one" interaction. In such a system, the only way to add more capabilities, from games to gardening, is to buy more programs, or plug-in modules from the manufacturer. Similarly, the BASIC programming language is attractive to many people because it seems that writing a simple, numbered list of instructions is the most convenient way to tell the computer what to do. (In many off-the-shelf computer systems, BASIC is the language you get by default.)

In the long run though, programming exclusively by menu or in BASIC will give you no contact with the powerful programming ideas and clean planning strategies possible with languages like Pascal, C, LISP, or LOGO. In addition, it will often be cheaper and more convenient to get new programs by swapping with your neighbors, professional contacts, or club mates, rather than being completely dependent on the plug-in suppliers. (You can't read the program in a plug-in module, or use the **substitution** method on it.) As you might suspect, the notion of computer literacy requires the acquisition of language, whether it is the "high level" ability to decompose problems and recognize patterns repeated with variation wherever they occur, or the nitty-gritty of communicating your ideas precisely enough to be translated (by yourself or others) into machine programs that function effectively, predictably, and reliably.

What you will find in the rest of this chapter will not be specific recommendations for the computer *you* should buy. The right computer for you depends on your interests and abilities, as well as such things as cost and availability which seem to change as rapidly as one can write them down. What you will find though, are some fundamental **guidelines** and considerations that you yourself can use in evaluating a variety of potential systems. Some valuable meta-advice: things are changing rapidly, but good information sources are available (including the magazines listed later in the chapter.) Beyond books and magazines, there are clubs and, of course, people you know. The best way to evaluate a computer system, with the guidelines you will find here and other criteria of your own, is by your own experience. Before you buy any computer:

- Ask (non sales)people about it.
- Watch someone use it, to do something you understand.
- Try doing something with it yourself.

There is no reason to forget all of the lessons you have learned the hard way in buying other equipment, from stereo sets to automobiles. The checklist used by *Infoworld* to rate computers could apply to other equipment of any type:

- How easy is it to unpack the equipment and actually get it going (setup)?
- How easy is it to use, once it is working? (You can't use your discs if the door is jammed shut, press keys your fingers won't fit on, or keep stopping to find loose wires.)
- How well does it perform? (Do you fall asleep waiting for it to do simple programs?)
- How clear are the instructions (documentation)?
- Who will fix it quickly, when it breaks (serviceability)?

The balance between price and features which makes one computer a better buy than another seems to change virtually from month to month, with manufacturers announcing price changes, new accessories becoming available, and so on. In the midst of all this innovation, it is worth remembering that new products, even with more power and options than established computers, will suffer initially from a lack of suitable programs, user experience, and independently developed accessories. If your need for computers is primarily practical, such as in a small business, you might be well advised to start with an established system, rather than the "most powerful, latest innovative" computer appearing in glossies. This first computer can then go to work for you immediately and reliably, paying for itself while you gain experience. If you miss out on the third generation of computers, you can always buy in again on the fourth.

Hardware: An Overview of Computer Anatomy

As an introduction to computer hardware, let me take you on an imaginary excursion to the housepaint department of your ordinary local hardware store. Here we will find some elementary components of the store's paint-mixing and delivery system, whose individual functions and relationships to each other should be familiar and obvious. Once you get your bearings in the paint department, we will move down the aisle to the information department, and show you the corresponding components of an information-mixing and delivery system, more commonly called a computer.

When you enter your local hardware store with a swatch of your deep orchid drapery, to buy some matching paint for the room, you will set in motion a whole chain of events.

> The paint clerk will go to the
> **stock shelves**
> And retrieve some basic white
> **paint**
> for mixing. This paint will be transferred to the
> **temporary holder**
> of the
> **pigment-mixing machine.**
> The clerk will adjust settings on the.
> **control knobs**
> on the pigment-mixing machine, which adds colors.
> You then go home and spread the paint with a
> **brush.**

The various components in the paint system have different roles, and **paint** is transferred between them. A computer system can be described by analogy with the paint setup, its own components performing specific jobs and transferring **information** (expressed in the **binary** language of high-low voltages) rather than paint, back and forth:

In the computer, large amounts of information can be stored on mass storage devices like
> **magnetic tape** or **magnetic** and **videodiscs.**
> *(stock shelves)*

When this information needs to be transformed in any way by logical processing, it is transferred from mass-storage to the computer's quick-access memory, often called
> **main memory,** or **random-access memory (RAM).**
> *(temporary holder)*

("random-access" will be described in more detail below.) Part of the information in this main memory will always be the instructions from a computer program. These instructions control the actions of the
> **central processing unit**
> *(pigment-mixing machine)*

which transforms the data in main memory, causes it to be sent back to mass storage or to other places, according to additional commands which you provide via an
> **input device,** like a **keyboard** or **light pen.**
> *(control knobs)*

In particular, the information can be communicated to the world outside the computer system by means of a
> **display device** like a **video screen** or **printer.**
> *(brush)*

Like all analogies, this one should not be pushed too far. (If you have heard of "white noise, " don't think it has anything to do with the paint on the stock shelves.) Nonetheless, the paint-store image should enable you to understand things like the need for both mass storage and RAM: In paint terms, all of the paint in the store will not fit in the mixing machine (central processing unit) at one time.

Later in this chapter, we will look at what each of these components of computer anatomy is like, in real machines you can buy off the shelf. The same basic structures are found in both the small computers now popular for home use and in the more powerful machines just beginning to be widely available. First though, I will tell you a few of the things to look for in each of the components, as well as how the components are described in standard terms. For those who know about hi-fi equipment, this review will resemble the way you would tell a novice about cartridges, woofers, tweeters, and tape decks, and explain the manufacturer's printed specifications. The importance of actually testing the equipment yourself before buying, regardless of its "specs," may be more important in hi-fi than in computers, but I will point out a few ways in which the "specs" for computers need to be examined critically.

Central Processors and the Bit Wars

The **central processing unit** or **CPU** (a.k.a. *pigment-mixer*) is the key element of any computer, and the fundamental reason why a home computer represents a radical departure from the simple storage of information (which your tape recorder can do) or the passive transmission of information by technology such as television. Admittedly useless without a lot of supporting elements, the CPU of a computer is nonetheless the component that makes all of the decisions, transformations, and other logical operations happen.

All other things being equal, the better computer for you is the one with the more powerful CPU. All sorts of capabilities, from the ability to do your programs quickly, provide instantaneous feedback even while performing complex operations, support graphical displays, and carry out many tasks simultaneously, all improve dramatically as more powerful CPUs are introduced into computers. The power of a CPU is determined by many things, including the repertoire of fundamental instructions or **instruction set** it knows how to carry out, and the degree to which various functions are coordinated for simultaneous processing. Two factors which determine a CPU's power, and which can always be immediately assessed, are the processor's **word size** and **speed**.

Word Size: The most fundamental thing about a CPU is its **word size**. The CPU is, after all, a processor like a sewage plant or a sawmill, and the wider the channel (for logs, sewage, or information), the faster things flow through the mill. (CPU's at one time were even called mills.) The bigger the word size of the CPU, the less time it needs to spend breaking down information, like external data or even the machine's own instructions to itself, into many small pieces. Eliminating this internal overhead is the reason why sixteen-bit processors are more than twice as effective as eight-bit processors. You may as well learn a disconcerting fact of life at this point: The home computer market has been built on the basis of 8-bit processors, and there is now an audible wrenching and shifting of gears in the whole industry as 16-bit and even 32-bit CPU's having the same small size, low electric power consumption, and affordability as the original 8-bit processors now enter full scale production. You can expect to see a whole new breed of home computers, built around these new 16-bit CPUs, start to appear, while hardware and software specialists agonize over cutting loose from their 8-bit machines to learn some new, and often quite different tricks.

Some numbers here, which you certainly can live without but will often hear mentioned, are the manufacturer's **names** for their CPUs. Maybe soon they will get around to calling them pintos, mustangs, and skylarks, but for now the "names" you will hear are:

- 6502, 6502A, 6502B—Three successive 8-bit models of the original 6502 microprocessor, and the basis for Apple, Atari, and PET computers.

- Z80, Z80A, etc.—Another 8-bit processor, which makes home computers like the TRS-80, Heath H89, and Osborne's all-in-one suitcase computer possible.

- 8086, Z8000—These two are "new wave" 16-bit processors with advanced design, as well as their large word size enabling them to greatly outperform the 8-bitters.

- MC68000—This 16-bit processor (by external connections) is actually a 32-bit processor internally. The 68000 is impressive in both its design and implementation, and can be used as the basis of a personal computer which is comparable to the early eighties main computer of many institutions and businesses.

Clock Speed: If you recall the backyard bucket memory example from Chapter Three, you know that **timing** is a critical part of the processing of binary signals. Both the sender and the receiver there needed to have clocks to synchronize their actions.

Similarly, a computer's central processing unit needs a clock, like a drill sergeant, to keep repeating "left, right, left, right..." while all of the data shuffles through the mill in lockstep. The faster the drill sergeant, the faster the troops move through the mill, and the more rapidly processing gets done. The big difference between the Z80 and the Z80A processors mentioned above, for example, is that the Z80 can keep up with a drill sergeant yelling left-right to the tune of two million steps per second (simple yes, but very fast), while the Z80A can keep up with four million per second. The "new breed" MC68000 is even more impressive than its 16/32 bit architecture suggests, since it can be clocked at eight million cycles per second or more. (The **electric power consumption** of most CPUs increases when the clock is speeded up, which tips you off that low power devices like the first pocket computers are typically much slower than the computers they are "lookalikes" for.)

Computer Memories: Speed or Size?

In Chapter Seven, we introduced a **desk clerk** actor to visualize the way that a computer system uses its memory. You will see references to three main kinds of memory hardware for computers, and the differences between them can be easily described in terms of what the desk clerk is allowed to do with his memory "pigeonholes." (If you skipped Chapter Seven, or weren't sufficiently impressed by the desk clerk the first time around, you might go back now and look at the Section called "Implementing Your Model.") The three kinds of memory are:

- **Mass Storage** (a.k.a. *stock shelves*)—This type of memory is comparatively slow, but has the advantages of being cheap and non volatile. (The usefulness of cassette tapes is greatly enhanced by the fact that the information stays there even if you turn the player off for a while. Not so, ordinarily, for the computer's main memory.) Mass storage memory is usually restricted to being accessed **serially**, at least to some extent. For example, you have to play through all of the programs on your **cassette tape** (or at least wind through them), in order to retrieve the last one. This is like having a desk clerk who manages mailboxes which are in one long row. The clerk must go past all of the boxes in the row to get to the last one, which would slow him down considerably in filing messages coming in at random for different boxes. Storage **discs**, whether **magnetic or optical (video)**, are arranged more like phonograph records, so you can skip to any "groove" or **track**, but things are still arranged serially within the track. (If your record player's needle is "stuck," it keeps repeating the same "track" on the record, and you hear over and over again the same music or string of words in order, "He lay face down in the desert sand, He lay face down in the desert sand, He lay face down . . ." or whatever.) Information on discs is much more rapidly accessible than cassette tapes, but still quite slow from the perspective of the million-ticks-per-second clocks used by CPUs.

- **Random-access Memory** or **RAM** (a.k.a. *temporary holding space*) is usually handled by an electronic device, and costs more than mass storage, since electronic devices are more expensive to fabricate, at least for the next few years, than magnetic tapes or optical discs. The advantage of RAM though, as the name suggests, is that the devices are constructed so that information can be retrieved in any (random) order, without going through any intermediate information. This arrangement is like having the desk clerk surrounded by a ring of pigeonholes, so that each pigeonhole is equally easy to reach, and the clerk doesn't have to walk past one pigeonhole to get to another one. Physically, the typical RAM stores information as patterns of empty-or-full charge buckets somewhere in the device, rather than as two kinds of magnetic regions on a tape or hole-or-no-hole burned by laser in the reflecting film of an optical disc.

- **Read-Only Memory** or **ROM** represents an attempt to have both the speed and random-access capability of ordinary RAM, with even greater stability than tape or disc. ROM devices are conceptually the same as ordinary random-access memory, with the same arrangement for the desk clerk. The only difference is that the desk clerk is only allowed to read the messages in the pigeonholes, and not change any of them. Physically, the yes-or-no bits in ROM are not stored as a charge which would leak away when the device was turned off, but in some manner which does not need electrical power to persist, and cannot be changed (ordinarily) by any signals coming from the CPU.

Each type of memory has its own place and usefulness, although if RAM and ROM were cheap enough, there would not be much demand for traditional mass storage. That is not likely to happen in the foreseeable future, but a step in this direction is **magnetic bubble** memory, which has the storage-and-retrieval structure of discs as well as their permanence, much greater storage capacity than typical RAM, and access speed intermediate between the two media.

When you are considering a computer, it is important to know *how much* memory capacity it has, of each of the three types mentioned above. If two computers are otherwise equivalent, but one has more memory capacity, or more of its memory capacity in a fast medium (RAM beats bubbles beats disc beats tape), the superior memory indicates the better choice.

Obviously, "how much" for information storage is not going to be measured in gallons like paint. The size of a memory is measured simply according to the number of different patterns or designs that can be made in it. Regardless of their physical size, two memories which can store the same number of distinct patterns are the same "size" in their capacity for information. The term **bit**, as you know, is used for a single yes-no piece of information, such as one empty-or-filled position in the backyard bucket array. The smallest memory imaginable for a computer would be a one-bit memory, which would be limited, but could be useful. In a smoke detector, this one-cell memory could signal the single bit of information that yes indeed, your house is on fire. Computers typically have so many bits worth of storage that no one wants to be bothered counting them, and so a larger unit of measure is used, just like dozens for eggs or reams for paper. The larger unit or group of bits is called a **byte**, and consists of **eight bits.**

The only reason you need to be concerned with any of this is to make some sense of the descriptions you will see of the **size** of computer memories. When you see something like **48K RAM** in the description of a computer, you know (now) that RAM means random-access memory, so what you are being told is that the size of the computer's fast (a.k.a.*temporary holding space*) memory is "48K." To finish interpreting this cryptic insider's jargon, you must be told that "K" stands for thousand, as in Kilogram, Kilometer, and so on, so we have 48 thousand of something. The something is **bytes** or eight-bit chunks of memory. In plain terms, which would take only marginally more ink to print but deprive computer folk of the warm feeling that comes from knowing things no one else can figure out, 48K RAM means "This computer has 48,000 bytes of fast, random-access memory, or 48 x 8 = 384 thousand bits." Three hundred eighty-four thousand buckets would fill up a sizable backyard, but the electronic version constitutes only a small electronic memory. Many 16-bit **microprocessors** (CPUs) available now will allow you to keep track of as much as a million bytes of fast memory space ("1M RAM" if you prefer being cryptic.) The size of disc memory is also measured in bytes. Disc storage capacity nowadays is commonly hundreds of thousands, millions or tens of millions of bytes. With optical disc technology, storage of hundreds of millions of bytes on disc may soon be as common.

The advantages of large amounts of memory space, other than the obvious attraction of having libraries full of books at your fingertips in a form where you can use, peruse, and utilize them as never before, is that **programs** as well as data, are stored in memory. The larger your computer's memory, especially the fast RAM and ROM, the larger and more sophisticated programs you will be able to carry out efficiently. For example, the programs that are used by the small Atari computer to interpret what you type in at the keyboard and to carry out commands in the BASIC language take up eighteen thousand bytes of fast memory (supplied to the customer as ROM, to prevent accidents). As you can imagine, such a computer, with an additional sixteen thousand bytes of RAM for programs and data you create, will do much more than the more primitive early computers, which might have less than one fourth of the memory needed just to store the program for *interpreting* your BASIC commands! One use of the freedom of large memories is that large and sophisticated "built-in" programs can be supplied to the user to make the communication process with the computer easier to manage. When you do something unexpected, the typical response of a small memory computer is to blank out and leave you to poke around in the gibberish it has made of its brain cells. A large-memory computer with a good operating system and interpreter programs will simply display an intelligible complaint.

Displays—Flaunting Your Figures

A variety of **display** (a.k.a. *paintbrush*) devices are commonly supplied with, or available for, personal computers. The options will increase dramatically as time goes on, but the list at present includes:

- **Video display**—this is presently the most common medium for display. Older displays were restricted to printing upper case letters in black and white. Nowadays, **color** video display is common, as well as and possibly along with full capability for displaying upper and lower case text. So-called "graphics terminals" are computer-controlled mosaics with hundreds or perhaps a thousand rows and as many columns, in black and white or color. As these **display terminals** improve, so that in the next few years realistic color images, text displays with hundred-line and variable style lettering, and real-time display of images for movie-style illusion become more common, computers will seem less like portholes on data than picture windows on the world.

- **Printers**—As with all things mechanical, printers cannot keep up with the dizzying progress of electronic logical circuits. Nonetheless, the great demand for printing devices compatible with computers and able to take advantage of computer-processing power has led to important developments. Pen-and-ink **plotters** capable of making color drawings for accurate scientific work or illustrations can now be obtained for a price comparable to video displays. Programs, such as the program which constructed the page images of this book, have been released for widespread use even by small computers and relatively simple printing devices to create high quality printed output. As print hammers, needles, and ribbons give way to lasers and mirrors, the printed page itself is becoming a more accurate mirror of the fine-grained logical mosaic.

- **Sound Production**—Sound has entered the computer picture with a boom, from the built-in music facilities of many small computers, to speech chips and other accessories, some capable of taking any written input and producing spoken output. Peripheral devices for speech in particular promise to radically alter the way in which humans interact with computers, and the way they learn, use, and think of their own languages in the near future.

Input Devices for Touch, Sound, or Sight

The progress of computer **input devices** (a.k.a. *control knobs*) has taken decades, going from the use of punched holes to electric switches to typewriter-style **keyboards**. In the short span of the last few years though, many more types of input devices have become available at personally affordable prices. Nowadays, you might get your thoughts translated into the computer's memory by many new routes:

- **Light-Pens, digitizing tablets**, or ballpoint mechanism **mice**, allow you to draw pictures for the computer to process. Rather than classic symbol oriented programs, entirely new programs are used, tailored to the creation, production, and display of graphics. These new routines do such things as automatically shrink, stretch, move, rotate, and repaint the pictures you draw, with various pens, brushes or colors.

- **Television Cameras** can be interfaced even to small home computers, along with the programs to automatically translate the patterns of light and dark which the camera sees into the computer's internal mosaic or **bit-map** representation. Less complicated and less expensive light sensors enable a computer to read data from bar codes, and programs are currently advancing rapidly to enable this technology to process handwriting automatically as well.

- **Voice Input** for computers is commercially available in off-the-shelf devices and their support programs, although presently restricted to understanding a small defined vocabulary from a single speaker. Greater sophistication, as well as simple "brute force" processing power, is bound to improve the value of voice input as time goes on.

Communication Links Expand Your View

For a beginning computer user, a key concept to be learned

about computer equipment and communication is the notion of a **standard**. We are all familiar with standards in sending ordinary communication through the postal service: The stamps have to be affixed in the proper place; the addresses of the sender and receiver must be distinguishable, and often a numerical "zip" code for the destination must be supplied as well. For computers, standards mean a widely agreed upon way to translate yes-no bits of information into electrical signals, and send these signals over a pair of wires or many wires together in a cable or over a phone line or a T.V.-antenna cable, and so on. The existence of standards enables computers made by a wide variety of manufacturers to communicate with each other, and also allows a variety of manufacturers to build accessories for computers made by others. As we all know, automobile parts have very little standardization, so that you can't salvage the tail-lights from your Edsel when you scrap it, as spares for your new Corvair. Although standardization among computers and their support devices is by no means universal, there are several widely used standardization schemes, and you would be wise both in the short run and the long to support these standards in your purchase of equipment.

Perhaps the most widely used communication standard and the most useful for your first efforts is the **RS-232** standard for sending data over a single pair of wires. The name certainly isn't catchy, but if you can't remember it, write it down on a piece of paper, and take it with you when you go to look at computers. A vast array of devices, from plotters to speech chips to telephone hookups, can be made to work with your computer, if it has the two-wire outlet from an RS-232 encoder. For example, your computer can be connected to the phone lines, starting with the RS-232 wires, by connecting them to an **acoustic coupler** device which holds the telephone handset, or directly through a **modem** into the telephone wall jack. An attractive accessory available with some computers is a completely automatic modem, which will answer the telephone and dial numbers automatically under the control of your programs. (See the "Supermarket Alert" section in Chapter Ten, if you need ideas for automatic dialing.) More and more "package deals" are appearing in computer stores and elsewhere, which offer you a computer, complete with RS-232 and telephone connections and a subscription to some banking, shopping, and remote information and computing services, such as The Source or Compuserve/Micronet. These offers will become more substantial, as the variety and usefulness of services available on computer networks increase. For the present, it is advisable to get a bona-fide computer with the RS-232 interface, rather than a simple data terminal. The computer will cost little or nothing more. There are also **community bulletin boards** which you can connect to once you have a telephone interface. A fairly recent listing of phone numbers from the Peoples' Message System of Santee California (714 449-5689) showed nearly three hundred and fifty community bulletin boards across the United States. These bulletin boards can handle notes of general and personal interest, as well as serve to transfer *programs* easily among participants.

Virtually every computer you will find has the capability to produce RS-232 output. The nitty-gritty question is whether or not the encoder is included in a computer's base price, or whether it's tacked on as an accessory like auto stereo. As with autos, you should look for computers with a good array of standard equipment like RS-232 encoding, and when accessories are required, realize that the original manufacturer may not be the cheapest or the best source to obtain them.

A single pair of wires carrying RS-232 encoded information is often not fast enough to carry data and signals for control at the rate computers can produce, communicate, and store them. For that reason, there are also **high speed bus** communication lines, involving many wires simultaneously rather than a single pair. A computer system uses its high speed bus to communicate both internally and with fast accessories such as the mass storage disc memory. Names (again not very catchy) to be aware of for standard bus encoding are:

- **S-100**—Computers which utilize the S-100 bus have many advantages over non-standard systems in the availability of versatile and affordable accessories. In addition, the acknowledged standard **operating system** for 8-bit computers (which keeps all of the computer's components, from the CPU to the disc and the keyboard, working harmoniously together) is **CP/M**, a system built for S-100 computers. The availability of accessories for input output and memory, and the value of the CP/M operating system with its extensive library of compatible programs (over forty discs' worth in the public domain, much of it available by phone) make the S-100 bus so valuable that off-the-shelf devices are widely sold to convert the signals of non-standard buses such as that of the TRS 80, Heath, and others into S-100 form. The main drawback of the S-100 bus is that it is oriented toward 8-bit machines, although a revision (the **IEEE S-100** bus) suitable for 16-bit machines such as Zilog's Z8000 CPU has been made. Whether or not the S-100 standard remains as important in the future as it is now, you may be well advised, for example if you contemplate an 8-bit workhorse system for business, to build with this bus as a starting point.

- **IEEE-488**—This standard seems a good bet to become progressively more important in the next few years. Historically oriented toward applications where laboratory instruments and other sensation and action devices needed to be connected, the IEEE 488 bus is now used by computers ranging from the suitcase-sized, 8-bit Osborne I to extremely powerful "personal workstations" based on Motorola's MC68000 processor. (Although the Apple computer has its own, non-standard bus, as does the PET, both of these buses are readily accessible, and both computers are easily connected to the IEEE 488 standard.)

Examples of the Main Components in Personal Computers							
Name	CPU	RAM	ROM	Disc	Input	Output	Interface
Apple II	6502	16-48K	12K	140-840K	k,GT,JS	C,S	RS*,IEEE*
Atari 400,800	6502	8-48K	10-26K	0-163K	k,JS	C	RS*
VIC 20	6502A	5-32K	16-32K	170K	k	C	RS,IEEE
Heath H89	Z-80	16-64K	8K	100K-1M	k	V	RS*
North Star Horizon	Z-80A	32-64K	8K	180-360K	k	V	S-100,RS*
TRS-80 Color	6809E	4-16K	8-16K		k,JS	C	RS
TI 99/4	TMS9900	16K	26-56K	90K	k,JS	C,S,Sp	RS*

(**Input:** k=keyboard, GT=graphics tablet, JS=joystick)
(**Output:** C=color graphics, V=video, S=sound, Sp=speech)
(**Interface:** RS=RS-232, IEEE=IEEE 488, *=option)

Software: Programs to Make Computers Useful

As you well realize by now, all of the structure and usefulness of computers depends completely on the **software** or programs, originated by humans, which occupy their silicon crania. The vast majority of the words in this book have been spent talking about programs, so that this section can be somewhat short. As a practical matter though, all computer users must be concerned with one type of program in particular, or rather a system of programs, which goes under the name of an **operating system**. Unless you want to go back to the bad old days of putting programs into the computer's memory by resetting the memory cells one by one, your intermediary for communicating with a computer, and getting your programs built, modified, and installed, will itself be a program, supplied by the manufacturer and automatically loaded into the computer's memory when you start it up. This **operating system** program determines so much of the computer's behavior, from the management of disc files and peripheral devices to the interpretation of commands you initiate, that it is often a more important factor to consider in choosing a computer system than the physical hardware.

Similarly, if you are considering a computer for a specific application, you should be much more impressed by the existence of programs for your computer that do accounts payable, tax consulting, elementary mathematics, or whatever your interest is, than shiny cabinets or even impressive CPU specifications. In particular, it may be better for you to use the "tried and true" 8-bit (preferably S-100) technology to get things done, while the bit wars rage around you and programs gradually accumulate for 16 bit, 32 bit, or even larger machines.

Language is a crucial element. If you buy a system which is developed in an offbeat language, or if you do not obtain the original **source** programs for systems you use, you have little chance to make modifications or corrections or even verify to your own satisfaction or that of independent experts that is working correctly.

Operating Systems You Should Try

There are about as many different operating systems around

nowadays as there are computers, and it is not practical or worthwhile to review them all here. There are two particular operating systems though, that have set the pace for a great deal of development. One of these, CP/M, has been mentioned already. CP/M is far and away the most widely used operating system for microcomputers. It was written by Digital Research of Pacific Grove, California, and has been updated several times as more sophisticated hardware became available to be managed. The principal distributor is Lifeboat Associates of New York, and you are sure to find the latest information about their services and prices in any major computer magazine. The other standout in the field of operating systems is **Unix**, developed at Bell Laboratories and now in its seventh version. Besides being designed by two superb computer scientists, Unix has the advantage of having been developed in the environment of powerful machines and a variety of peripherals, for a sophisticated and demanding user community. Developers of the new breed of personal computers in the 16-bit world and beyond are taking to Unix like ducks to water. The result is that either Unix or a look-alike operating system is what you are likely to be offered, if you wait and take the plunge with the new machines. It is hardly fair to compare CP/M and Unix, since the machines and the times in which Unix was developed were so much more congenial. CP/M and its more sophisticated descendant **MP/M** undeniably will have their place for quite some time, but Unix and "unix-like" operating systems appear to be the newly developing standard. Powerful computers make Unix's flexible command structure, file system management, and multiprocessing, multiuser capabilities irresistably attractive.

You can obtain more information about both CP/M and Unix systems from the frequent discussions of these systems in computer magazines, as well as from the **users groups** which are active for both systems. For CP/M, the users group is called CPMUG, and they publish a magazine of their own called *Lifelines*. The user's group for Unix and its lookalikes is called Usenix.

Programs by the Megabit

As we have stressed, the *planning* of computer programs is much more important than the more mechanical translation into program codes. There are a variety of language dialects and approaches for you to choose from. The distinguishing features of a good language are the ease with which you can implement top-down, hierarchical planning and the cleanness of the language's control structures, so that the route and progress of the program's execution are clear and provably correct. In an excellent article in *Byte* magazine of August 1979, Vaughan Pratt (making a strong case for the LISP language), gives four criteria for evaluating a language:

- Mobility of data—How much fuss does the language require you to make to move data around between variables, functions, and input-output ports?

- Modularity of Function—A programming language should be like a hardware store full of parts which you can pick and choose from independently of each other, to use as you need, rather than having its facilities structured into the form of a monolithic grammar.

- Declarative programming—Programs should be written in terms of the facts underlying the algorithm, letting the computer derive the algorithm itself automatically.

- Metalinguistics—Since programs often deal with languages, (including the same language the program is written in), languages like LISP which are well suited to talking about language are extremely useful.

In acquiring a language yourself, the best strategy is to find some "natives" who speak the various languages well, including the authors of the books listed in the bibliography but in addition some real people who can sit down with you at a keyboard and show you things *by doing*. The most effective way to learn any language is by communicating with a computer, so that the text can say, "All right, now try *doing* a few things with the commands we have just discussed." It would be enlightening for you to make up a task for a computer to do something *you* are interested in, and have several language experts describe how they would plan it in their own languages, or perhaps even show you the programs that could do it. You can then decide for yourself which explanations and language structures are easier to follow, verify for correct operation, and modify as will always happen eventually.

How To Find Out More

The bibliography of this book contains many entries which can help you follow up on topics touched only lightly here. In order to keep up with current information on the availability of products and systems, as well as to tune in to the programming strategies, applications, and other ideas which are being developed daily, the computer magazines are invaluable. By browsing through several of the ones listed below, you should be able to find one that agrees with your interests and level of experience. Frequently, the advertisements in these magazines are as interesting to follow as the articles, whether announcing new products or significant price reductions in old favorites. The **Datapro Directory of Small Computers**, a yearly volume with monthly updates, is a valuable publication, although expensive enough to be a good investment for libraries rather than individuals. Beyond books and magazines, there are clubs and users' groups for nearly every computer topic imaginable. *Byte* magazine, in particular, regularly prints an updated list of clubs and directions for contacting them by mail or telephone.

Computer Magazines and Publications

Byte
Co-Evolution Quarterly
Compute!
Creative Computing
Dr. Dobbs Journal
Electronics
Infosystems
Infoworld
Interface Age
Microcomputing
OnComputing
Personal Computing
Practical Computing
Popular Computing
Recreational Computing
ROM
Robotics Age

Bibliography

Allen, John R., *Anatomy of Lisp.* McGraw Hill (New York) 1978.

American Federation of Information Processing Societies, *Annals of the History of Computing.* (Arlington, Va.) periodical.

Basmajian, John V., ed., *Biofeedback - Principles and Practice for Clinicians.* Williams and Wilkins Company (Baltimore) 1979.

Bowles, Kenneth, *Beginner's Guide for the UCSD Pascal System.* Byte Books (Peterborough N.H.)1979.

Cherry, George W., *Pascal Programming Structures: An Introduction to Systematic Programming.* Reston Publishing Co. (Reston,Va.) 1980.

Ciarcia, Steve, *Build Your Own Z80 Computer.* Byte Books (Peterborough N.H.) 1979.

Ciarcia, Steve, *Ciarcia's Circuit Cellar,* volumes 1,2... Byte Books (Peterborough N.H.) 1979.

Conway, J. H., *On Numbers and Games.* Academic Press (London) 1976.

Datapro Research Corp., *Datapro Directory of Small Computers.* (Delran New Jersey) yearly with monthly updates.

Datapro Research Corp., *All About Personal Computers.* (Delran, N.J.) 1981.

Dutton, J. and Starbuck, W., *Computer Simulation of Human Behavior.* Wiley (New York)1971.

Everitt, B.S., *Graphical Techniques for Multivariate Data.* North-Holland, (New York) 1978.

Fisher, E. and Jensen, C.W., *PET and the IEEE-488 Bus.* Osborne/McGraw Hill (Berkeley) 1980.

Genesereth, M.R., "The Role of Plans in Intelligent Teaching Systems." HPP memo 80-4 Stanford University, March 1980.

Gnanadesikan, R., *Statistical Data Analysis of Multivariate Observations.* Wiley (New York) 1977.

Harville, David, Predictions for National Football League Games Via Linear-Model Methodology. *Journal of the American Statistical Assoc..* v. 75 no. 31, September, 1980.

Ira Goldstein, *Developing a Computational Representation for Problem Solving Skills.* MIT-AI Memo 495 October 1978.

Jensen,K. and Wirth, N., *Pascal User Manual and Report.* Springer-Verlag (New York) 1978.

Keller, Arthur, *A First Course in Computer Programming Using Pascal.* McGraw Hill, (New York) 1982.

Kelley, J.L. Jr., A New Interpretation of Information Rate. *Bell System Technical Journal,* July 1956.

Kernighan, B. and Richie, D., *The C Programming Language.* Prentice-Hall 1978.

Libes, Sol, *Fundamentals and Application of Digital Logic Circuits,* Hayden Book Company (Rochelle Park, N.J.) 1980.

Mateosian, Richard, *Inside BASIC Games.* Sybex (Berkeley) 1981.

McCracken, Daniel D., *A Simplified Guide to Structured Cobol Programming.* Wiley (New York) 1976.

Melzak, Z.A., *Mathematical Ideas, Modeling & Applications.* Wiley (New York) 1976.

Mezzich, Juan E. and Solomon, Herbert, *Taxonomy and Behavioral Science.* Academic Press (New York) 1980.

Mosteller F. and Tukey, J.W., *Data Analysis and Regression.* Addison-Wesley (Reading,Mass.) 1977.

Noyce, Robert N., Microelectronics. *Scientific American.* v. **237**, no. 3, August 1977 (available as a reprint).

Papert, Seymour, *Mindstorms: Children, Computers and Powerful Ideas.* Basic Books (N.Y.) 1980.

Pattis, Richard E., *Karel the Robot.* Wiley (New York) 1981.

Riddell, Brian, *The Origins of Digital Computers.* Springer-Verlag (New York) 1975.

Roberts, Fred S., *Discrete Mathematical Models.* Prentice-Hall (Englewood Cliffs, N.J.) 1976.

Safford, Edward L. Jr., *The Complete Handbook of Robotics.* TAB Books (Blue Ridge Summit, Pa.) 1980.

Shepp, L. A. and Kruskal, J. B., Computerized Tomography: The New Medical X-Ray Technology. *American Mathematical Monthly* v. **85** no. 6 June-July 1978 420-439.

Tanur, J. M., Mosteller, F.M.,et al., *Statistics: A Guide to the Unknown.* Holden Day Inc. 1972.

Tukey, J.W., *Exploratory Data Analysis.* Addison-Wesley (Reading, Mass.) 1977.

Tversky, Amos and Kahneman, Daniel, The Framing of Decisions and the Psychology of Choice. *Science.* v. **211** no. 4481, 1981.

Index

Personal Notes

This spot in a book is usually reserved for the author, in the third person, to trot out his credentials and otherwise effuse. In my case, a list of my credentials is a list of my debts, and there is an economy in presenting one and acknowledging the other simultaneously. You'll pardon the affectation of speaking as if I were myself.

My experience with computers began in 1964 with a summer Science Training Program sponsored by the National Science Foundation at Kansas State Teacher's College in Emporia, Kansas. Besides the chance for me to leave St. Louis and see the world, the summer program gave me the opportunity, commonplace now but rare indeed then, to learn about and use computers in high school. I am indebted to my early mentors, the Revs. Emmett Collins, Martin Coyne, and Patrick Kaler in particular, who brought this program to my attention and consistently encouraged my academic efforts. In 1970, I received an A.B. in physics (*summa cum laude*, Phi Beta Kappa, etc.—let's not forget one reason this is being written), from Washington University in St. Louis. Without the initial welcome and continuing support of my advisor, Dr. Dan Bolef, that program would never have begun. In 1976, I completed a Ph.D. in Statistics at Stanford University, and joined the faculty of the Statistics Department at Princeton University. In the rare air of academe, I owe debts to many and ideas to more, but relative to this book, Bill Gosper and Peter Bloomfield deserve special mention for the influence of their varied and inspiring talents with computing. Equally exemplary has been the influence of the MACSYMA group at M.I.T., (particularly Joel Moses and Ellen and Jeff Golden), whose development and support of research computational facilities sets a high standard for scientific cooperation. The list here ends with the National Science Foundation, as it began, for their support of my academic research for the past two years at Stanford. In the Fall of 1981, I will return to teaching, with the faculty of the Statistics, Operations Research, and Data Processing Division of the School of Business at the University of Texas, Austin.

The chronicle of this book begins with Maria Guarnaschelli, who suggested I write it, and would have no continuation or conclusion except for the efforts of many others as well. It would probably save ink in the future if only those books which did *not* acknowledge Don Knuth's work in font design and typesetting made mention of him, but I thank him here, until the tradition is established. Max Diaz is also to be thanked in numerous ways for the physical appearance of the book, which in large part represents my **substitutions** in programs of his design. Greg Brown, whose murals are known by everyone in Palo Alto who has ever tried to shake hands with them, risked a small portion of his sanity to contribute the opening Chapter pictures. You may espy my own eccentric hand in some of the remaining illustrations; where you do not, thanks most likely go to Julie Brown and Jan Chambers.

Though I echo Marvell and think that a book's a fine and proper place, not suited for larger debts and stronger feelings, I will put two lines here, with no better opportunity elsewhere.

Still Kate your mask persists, why mad court pain?
The sky is black. The living love-stars rain.

Last to say and best...

...**Here's to friends.**